In Statu Nascendi

Journal of Political Philosophy and International Relation

Vol. 6, No. 1 (2023)

Special Edition: On Continental Philosophy

About In Statu Nascendi

In Statu Nascendi *(ISN) is a peer-reviewed journal that aspires to be a world-class scholarly platform encompassing original academic research dedicated to the circle of Political Philosophy, Cultural Studies, Theory of International Relations, Foreign Policy, and the political Decision-making process. The journal investigates specific issues through a socio-cultural, philosophical, and anthropological approach to raise a new type of civic awareness about the complexity of contemporary crisis, instability, and warfare situations, where the "stage-of-becoming" plays a vital role.*

Any views expressed in this publication are the views of the authors and are not necessarily shared by the editorial board of this journal. In Statu Nascendi is committed to freedom, liberty, and pluralism of opinions and endeavors to contribute to unconstrained public discourse and debate on relevant social, political and philosophical matters.

ISN welcomes all types of partnership and collaboration for fostering a knowledge-based society, organizing events, and framing new projects. If you are an academic institution, research institute andinvestigation team or group, a non-profitorganization, research center, research funder and you are willing to become a long-term partner for ISN's activities, please contact us on *irinstatunascendi@yahoo.com,* and we will get back to you as soon as we can.

More information about ISN, including information on the editorial board, membership information, and on all our initiatives can be found on the ISN website at

https://irinstatunascendi.wixsite.com/journal

Bibliographic information published by the Deutsche Nationalbibliothek
The Deutsche Nationalbibliothek lists this publication in the Deutsche
Nationalbibliografie; detailed bibliographic data are available on the Internet at
http://dnb.dnb.de.

Bibliografische Information der DeutschenNationalbibliothek
Die Deutsche Nationalbibliothek verzeichnet diese Publikation in der Deutschen
Nationalbibliografie; detaillierte bibliografische Daten sind im Internet über
http://dnb.d-nb.de abrufbar.

**In Statu Nascendi—Journal of Political Philosophy and International Relations
Vol. 6, No. 1 (2023)**

Stuttgart: *ibidem*-Verlag / *ibidem* Press

Erscheinungsweise: halbjährlich / Frequency: biannual

ISSN 2568-7638

ISBN-13: 978-3-8382-1782-6

Ordering Information:
PRINT: Subscription (two copies per year): €72.00/year (+ S&H: €4.00/year within Germany,
€7.00/year international). The subscription can be canceled at any time.

Single copy or back issue: €44.00/copy (+ S&H: €2.00 within Germany, €3.50 international).

E-BOOK: Subscription (two copies per year): €49.99/year and concurrent user. The subscription
can be canceled at any time. Access for libraries (no user limit): €150.00/year.

Single copy or back issue: €28.99/copy. Available via amazon.com or google.books.

For further information please visit www.ibidem.eu

In statu nascendi (Latin)

In the process of creation, emerging, becoming

Table of Contents

EDITORIAL

Dear Readers, Dear Publishers, Dear Colleagues,

Welcome to **Vol. 6, No. 1**, which accounts for our special edition, dedicated to **continental philosophy** and its incredible interdisciplinary link with quite a diversified collection of seemingly unrelated disciplines such as international relations theory, economics, literature, and culture. This volume accounts for an essential milestone in the process we launched in 2017, for it interlinks debates covered in our previous editions.

The work on this volume coincided with unprecedented global and regional turmoil, the ongoing global energy crisis, the preparations for the Ukrainian counteroffensive in the Russian war in Ukraine, and the outbreak of new tension in the Middle East, the Balkans (especially in north Kosovo), Ethiopia, Sudan, and between China and Taiwan. Various post-pandemic-related repercussions in macroeconomics, geopolitics, and society at large have reshaped the foundation of our everyday lives.

On top of that, BRICS countries started to become quite persistent about their idea of launching an alternative currency for global transactions that may supersede traditionally accepted forms of payment, and this is slowly but surely attracting other countries to join this organization to counterweight Western influence and power projection capacity. We most certainly have entered an unbelievable period of fast-paced changes in the field of new technologies, new software-fueled weapons advancements in aerospace engineering, new developments in artificial intelligence and robotics, and cutting-edge research in the biomedical sphere while ethics tries to catch up with these developments. Cryptocurrency, and NTF-blockchain technologies have accelerated in recent years beyond what the old-guard futurologists may have imagined some thirty years ago.

The journal *In Statu Nascendi* always wanted to understand and meet those new challenges head-on. This also will be the case with the **In Statu Nascendi Think Tank**, but let us first introduce to you this edition:

My humble self writes the first paper in our Continental Philosophy, Literature & Culture section. It is dedicated to the ethics of AI and robotics from a non-zoomorphic and non-anthropomorphic perspective. It is an attempt to reach a different conception of ethics in AI and robotics that emphasizes the importance of the vulnerability of AI, the asymmetrical relations between humans and AI, and a general reconsideration of human and non-human entities' interactions based on an expanded environment of coexistence, while preserving the distinction between the living and the machine.

Subsequently, the second article is written by **Myron Vourakis**, who deliberates on the very complex, multidimensional, and very pressing issue of Gödel's incompleteness theorems as an example of scientific thinking that brings to the fore a unique fusion of the philosophy of mathematics and the philosophy of general science and technology. It is a proposition for scientific thinking beyond the limits of so-called formal logic, which also touches on the critical issue of technique.

The third article in this section belongs to **Artemis Papachristou,** who brings to the fore an incredible paper titled "God did not die; he was transformed into Big Data", which is a parallelism between the concept of Spinozian *conatus*, also known as *deus sive natura*, and the knowledge acquired from Big Data analysis. She works at the limits of Western classical metaphysics and the new trends in philosophy of the 21st century.

This article is followed by **Alma Dema & Risvan Tërshall**'s fascinating paper related to an inherent connection between folklore and culture ("E madhe gjëma e mëkatit, Tat Tanushi i Bubutimës"). This paper deals with the philosophy of literature and culture as well as theoretical linguistics through significant works of Balkan poetry and literature, mainly those of Mitrush Kuteli, and presents various forms of interconnection between folklore and oral, mythic, linguistic, and ethnographic culture.

The fifth paper in this section is by **Eriola Qafzezi**, who introduces us to the concept of "Hindered With(in) Hedges that Explores Hedging as Stylistic Devices Employed by Detective Writers: The Case of Agatha Christie in Translation into the Albanian Language", which relates to translation and, more specifically, the hedging as used in the translation of Agatha Christie into Albanian.

This article is followed by **Venera Russo**'s review of Will Durant's *The Story of Philosophy: The Lives and Opinions of the Greater Philosophers*—one of the most comprehensive academic reviews that *In Statu Nascendi* has published.

Our "Politics, Economy, and Theory of International Relations" section begins with the exceptionally fascinating and comprehensive piece dedicated to approaching regional conflicts through the prism of ontology *in statu nascendi*—the new compartmentalization of IR theory written by **Piotr Pietrzak**, who suggests a new way of approaching contemporary conflict by embracing much stronger ontological roots in an international relations theory that reinvigorates the pursuit of the truth about international relations.

This paper is followed by **Baba Seidu Abdul Rahman**, who offers us a remarkable opportunity to investigate the "Negative Impacts of Economic Globalization on Africa's Economy Through Regional Economic Integration. Tension in Sudan and the Role of South Africa and BRICS".

The third article in this section belongs to **Yunus Emre Özigci**, who dedicated his paper to explaining to us the intricateness of German foreign policy through the prism of the concept of Sonderweg, The Mittellage and the Mitteleuropa are phenomenologically reducible to interactional individuality and meaning ground in bracketing contents and judgments ascribed to them.

The fourth item in this section accounts for an interview with **Dr. Begüm Burak** on her creation process and her take on a number of sociopolitical developments in Turkey under Recep Tayyip Erdoğan. The interview was conducted before the devastating earthquakes and the 2023 elections, which is why it is so valuable from an empirical perspective.

Finally, you are offered a special treat, for the fourth and fifth pieces in this part account for fascinating book reviews by **Violeta Nikolova** on Peter Frankopan's *The Silk Roads: A New History of the World* (Alfred A. Knopf, 2019) and by **Dobromir Gyulev** on Peter Zeihan's *the End of the World Is Just the Beginning: Mapping the Collapse of Globalization*. First ed. New York NY: Harper Collins Publishers. (2022)

Thank you all for contributing to our project: In this respect, I would like to express my special gratitude to **Piotr Pietrzak,** editor-in-chief and one of the co-founders of *In Statu Nascendi*, who put his heart and soul into this project and assisted me with this project since the very beginning. Thank you for giving me this opportunity to co-edit this special edition. It was the adventure of a lifetime, a learning curve, and an eye-opener. We embarked upon it a few years ago and completed it with a solid collection of papers. We learned. We deliberated. We had lots of fun dealing with discovering the beauty of the creation process of every one of us. We made tons of friends throughout the process and will continue doing so in the decades to come.

Speaking of friends, the composition of this edition was possible thanks to the valuable suggestions of the members of the Editorial and Advisory Board: **Zoran Kojcic, Joseph Thomas Milburn, Marcin Grabowski, Stavros S. Panayiotou, Galina Raykova, Venera Russo, Magdalena Tomala, Bálint Tóth,** and **Krzysztof Żęgota.** Our initiative may change its profile, but our network is still expanding, and we will not give up on our dreams or aspirations.

My special thank you goes to **Artemis Papachristou** for her contribution to this volume and participation in the first interdisciplinary conference of *In Statu Nascendi* in 2019. She was the primary representative and connection with the New Center of Research and Practice in New York City. Thanks to her we invited some members of the New Center of Research and Practice to our conference, such as **Andrea Guisepe Ragno**, **Reza Negarestani**, **Anne Françoise Schmid,** and **Katerina Kolozova**, as well as many of their students. My thanks also go to **Myron Vourakis** for all the ideas we have exchanged through the years related to our shared passion for the philosophy of science, first in Paris and subsequently in Athens.

My next thank you is reserved for **Matthew Gill** for his exceptional support with various proofreading jobs over the last few years, his professionalism, his honest opinions, and, most importantly, for the breathtaking speed with which he usually responds. Thanks to Matthew, our communication with our readers has become more precise than it was in 2017 when we embarked on this journey. If you are a writer who needs some support with your papers or dissertations, I strongly recommend you contact him.

Our deepest thanks go to *Ibidem Press* and **Columbia University Press** for their fantastic cooperation. And to all of you, the readers, and the authors who contributed to this initiative for the last six years, without you, this whole initiative would be without any meaning.

Indeed, when it comes to meaning, we would like to inform you that our nonprofit is transitioning to a think tank, and that is why this special edition's main message was chosen to be *Finis Origine Pendet.* The End Depends Upon the Beginning; for more information in this respect, please see a short letter that is published in the last pages of this edition from the man who earned himself the right to call himself **Mr. In Statu Nascendi**.

Thank you for purchasing this volume.
We hope that you enjoy it.

Yours sincerely,

Koumparoudis Evangelos, Ph.D.
Co-editor of this volume, and a Member of the
Editorial Board of *In Statu Nascendi.—Journal of
Political Philosophy and International Relations*

Part I:
Continental Philosophy &
Literature &
Culture

Koumparoudis Evangelos

Ethics of AI and Robotics from a Non-Antropomorphic and Non-Zoomorphic Perspective

Introduction

We move the history backward, to the point that Argonauts were approaching Crete and attacked by the first probably robot Talos.[1] Talos was created by Hephaestus and was given to king Minos of Crete as a gift. Talos was a human-like, let it say robot made of bronze, responsible for eliminating all the possible threats to the kingdom of Crete. The right imposition of the law was also one of his responsibilities. Talos while strolling (or fling) around Crete had together with him all the legislation carved in stones. The end of Talos came during the battle between the Argonauts and Cretans. The sorceress Medea in a way controlled Talos "mind" and managed to remove a rivet from his foot, which was the only way to drain away the life fluid (Ihor) running in his "vein." What can we derive from this mythological narration? Firstly, the issue of anthropomorphism in robotics and AI is very old, Talos was not only human-like but as it seems had a form of "sentience" and also a kind of circularity system. The other equally important feature is that the imposition of the law and the keeping of the legislation are assigned to a machine. Contemporary ethical debates concerning AI and robotics deal with the possible elimination of the risk when a demanding task is performed not by a human but through an automatic or semi-automatic algorithmic procedure. Face, voice, and DNA recognition of a suspect at the borders is one of the many examples that we could give. There are also plenty of applications and programs used for military reasons surveillance systems, self-diving armed drones, etc.,[2] The third feature is that mythological and cultural representations of the literature, spectacle, and mass media, usually attribute

---

1 Oliver Korn et.al., "Perspectives on Social Robots: From the Historic Background to an Experts View on Future Developments," Conference: 11th PErvasive Technologies Related to Assistive Environments Conference, At: Corfu, Greece, June 2018, DOI: 10.1145/3197768.3197774.

2 Simon Peter van Rysewyk and Matthijs Pontier, A Hybrid Bottom-Up and Top-Down Approach to Machine Medical Ethics: Theory and Data, in *Machine Medical Ethics* ed. Simon Peter van Ryswyk and Matthijs Pontier (Switzerland: Springer International,2015) 93-110.

characteristics of a possible dystopian even future, where robots and AI will take the driving seat and be responsible for not only decision-making but the regulation of political and social life.[3]

This paper examines the ethics of AI and Robotics (although today everything tends to be meshed up as AI ethics), from a non-anthropomorphic and zoomorphic perspective. The first term has a threefold meaning, firstly the fact that we approach other non-human entities starting from the fact that may have human characteristics, like shape, possibly face, cognition, speech, self-moving capacity, etc., therefore could act as moral agents. Secondly that humans tend to empathize with non-human entities mainly social robots used as companion pets, or in the care of the elderly, for sexual pleasure, etc., there are cases in which people react when for example someone tries to kick or harm a robot, or if we speak for sexual pleasure the empathetic relationship may turn to intimacy and even love. Thirdly, AI and robots are seen from an anthropocentric point of view, in which the human has the leading role and AI and robotics in under his servitude, equal to a slave. Zoomorphism has a double essence either it refers to the conception of social mainly robots as companion species, having characteristics similar to an animal or a pet, or as applications and machines used for exploitation (not as slaves) but in a way closer to the mass industry of domestic animals. In the first section we will deal with an overview of the ethical theories proposed for AI and robotics, deontological and utilitarian mainly after Luciano Floridi and J.W.Sanders, Sullins etc., In the second section we will expand the debate to medical AI ethics in which we will explore the above theories on an applied level mainly after Oliver Bendel, William Andrew Drust. In the third section we seek to unravel the issue of animality with zoomorphism of AI by analyzing the work of Jacques Derrida, Giorgio Agamben and Rosi Braidotti. In the fourth section we emphasize how we could surpass the ethical theories with an anthropomorphic (and anthropocentric) background as well as zoomorphic and propose an alternative that speaks for a possible vulnerability of AI and robotics and radical alterity after the work of Mark Coeckelbergh and Nicola Liberati and Shoji Nagataki etc., In the final section we will present and compare at least three theories these of Floridi's Inforgs, Braidotti "Life Itself" and J.Parvianinen and J.Turja abiozoomorphism, all these theories relate to either an expansion of the relation between the living and the machine

---

3   Vasilis Galanos, "Teratological Aspects in Artificial Intelligence and Robotics: From Monstrus Threats to Rorschach Opportunities", in *Monsters, Monstrosities, and the Monstrous in Culture and Society* ed. Diego Compagna and Stefanie Steinhart (Delaware: Vernon Press, 2020), 101-129.

in a place of mutual co-existence or underline the fact that the distinction between the living and the machine is still valid.

Overview of the Ethical Theories Utilitarian and Deontological Ethics

As we mentioned in the introduction, there are many AI and robotics ethical theories proposed, one of them is consequalism, in rough words is means that ethics should be based on the consequences of an action, and in our case the consequences performed either by an algorithm or a robot. A subcategory of consequalism is rule utilitarian ethics. A rule should be followed and then we attain the best results. The results may refer to a general good/harm output and concern members of the ethical community (humans, animals, and non-human entities). Accountability for future consequences should also be part of the rule. The combinational capacity of the algorithm is relevant to the rule. If for example, we speak for a weak capacity then we could implement a rule with some practical limits of utility, if is higher anticipatory or indented consequences can also be part of the rule.[4] Contrary to utilitarian consequalism, deontology or deontological ethics seeks to explore the issue of moral agency in AI and robotics. These theories and their supporters usually have a Kantian basis. This basis refers to direct and indirect duties that a machine should have. Direct moral standing is deeply connected with anthropomorphism. Anthropomorphism as we pose has to do mainly with the empathetic feelings of humans to robots or better non-human entities, in a manner is connected to possible intrinsic properties that robots may have (although they do not exactly have) like speech, cognition etc., and deserve direct moral standing.

Floridi and Sanders in their 2004 paper,[5] propose an ethical theory from a non-anthropocentric view. This theory divides moral agents (class A) which are entities with direct moral action and moral patients (class P) which are the receivers of a moral action. Between A and P, there are at least five logical relationships, three unrealistic, and two others remaining. The first alternative is that A and P are equal, therefore a moral agent can be a moral patient and vice versa. The second alternative is that A can be a subset for P, in this case some entities can be moral agents, but some others cannot. Floridi and

---

4   Simon Peter van Rysewyk and Matthijs Pontier, "A Hybrid Bottom-Up and Top-Down Approach to Machine Medical Ethics: Theory and Data", in *Machine Medical Ethics* ed. Simon Peter van Rysewyk and Matthijs Pontier (Switzerland: *Springer International*, 2015), 93-110.

5   Luciano Floridi and J.W. Sanders, "On the Morality of artificial agents", *Minds and Machines*, No. 14(2004): 349-79.

Sanders, speak for a post-environmentalist approach that does not only account for animals or the environment but is expanded to corporations as direct moral agents and other non-human entities like algorithms and robots (MENACE, Webott, Futurist Thermostat, Smart Paint) or organizations which can serve as moral patients (or agents). They implement an analysis based on levels of abstraction (LoA). LoA: " *is a finite but non-empty set of observables, which are expected to be the building blocks in a theory characterized by their very choice* ". The authors give us the three criteria of a right LoA: a) Interactivity between the agent and its environment, b) Autonomy which means that the agents can change state without direct response to an interaction and c) Adaptability which refers to the capacity of an agent to change the transition rules by which it changes state during an interaction. According to the level of abstraction, an entity can or cannot be considered an agent or patient.

Sullins in his 2006 paper[6] speaks about the three presuppositions for a robot to be a moral agent, autonomy, intentionality, and responsibility. The concept of autonomy is used in an engineering sense when a robot or a machine is not used by direct control of another agency. The level of moral agency that we can ascribe to a machine is relevant to its ability to perform tasks and achieve goals. The intentional way that a robot can act refers to a possible beneficial or harmful result, after a moral calculation of these acts then a robot can be considered a moral agent. Finally, responsibility is about the possible responsibility that a robot as a moral agent can carry, for example a social robot responsible for caring for the elderly.

Medical AI and Robotics

Medical AI and Robotics can expand in many fields, from electronic health records up to specialized algorithms in diagnostics and epidemiology, robotic surgery or robotically assisted medical praxis and care or issues that refer to big data from biomarkers, omic revolution, and the advancements in synthetic biology. Additionally, information and disinformation in medical platforms and the changes in the doctor and patient relationship in the information age. Of course, the scope of this paper is not to analyze these issues in greater detail for obvious reasons, this would demand much more pages and time but many of those ideas can be found in Evangelos Koumparoudis *Medicine in the Post Consumerist Society*, Ibidem, 2023. In any case, we could

---

6   John P. Sullins, "When is a robot a moral agent," *International Review of Information Ethics* No. 6 (2016): 23-30.

proceed to a bibliographical and philosophical overview of all these issues listed above.

Electronic health records are used to a greater extent today for the management of hospitals and care units up to private medical practice. They can be used for patients' medical history recording something quite simple, but with greater algorithmic and (bio)statistical analysis for personalized and precision medicine for example personal files of drug administration, and personalized interventions, etc., This kind of personalization can be assisted by the extraordinary progress in omic technologies[7] (genomics, metabolomics, proteomics, biomarkers), something that leads us to rethink the usual classification of a disease based on symptoms and nosology and speak for classification on a molecular level.[8] From a telescopic view, these data can be used for the reduction of health care expenses, and elimination of risk, but also can be a perfect material for the state, big pharma corporations, insurance companies, and various policymakers, for a new public health policy or their next campaign for promotion of a new drug or therapy. The latter opens the very serious issue of privacy; consent and ethical use of medical data, furthermore is the danger of the patient becoming a statistical unit and so we could speak for treating *a patient* in general and not *this particular* patient[9].

The concept of personalized and precision medicine (more precision) has been enriched by the use of algorithmic processes in diagnostics and epidemiology. There are many methods for data analysis we will briefly enumerate some of them with the respected bibliography concerning their medical effect. A) Clustering in phylogenetic and microarray analysis [10]b) Linear Regression on diabetes mellitus and cancer[11] c) Logistic Regresion on iatrogenic

---

7   A detailed overview, both of the history of the rise of omics data and the methods of their analysis and the associated problems is found in the work of C. Manzoni, D. Kia, J. Vandrovcova, J. Hardy, N. Wood, P. Lewis, & R. Ferrari, "Genome, transcriptome and proteome: the rise of omics data and their integration in biomedical sciences," *Briefings In Bioinformatics*, no. 19 (2016): 286-302.

8   National Research Council. *2011. Toward Precision Medicine: Building a Knowledge Network for Biomedical Research and a New Taxonomy of Disease* (Washington, DC: The National Academies Press, p. 12.

9   Gungov, Alexander. 2018. *Patient Safety: The Relevance of Logic In Medical Care*, Stuttgart: ibidem Press, p. 60.

10   Alizadeh, MB Eisen, RE Davis, C Ma, IS, Lossos , A. Rosenwald , et al, " Distinct types of diffuse large B-cell lymphoma identified by gene expression profiling, "*Nature* , no.11 (2000):403-503.

11   M.Reed, J.Huang, R.Brand, I.Graetz, R.Neugebauer, B.Fireman, et al., "Implementation of an outpatient electronic health record and emergency department visits, hospitalizations, and office visits among patients with diabetes, "*JAMA, no.*310 (2013):1060-65. T Yuasa, S Urakami, S Yamamoto, J Yonese, K Nakano , M Kodaira, et al., "Tumor size is

diseases out of the operation room[12] d) Epigenetics on DNA methylation[13] e) Deep Learing on dermatological cancer, Google Flu trends, and Retinal Disease.[14]

According to Oliver Bendel, robotics in medical care could be divided into at least four categories a) Surgical Robots b) Therapeutic robots c) Nursing robots d) Sex robots. Surgical robots (ZEUS, da Vinci, Amigo, Cyber-Knife) can usually perform surgery under the control of a surgeon, but there are opportunities for telemedical use even possibly autonomous. The biggest advantage is that they can be more accurate in incisions, drilling, or penetration according to the form of the surgery, although da Vinci, seems to be responsible for neuron traumas during mainly surgeries of the urinary system. The biggest disadvantage is the cost and the specialized training needed for performing such kinds of surgeries. [15]Although that is quite similar to laparoscopic surgery, the camera in that case is incorporated in the surgical system and does not need the direction of the surgeon or an assistant, of course, there are always nurses, anesthesiologists, and in most cases the doctor who uses the robot from a certain distance. The use of the camera, contrary to laparoscopic surgery on the one hand demands the participation of fewer people, on the other permits better focusing and resolution, also the robotic arm can eliminate tremors of the surgeon and other possible complications such as extensive bleeding, etc., One of the possible disadvantages is that it creates a quite disembodying experience to the operator since everything is under the mediation of the camera and the screen. [16] There are serious ethical questions linked to the use of robotic surgical systems according to Bendel[17]:

---

a potential predictor of response to tyrosine kinase inhibitors in renal cell cancer, *"Urology,* no77 (2001):831-5.

12   DC Peterson, C Martin-Gill, FX Guyette, AZ Tobias, CE McCarthy, ST Harrington , et al., "Outcomes of medical emergencies on commercial airline flights," *N Engl J Med,* no.368(2011):2075-83.

13   AQ Fu, DP Genereux, R Stoger, CD Laird, M Stephens, "Statistical inference of transmission fidelity of DNA methylation patterns over somatic cell divisions in mammals," Ann Appl Stat, no.4(2010), p. 871-92.

14   Simon Pollett, W. John Boscardin, Eduardo Azziz-Baumgartner, Yeny O. Tinoco, Giselle Soto, Candice Romero, Jen Kok, Matthew Biggerstaff, Cecile Viboud, George W. Rutherford, "Evaluating Google Flu Trends in Latin America: Important Lessons for the Next Phase of Digital Disease Detection, *"Clinical Infectious Diseases,* no. 64 (2017):34-41. Cf. V Gulshan. et al., "Development and validation of a deep learning algorithm for detection of diabetic retinopathy in retinal fundus photographs, *"JAMA*(2016).

15   Cf. William Andrew Drust, "Embodied Care, Spatiality and Ethics of Robotic Surgery," *Master dissertation,* (Drexel University, 2015).

16   Ibid.

17   Oliver Bendel, "Surgical Therapeutic, Nursing and Sex Robots in Machine and Information Ethics," in *Machine Medical Ethics* ed. Simon Peter van Rysewyk and Matthijs *Pontier* (Switzerland: Springer International,2015), 23-37.

Should the surgical robot have moral skills, and if so, what skills? • *Should it follow defined duties only (deontological ethics), or should it be able to estimate the consequences of its actions (consequentialist ethics) and weigh the pros and cons in decision-making?* • *Do other normative models apply, for instance, a materialistic concept?* • *How autonomous should it be?* Therapeutic robots such as Paro and Keepon, according again to Bendel make us consider: *Must therapeutic robots implement certain therapeutic concepts and models?* • *Do they have to consider patient needs and parameters?* • *How to handle that the robot normally will not be able to adequately respond to uncertainty and worries?* The use of robots for elders with mobility problems or dementia raises questions about the different roles of the caregiver, the care receiver, and robots in care praxis. Can the human-machine interaction supplement the embodying experience created by the nurse when he touches or lifts the patient and the oral communication and thus interaction and socialization, which may also include games or songs for maintaining the verbal capacity of elders? Is the interaction between the nurse and the patient an interplay between two living bodies, and thus more profound, while robots can provide only more relational autonomy to the patient (actions which are linked to the affordances of the agent's environment)[18] Sex robots may have the shape of a woman, called fembots, or of both genders even transgender. They are usually made of medical silicone and during this time it can resemble an almost perfect android. During the sexual act, they can respond or can change modes of activity to pleasure their partner. The ethical debate consists of the autonomous agency that they may take for example force the partner to an action, or refuse an action, etc., Furthermore, if empathy or even intimacy is possible and under which circumstances and consequently if a partner stops the use of the robot or harms it, etc., this action should be considered as something with more ethical burden than other social robots? Should the latter be considered as attributing extreme anthropomorphic agency to sex robots, over the requirements that Sullins proposes autonomy, intentionality, and responsibility?

Deborah Lupton[19] research focuses on the patients and caregivers who interact on digital platforms. In these cases, they share information about the subjective feeling of their condition and either act as health seekers for more advice on their issues, or the place of caregivers to promote their services.

---

18   Jaana Parviainen and Jari Pirhonen, "Vulnerable Bodies in Human-Robot Interactions: Embodiment as Ethical Issue in Robot Care for the Elderly," *Transformations Issue*, no. 27 (2017).

19   Deborah Lupton, "The commodification of patient opinion: the digital patient experience economy in the age of big data," *Sociology of Health and Ilness* 36, no.5 (2014): 856-69.

She also speaks about digitally engaged patients, who measure parameters from wearable devices and electronic health records; consequently, they become more knowledgeable about their condition. These actions are encapsulated by the term "digital patent experience economy," and are also linked with what Lupton calls presumption (the combination of content consumption and production in web 2.0). This information has in the first place no real value, but it can be exploited by policymakers and big pharma for promotion.

Marion Ball and Jennifer Lillis describe at least three characteristics of modern e-health consumers.[20] First, they seek convenience. Second, they wish to have control of their health or at least play a significant role in it, so they seek internet resources to supplement the information they receive from their physicians. Third, they demand to have a wide variety of choices for every service and product they require. Ball also refers to the administrative efficiency that computerization in health care delivered, like the reduction of waste of time and paper, since all the necessary documents are shared directly in a digital form, the improvement of outcomes through online prescription systems, and cost reduction by the use of simple automatic processes. She also makes some propositions for the doctor-patient relationship in the information age to follow a better path. Ball suggests that physicians recommend appropriate websites to their patients to prevent them from relying on faulty medical information; for example, in the US, reputable medical websites display the HONcode logo. Doctors' recommendations are seen as the most important factor in building consumer trust in online information.

Miriam McMullan proposes three scenarios concerning the doctor-patient relationship in the information age.[21] The first scenario is health professional-centered. The doctor may feel that his knowledge and authority are threatened; thus, he responds defensively and asserts his expert opinion. The second scenario is more patient-centered; in this scenario, the doctor and patient collaborate. In the third scenario, doctors recommend websites to their patients to educate them so they can filter the information gained from their web searches.

---

20   Marion J. Ball and Jennifer Lillis, "E-Health: transforming the physician/patient relationship," *International Journal of Medical Informatics* 61, (2001):1-10.

21   McMullan, Miriam. 2006. "Patients using the Internet to obtain health information: How this affects the patient–health professional relationship," *Patient Education and Counselling* 63. 2006: 24-28.

The Concept of Animality with Zoomorphism

In this section, we will try to explore the relationship between humans and the animal, not in their general essence for example the interaction of a human with a pet or a domestic animal concerning only its breeding, but we will try to expand it in a broader sense to cases that a human can or cannot adopt characteristics usually attributed to animals. As we briefly exposed in the introduction the concept of Zoomorphism in AI (and Robotics) either refers to the conception of a social robot as a pet having autonomy, self-moving capacity, etc., or more crucially cases in which robots are equated by a slave. Is this position of a slave when we first consider a human being similar to a form of life that could be taken as inferior, closer to an animal or animality? Furthermore, the advancements in genetic engineering and synthetic biology make us rethink the concept of the organism and the species or the living in general, for example, which is the standing o a genetically modified organism or even more of a cloned animal if we think of Dolly the sheep? We will expose briefly the ideas of Derrida, mainly after his *The Animal Therefore I am*, Agamben's *Homo Sacer*, and Braidotti's the *Posthuman*.

Derrida [22]starts from the concept of nudity or nakedness, the image of a naked human being embarrassed in the eyes of a strolling cat in the room. This nakedness has at least two essences first it refers to clothing as a purely human cultural property as it is the mourning, the tear, the burial of the dead, the gift, etc., contrary to completely naked animals if we do not account for their fur. The second essence has a mainly biblical and mythological basis, for example, Adam and Eve were naked in heaven, before the coming of Evil before the bite of the apple they seem to be in a harmonious co-living with the other animals, but since the evil came to the covering of their bodies, the becoming dressed is deeply linked with that major embarrassment. The other similar mythological representation is that of naked Prometheus, the one who brought the fire and knowledge to the humans is doomed naked, bondage to a rock and an eagle devours gradually his liver. Derrida continues by supporting that all the philosophical theories from Rene Descartes to Kant, Nietzsche, Heidegger, Levinas, and Lacan made a distinction between the rational animal the *zoon logon exon* the human being or *Anthropos*, and the animals that cannot respond and have no speaking capacity and, in some cases, no rational capacity at least in the grade that a human has. Descartes, for example, conceives an animal close to an animal machine because of its self-moving capacity and behavior one of the first let it say equations of an animal to

---

22   Derrida, Jacques. 2008. *The Animal Therefore I am*. New York: Fordam University Press.

a machine and a preliminary zoomorphism that we could speak about. Kant related human cognition with Ratio (*Reason, Vernuft*), consequently morality can be based mainly on Ratio, then the animals since they do not have such an intrinsic property, they do not have direct moral standing, and then humans should follow only deontological ethics concerning their behavior to them. Nietzsche in his *Genealogy of Morals* refers to the domestication of animals. Heidegger proceeds to the ontological distinction between the entity (Dasein) which can ascribe meaning to his life and the other entities including animals that cannot. Levinas, in his theory of the trace as the trace of the Other, refers purely to humans (the orphan, the widow, the poor) and not in any case to animals, although Derrida makes some references to the naked eye of the animal resembling the depths of the sight of the Other (something close to a human animality). Lacan (Derrida refers to Autobiography and the autobiographical animal that a human can be, thus leaving written traces or traces linked to psychology-psychoanalysis) supports that an animal can never eliminate or erase these kinds of traces. Derrida poses the question, coming from the tradition of utilitarianism and Jeremy Bentham, if the animals, at last, do not have a rational capacity if they can suffer. Based on that speaks about the mass exploitation of the animal industry and genetic engineering. His second task is the deconstruction of the conception of the word animal, based on the philosophical tradition just described above by saying that is a just mot (word in French) and introduces the term *animot. Animot* is: *Neither a species nor a gender nor an individual, it is an irreducible living multiplicity of mortals, and rather than a double clone or a portmanteau word, a sort of monstrous hybrid, a chimera waiting to be put to death by its Bellerophon.* [23]

Agamben in his *Homo Sacer,*[24] describes a form of life that is neither *bios* that is a human life with purpose *nor Zoe* that is "life" common in humans and animals, but a state close to animality and is called bare life. The example that he gives for the contemporary biopolitical society is the collection of biometric data in control points like borders or airports which is similar to the tattooing of the Jews during the holocaust. The holocaust itself is one of the most common examples of Agamben, in the Nazi camps, the prisoners were at a place of second-class citizens or inferior without actual political rights, something similar to the state of the immigrants at the borders waiting for asylum in various camps. Homo Sacer comes from ancient Rome to describe someone who commits a crime and then he can be killed, without any

---

23   Ibid., 47.
24   Agamben, Gorgio. 1998. *Homo Sacer.* Stanford, Calif.: Stanford University Press.

consequences for his killer, this is the form of bare life that Agamben describes. In his, *The Open Man and the Animal*[25], strives his theory in the relationship between humans and animals to evolutionary biology and of course the issue of social Darwinism, the anthropological machine of evolution, and the examples of the ape-man that becomes homo sapiens having the capacity to speak and thus differentiate from the animal state, although Agamben still speaks for the bare life that is in the borderline zone of animality. He continues with paradigms from the Heiddegerian notion of boredom, the existential position to be always in suspense something prevailing in our post-industrial (post-consumerist) society. Agamben states[26]:

Being, the world, and the open are not, however, something other for the animal environment and life: they are nothing but the interruption and capture of the living being's relationship with its disinhibitor. The open is nothing but a grasping of the animal not open. Man suspends his animality and, in this way, opens a "free and empty" zone in which life is captured and a-bandoned {ab-bandonata} in a zone of exception. At this point, two scenarios are possible from Heidegger's perspective: (a) posthistorical man no longer preserves his own animality as undisclosable, but rather seeks to take it on and govern it by means of technology; (b) man, the shepherd of being, appropriates his own concealedness, his own animality, which neither remains hidden nor is made an object of mastery, but is thought as such, as pure abandonment.

Braidotti in her *The Posthuman*[27] speaks for the post-anthropocentric ontological gap that was created on the notion of species hierarchy of a single common standard of "Man". Anthopos and anthropocentricity model the ideals of masculinity, the perfectly functioning body, normality, youth, and health and excludes the non-masculine, non-normal, etc., Anthrpos has an oedipal relationship with animals, since it is permitted to have access to all kind of bodies including animals. Derrida uses the term carno-phallocentricsm to describe this relationship. Braidotti refers to the Donna Haraway's Manifesto of Companion species in which she describes the relationship of loyalty between dogs and humans, this kind of relationship could be expanded to non-human entities like AI and robots. The animals are no more the satisfying systems of human self-projection and aspirations, thus a "zo-ontology" has to be created as a code system. The second important is the

---

25   Agamben, Giorgio. 2020. *The Open Man and the Animal.* Stanford, Calif.: Stanford University Press.
26   Ibid., 79.
27   Braidotti, Rosi. 2013. *The Posthuman.* Cambridge UK: Polity Press.

exploitation of the animals as labor and market forces, a term encapsulated as "zooproletatiat." Is there something similar with the use of robots as a possible "robotproletariat"? In the post-industrial society, the informatization and robotization of production is something fundamental, beyond the apparent problem of replacing human workers with machines in different tasks, there is the problem of possible exploitation of robots equal to a slave, from this zoomorphic perspective. Rosi Braidotti criticizes the anthropocentric and anthropomorphic conception of the *person* which privileges humans over other non-human living entities. This critique does not abandon the idea of cumulative terrestrial evolution. She calls us to rethink human life (*Zoe*, in her words) as a complex ensemble of functions, relations, and processes of a system of evolution that goes in parallel with other technological systems. These systems are characterized by auto-organization, auto-poiesis, and interdependence.

Vulnerability and Phenomenological Perspectives in AI and Robotics

Anthropomorphism and second-grade zoomorphism, are responsible for the debate over the direct and indirect or relational approaches to the ethics of AI and Robotics. The possibility of a direct moral standing of AI and robots was given in our first section. There seems to be a gap between the two approaches. Mark Coeckelbergh in his *Should We Treat Teddy Bear 2.0 as a Kantian Dog? Four Arguments for the Indirect Moral Standing of Personal Social Robots, with Implications for Thinking About Animals and Humans*[28], tries to provide a solution for the indirect moral standing based on Kantianism, Levinas, and Dewey. He uses the example of the Kantian Dog to expand the ethical relation to non-human entities. Kant speaks clearly about direct and indirect moral standing over animals. Briefly, since the animal is not rational, human beings as rational entities have only duties, the duties to respect and protect the animals. Coeckelbergh provides us with four premises in his expanded approach: *1. If a human who would do something bad to the robot would be seen by other humans as having a bad personality, as being a bad person (in virtue ethics language: not virtuous, or as being in danger of doing bad things to humans; 2. If the human user has a (one-directional) relationship with the robot and has developed feelings of attachment and empathy towards the robot; 3. If the robot is part of a human–the robot joint action and collaboration and it is desirable or necessary that this collaboration continues; 4. If there is*

---

28   Coeckelbergh, M. Should We Treat Teddy Bear 2.0 as a Kantian Dog? Four Arguments for the Indirect Moral Standing of Personal Social Robots, with Implications for Thinking About Animals and Humans. *Minds & Machines* 31, 337–360 (2021).

serious doubt about the robot's moral standing on the part of the user(s). Coeckelbergh continues with some aspects of Levinasian philosophy, based on indirect moral standing with possible application to AI ethics. According to Levinas there is always an ethical relationship with the Other which is not symmetrical and reciprocal. Am always more responsible than the Other, I have to respond to the Other's appeal to me in a responsible way. So, in this case, we do not give moral standing due to the intrinsic properties of the Other (in our case a robot) but the encounter is a kind of experience that creates and appeals to my feelings, the Other always interrupts me, and asks for a response. Thus, the relationship turns from other-based (intrinsic properties) to Other-directed. At last, Dewey speaks for moral imagination. The moral imagination broadens our ethical horizon to situations that demand moral standing not in present but in a different time and place. By this approach, we can expand our feelings and our standing to all the possible relations that we could have with other non-human entities elsewhere in the future.

Nicola Liberati and Shoji Nagataki[29], approach human vulnerability from its historical sense. They refer to all the obstacles that humans faced during their evolution, threats by diseases, animals, nature, etc., From this starting point, the fact that humans are vulnerable and fragile, by the use of Levinas, Sartre, Merleau Ponty, and Habermas, propose the idea of creation of vulnerable robots so as a non-anthropomorphic ethical relationship be established. They provide us with at least two examples of vulnerable robots, the one is the trash collector which, while collecting trash motivates the human participants to the trash collection to collect more trash, and the robot that can recognize human arousal before sexual action. In these cases, the vulnerable robots in a manner shape our moral standing in a place of co-existence and dwelling.

Humans and non-living entities: Flordi, Braidotti, Parviannen and Turja

The human and non-entities interaction, beyond the ethical aspects that we exposed above, lead us to reconsider the concept of life, death, and as well as the general co-existence of human and non-human entities in a form of an extended environment. Floridi[30] speaks for such an extended environment that contains humans, smartphones, tablets and various forms of robots and

---

29   Liberati, N., Nagataki, S. Vulnerability under the gaze of robots: relations among humans and robots. AI & Soc 34, 333–342 (2019). https://doi.org/10.1007/s00146-018-0849-1.

30   Floridi Luciano. 2013. *The Philosophy of Information.* Oxford England: Oxford University Press.

cyborgs. These are inforgs of an infosphere. The infosphere contains information rather than matter and has as its main rules of preservation are based in Shannon's information theory. Braidotti[31], speaks in her theory about the reconsideration of zoe or life. Zoe turns to a form of "Life itself", in which emerging biopower and the new vitalist materialism of genetic engineering and medicine, all the mediated aspects of life and death through the information systems and robotics making human life dependent on them, but also forms of bodily governance such as DNA recoding and surveillance, or forms of body subjugation such as specialized diets, medical interventions to the body for reshaping all mediated by the mass spectacle, create the conditions of o a form of life that balances in the borderline between the living and the dead. Finally, Parviannen and Turja[32], trying to pass beyond anthropomorphism and zoomorphism in AI and Robotics, propose the term abiozoomorphism which proposes that the distinction between the living and the non-living entities is still valid while maintaining the animal-like qualities in social robotics. They also propose four premises for not treating social robots as companion species: a) People Look for Intrinsic Motivation from Their Interactional Counterparts b) The Former Premise Is the Reason That People Are Prone to View Robots as Having Traits and Intentions of a Living Entity c) Humans and Animals Are Driven by Their Intrinsic Motivations d) Robots Are Not Capable of Having Intrinsic Motivation.

Conclusions

The purpose of this paper was to present the ethics of AI and Robotics from a non-anthropomorphic and zoomorphic perspective. For this reason, we proceded to an overview of the basic theories concerning AI ethics, deontological and utilitarian ethics, our basic assumption was if AI and robots deserve direct moral standing. This was achieved by the non-anthropocentric theory of Floridi and Sander who propose an ethical theory based on Low Levels of Abstraction as well as Sullins who speaks for the three presuppositions of a robot to be a moral agent, autonomy, intentionality, and responsibility. We chose medical AI and robotics for the application of these theories, for two reasons first that medical AI and Robotics are forms of robotics that

---

31   Rosi Braidotti, "The Politics of Life Itself" and "New Ways of Dying", in Coole Diana H and Samantha Frost. 2010. *New Materialisms: Ontology Agency and Politics.* Durham NC: Duke University Press, 201-219.

32   Parviainen, J. & Turja, T. 2021. "Toward Abiozoomorphism in Social Robotics? Discussion of a New Category between Mechanical Entities and Living Beings." *Journal of Posthuman Studies* 5(2): 15–168. doi: 10.5325/jpoststud.5.2.0150.

are directly relevant with a more crucial role in the human-machine interaction since it relates to health and health care but also in some cases mainly in surgical robotics either we speak for intervention and is quite different for a technology to have an effect on the human body or for the possible quantification of the self through the collection of biometric data from wearable devices and Electronic Health Records or more especially after the rise of the omic revolution and the danger of becoming a statistical unit. We continued with the changes in the doctor-patient relationship in the information age, the use of medical platforms, and the possible disinformation in them by proposing some solutions mainly based on the work of Lupton, Ball, and Lillies, McMullan Then we tried to explore forms of human life that are closer to an animal state with zoomorphism following the work of Derrida, Agamben, and Braidotti. Far from classical utilitarian and deontological ethics, we insisted that there are also forms for indirect moral standing of the AI and Robots, voices like these of Coeckelbergh, Liberatti and Nagataki, propose theories based on Kantianism and phenomenology for the possibility of vulnerable robotic Other and the ethics of alterity and radical asymmetry in which it is the Other-robots which shapes or moral standing and not the human or the robots with some intrinsic properties that act as moral agent. The relation then turns from other-based to Other-directed. Finally, we exposed some views for a general reconsideration of human-non-human entities interaction on a basis of an expanded environment of co-existence like the infosphere or Floridi. In addition, we emphasized the new forms of vitalistic materialism and the idea of "Life Itself" using the work of Braidotti. We closed our last section with the idea of "abiozomorphism" proposed by Parvianinen and Turja which speaks for the still valid distinction between living and non-living entities.

Bibliography

Agamben, Gorgio. 1998. *Homo Sacer.* Stanford, Calif.: Stanford University Press.

Agamben, Giorgio. 2020. *The Open Man and the Animal* (Stanford, Calif.: Stanford University Press.

Alizadeh, MB Eisen, RE Davis, C Ma, IS Lossos, A. Rosenwald, "Distinct types of diffuse large B-cell lymphoma identified by gene expression profiling," *Nature.* No.11 (2000):403-503.

Ball, Marion J. and Jennifer Lillis, "E-Health: transforming the physician/patient relationship," *International Journal of Medical Informatics* 61, (2001):1-10.

Bendel, Oliver, "Surgical Therapeutic, Nursing and Sex Robots in Machine and Information Ethics," in *Machine Medical Ethics* ed. Simon Peter van Rysewyk and Matthijs

Braidotti, Rosi. 2013. *The Posthuman.* Cambridge: Polity.

Coole, Diana H. and Samantha Frost. 2010. *New Materialisms : Ontology Agency and Politics.* Durham NC: Duke University Press, 201-219.

Coeckelbergh, Mark, "Should We Treat Teddy Bear 2.0 as a Kantian Dog? Four Arguments for the Indirect Moral Standing of Personal Social Robots, with Implications for Thinking About Animals and Humans," *Minds and Machines* , no.31 (2021): 337-360.

Derrida, Jacques. 2008. *The Animal Therefore I am.* New York: Fordam University Pres.

Drust, William Andrew. 2015. *Embodied Care, Spatiality and Ethics of Robotic Surgery,* Master dissertation. Drexel University.

Floridi, Luciano and JW Sanders, "On the Morality of artificial agents," *Minds and Machines,* No. 14(2004): 349-79.

Floridi, Luciano. 2013. *Philosophy of Information.* Oxford: Oxford University Press.

Fu, AQ, DP Genereux, R. Stoger, CD Laird, M. Stephens, "Statistical inference of transmission fidelity of DNA methylation patterns over somatic cell divisions in mammals," *Ann Appl Stat,* no.4(2010):871-92.

Galanos, Vasilis, "Teratological Aspects in Artificial Intelligence and Robotics : From Monstrus Threats to Rorschach Opportunities," in *Monsters, Monstrosities, and the Monstrous in Culture and Society* ed. Diego Compagna and Stefanie Steinhart. Delaware: Vernont,2020) Press, 2020.

Gungov, Alexander. 2017. *Patient Safety: The Relevance Of Logic In Medical Care.* Sttugard: ibidem Press.

Gulshan, V, L. Peng, M. Coram, et al., Development and Validation of a Deep Learning Algorithm for Detection of Diabetic Retinopathy in Retinal Fundus Photographs. JAMA. 2016; 316(22):2402–2410. doi:10.1001/jama.2016.17216.

Korn, Oliver et.al., "Perspectives on Social Robots: From the Historic Background to an Experts View on Future Developments," *Conference: 11th PErvasive Technologies Related to Assistive Environments Conference,* At: Corfu, Greece, June 2018, DOI: 10.1145/3197768.3197774.

Liberati, Nicola and Shoji Nagataki, "Vulnerability under the gaze of robots: relations among humans and robots," *AI&SOCIETY* , 2018.

Lupton, Deborah. 2014. "The commodification of patient opinion: the digital patient experience economy in the age of big data," *Sociology of Health & Illness* Vol. 36 No. 6 2014 ISSN 0141-9889, pp. 856–869, doi: 10.1111/1467-9566.12109.

Manzoni, C, D. Kia, J. Vandrovcova, J. Hardy, N. Wood, P. Lewis, & R. Ferrari. 2016. "Genome, transcriptome and proteome: the rise of omics data and their integration in biomedical sciences," *Briefings In Bioinformatics*, no. 19: 286-302.

McMullan, Miriam. 2006. "Patients using the Internet to obtain health information: How this affects the patient–health professional relationship," *Patient Education and Counselling* 63: 24-28.

National Research Council (U.S.). 2011. Toward Precision Medicine: Building a Knowledge Network for Biomedical Research and a New Taxonomy of Disease. Washington D.C: National Academies Press. http://site.ebrary.com/id/10531105., 12.

Parviainen, Jaana and Jari Pirhonen. 2017. "Vulnerable Bodies in Human-Robot Interactions: Embodiment as Ethical Issue in Robot Care for the Elderly," *Transformations Issue*, no. 27.

Parviainen, J. and T Turja. 2021. Toward Abiozoomorphism in Social Robotics? Discussion of a New Category between Mechanical Entities and Living Beings. *Journal of Posthuman Studies* 5(2): 15–168. doi: 10.5325/jpoststud.5.2.0150.

Peterson, Drew C., Christian Martin-Gill, Francis X. Guyette, Adam Z. Tobias, Catherine E. McCarthy, Scott T. Harrington, Theodore R Delbridge and Donald M. Yealy. 2013. *Outcomes of Medical Emergencies on Commercial Airline Flights*. Emmitsburg MD: National Emergency Training Center. https://doi.org/10.1056/NEJMoa1212052. 2075-83.

Pollett S., WJ Boscardin, E. Azziz-Baumgartner, YO Tinoco, G. Soto, C. Romero, J. Kok, M. Biggerstaff, C. Viboud, GW Rutherford. Evaluating Google Flu Trends in Latin America: Important Lessons for the Next Phase of Digital Disease Detection. Clin Infect Dis. 2017 Jan 1;64(1):34-41. doi: 10.1093/cid/ciw657. Epub 2016 Sep 26. PMID: 27678084; PMCID: PMC6394128.

Reed, M., J. Huang, R. Brand, I. Graetz, R. Neugebauer, B. Fireman, M. Jaffe, DW Ballard, J. Hsu. Implementation of an outpatient electronic health record and emergency department visits, hospitalizations, and office visits among patients with diabetes. JAMA. 2013 Sep 11;310(10):1060-5. doi: 10.1001/jama.2013.276733. PMID: 24026601; PMCID: PMC 4503235: 1060-65.

Sullins, John P. 2016. "When is a robot a moral agent," *International Review of Information Ethics* No.6: 23-30.

van Rysewyk, Simon Peter and Matthijs Pontier. 2015. "A Hybrid Bottom-Up and Top-Down Approach to Machine Medical Ethics : Theory and Data," in *Machine Medical Ethics* ed. Simon Peter van Rysewyk and Matthijs Pontier Switzerland : *Springer International*: 93-110.

Yuasa, T., Urakami S, Yamamoto S, Yonese J, Nakano K, Kodaira M, Takahashi S, Hatake K, Inamura K, Ishikwa Y, Fukui I. 2011. "Tumor size is a potential predictor of response to tyrosine kinase inhibitors in renal cell cancer," *Urology*. Apr;77(4): 831-5. doi: 10.1016/j.urology. 2010.12.008. Epub 2011 Feb 12. PMID: 21316083: 831-5.

ABOUT THE AUTHOR

KOUMPAROUDIS EVANGELOS holds a PhD degree in Philosophy from Sofia University "St. KlimentOhridiski". He was awarded an Erasmus Scholarship in 2019 to the Sorbonne University, Paris. Evangelos looks after a column on Bibliotheque.gr where he frequently publishes original essays and short stories (literature). Additionally, he writes dramas and black comedies for the theatre.

ORCID: http://orcid.org/0000-0002-1068-4376
Email: vaggelis3@yahoo.gr

Myron Vourakis

Gödel's Incompleteness Theorems as an Example of Scientific Thinking

Introduction

In this paper I am going to examine Gödel's incompleteness theorems from a philosophical point of view and more precisely, as an example of thinking in a Heideggerian sense. Gödel's two theorems of incompleteness can be considered as the two most profound theorems of mathematical logic, even though they could be considered "useless", as they only affirm an impossibility, rather than a possibility or a methodology. In a way then, their essence is negative. Although their uselessness for calculation purposes, they do form a new sort of mathematical intuition, which is twofold. One aspect is the more self-evident, that of philosophy of mathematics: they treat the notions of truth, provability and first and foremost the limits of mathematical systems, they shed a new light on their nature. The second aspect, which is the one that incarnates a new mathematical intuition, is the one that shows the internal limits of the mathematical production in an immanent way. It is in this second aspect that we are going to elaborate our proposition, that the two theorems of Gödel constitute thinking in a Heideggerian sense and at the same time a true example of mathematical thinking.

Heidegger states that "Science does not think"[1], at his seminar *What is called Thinking?*. This proposition is one of the most critiqued and not well understood of his entire work. This paper is also a criticism on Heidegger's view of science, but a criticism that hopes to take a closer and more nuanced look at this proposition. We must first and foremost understand what "science" and what "thinking" is in the Heideggerian context. For Heidegger, science can be considered a self-generating corpus of knowledge whose purpose is to fix contexts, frames better yet, so that everything can fall into some of them. Frames of usage of course, since for Heidegger the essence of science is the Technique. On that note, one could clearly see it both from Heidegger's works where he criticizes science, as a "theory of the real" i.e. fixing a "real" via objectivity and hence demystifying Being as a source of

---

1   Heidegger, Martin, *What is Called Thinking?* (1968, transl. Fred D. Wieck and J. Glenn Gray, ed. Harper & Row, Publishers) p. 8.

energy and decontextualizing beings as objects, as well as from articles on the subject[2]. I will elaborate on the sense of "thinking" further down.

My elaboration and criticism are based mainly on two texts of Heidegger: the conference *The Question Concerning Technology*[3] and his seminar *What is called Thinking?* I consider the Heideggerian sense of thinking the most apt to properly give the essence of this word. On the other hand, I would like to contest the meaning Heidegger gives to science and its value. If I consider science as only a self-generating corpus of knowledge, that aspires to control Being and beings, Heidegger's proposition is true. That is to say that science under that perspective indeed cannot and does not think, it only calculates. I do agree with him, in the context of pure calculation, but I think that there is another aspect in science as well. This second aspect, which is indeed scientific, has a value towards the exceeding of the Technique,[4] in the sense of appropriation/expropriation *(Ereignis/EnteignisI)*.[2] It's the aspect of science that showcases in an immanent way its own limits, that is to say that these limits are shown via each science's means and ways. The example showcased here, from mathematics, has the aforementioned characteristics.

Heidegger admits that scientists can think, but as humans, and that this thinking is never scientific. This is important, because we could very well interpret it as follows: the idea, that a scientist came up with, doesn't constitute scientific thinking, or any sort of scientific oriented mental faculties, but rather what is properly scientific is how this idea will be translated in the formalistic terms of the science in question. The process via how a scientist has an idea or a conception is not the field upon which we will try to argue for a scientific thinking in Heideggerian terms (although that would be very interesting to be done, my intuition is that there are scientific elements in the conception of an idea), but rather in this process of translation itself and always

---

2   Some relevant Heideggerian sources on the subject of science would be: *Science and Reflexion* in Martin Heidegger, *The Question Concerning Technology and Other Essays*, 1977 transl. William Lovitt, ed. Garland Publishing and the relevant parts of his seminar *What is a thing?* 1967 transl. W. B. Barton, Jr. and Vera Deutsch on Gateway Editions. As a secondary reading, I found the article of Marián Ambrozy very interesting: Heidegger's View and Approach to Science and its Similarities and Differences Before and After the "Turn", published on Φιλοσοφια vol.22 2021.

3   Heidegger, Martin, *The Question Concerning Technology and Other Essays* (1977 transl. William Lovitt, ed. Garland Publishing).

4   In this paper I refrain from the use of the term technology, commonly found in English translations of Heidegger's works. The reason for that is that we prefer to keep the word Technique, as it resounds closer to both the Greek word τέχνη (from which Heidegger derives his notion) and to the sense of the Technique according to its essence the *Gestell* (Enframing). On the other hand I consider technology a result of the Technique, at least in its modern sense.

through the experience of the scientist. This sort of translation is not something calculable, but rather a passing from one form of thinking (Heidegger would call it philosophical) to another, which can be considered properly scientific. This is the case at least of Gödel's theorems: it is not the conception of truth and provability that Gödel had in mind (conception which would be rather philosophical, as it was thanks to these theorems that a properly mathematical conception could be formed to begin with), but rather how he translated them into mathematics. It is this "how" the properly questions the limits of formatting and the Technique itself, in a profound manner.

With the example studied here, I hope to show how science can show the possibilities and limits of the Technique and its modalities. In a very profound manner, these theorems destroy the conception of an all-mighty scientific knowledge, conception according to which human power can understand everything, predict everything and finally manipulate everything. This destruction is accomplished already because these theorems showcase the limits of mathematical provability, all the while being mathematical theorems, that is proposition that hold the highest form of "certainty". I will begin by an examination of the Heideggerian concept of thinking, especially of thinking in the Technique, with the help of Reiner Scürmann and also elaborate further on Heidegger's conception of science. Afterwards, we will discuss the two theorems in question, along with their historical context and how they could not be included in Heidegger's conception of science. It is then, that we will treat the great book of Jean-Michel Salanskis *L'herméneutique formelle* in this questioning. It is thanks to this book, which is a very well-constructed immanent criticism of Heidegger's proposition for science, that we could treat this question at all, even though our analysis goes to other directions from that of Salanskis, it is thanks to him that we could do it at all.

Thinking according to Heidegger

It would be impossible to understand the term "thinking" in Heideggerian context without what is "Most thought-provoking in our thought-provoking time is that we are still not thinking."[5] On the other hand what gives most to think and that we don't think yet, is the proper of the end of metaphysics in Heidegger, that is to say: the Technique. Although tempting, a proper analysis of the Heideggerian Technique is out of the scope of my paper, as it would need a lot of space, rather we will treat some characteristics of it that could

---

5   Heidegger, Martin, *What is Called Thinking?* (1968, transl. Fred D. Wieck and J. Glenn Gray, editions Harper & Row, Publishers) p. 6.

be considered as guideposts to my questioning. Firstly, it is important to keep in mind that thinking for Heidegger is thanking[6] for a gift, rather than a spiritual faculty. The gift is the gift of Being, which has found itself in the final epoch of metaphysics. Thus thinking comes to one as a reaction in a way, one can only think when one finds themselves in the midst of Being. Thinking is a path towards Being, one merely find ourselves on it, if at all. This analogy will be more concretely explained thanks to both Scürmann and Salanskis later on. In the age of the Technique, where it is impossible to pose/impose a new archic principle (i.e. a new metaphysics) we find ourselves in the Technique, or how Scürmann characterizes it: the principle of anarchy. There is no possible new archic economy of presence, hence Scürmann advocates for a new, anarchic economy of presence as the only possibility after the Technique. While there is no concrete absolute principle as the essence of the Technique there is a principle, that of anarchy i.e. the a-la-carte conception of beings, always with a scope of "doing something with them". Another characteristic of the Technique in Heidegger's works is the kingdom of doing. Hence this doing, deprives Being of its essence, all the while opening it up the multiple. It is towards that multiple that the event of appropriation/expropriation would go. Being without archic principles, anarchic Being, that is Scürmann's conception for the new beginning. Thinking here, for both Scürmann and Heidegger, is what makes possible that new beginning and meanwhile it is the most intrinsically human capacity.

We will begin with four characterizations of what thinking is not/does not, that Heidegger gives in his famous seminar *What is called Thinking?*: " 1. Thinking does not bring knowledge as do the sciences. 2. Thinking does not produce usable practical wisdom. 3. Thinking solves no cosmic riddles. 4. Thinking does not endow us directly with the power to act."[7]. These four propositions already show thinking's character as a path, and not as a process to get immediate results from. One can also somewhat see Heidegger's conception of science as a contrast to thinking behind these propositions, but more on that further down. So now there are some positive characterizations of thinking (path, thanking for a gift) and some negative.

---

6   In his seminar *What is Called Thinking?* Heidegger derives the essence of thinking via an etymological argument between the German verb Denken, meaning thinking, and Gedanken, meaning thanking. He means to show that thinking comes as human's response to Being and its essence, hence it is rather a human action, after he is bestowed the gift of being.

7   Heidegger, Martin, *What is Called Thinking?* 1968, transl. Fred D. Wieck and J. Glenn Gray, editions Harper & Row, Publishers, p. 159.

Here Scürmann's distiction between thinking-that-attends and thinking-that-is-attended is very helpful, because our characterizations needed a little push. Here we will treat the thinking-that- attends, that is questions, clears out and prepares the place for the thinking-that-is-attended to come. In the context of the event of appropriation/expropriation, this distinction makes a lot of sense, as the expropriation is essentially first, before the appropriation and the thinking that is its own is the questioning thinking i.e., hermeneutics. The hermeneutic circle, as exposed by Heidegger and after (Gadamer, Salanskis and many more), is the schema that showcases how questioning is possible at all and also how it moves. This questioning does not arrive to any final answer, hence it destroys the conception of a "final answer, first/absolute principle" as the ultimate purpose. The attending thinking is fundamentally destructive (in the sense of Heidegger's *Destruktion*). It is this aspect of thinking that we will treat here, as it is more apt for our example and helps make our point towards the cracks of the Technique that get deeper via science. It is this thinking after all that clears out and prepares the openness towards the multiple Being.

Technique and Science according to Heidegger

According to the first of the negative propositions cited above, science does not lead to any scientific knowledge. But what is science according to Heidegger? Heidegger states that the essence of science is the Technique, then our questioning should turn towards the Technique. As has become clear the Technique mentioned here does not refer to a specific technique for something, but rather is the Heideggerian term for a coming together of horizons of understanding, it is an era of Being: "The Technique is neither a "mean" neither a purpose, but rather, more originally, the adjointement of the domain of the revealed and the "purposes" it allows for itself. The Technique is the accomplissement, from a long time ago, of the essence of the "culture"; the last one—still misunderstood—is in its essence "Technique"; which is the reason for which it would be nonsensical what is the place of the latter in the interior of modern culture!".[8] Technique's essence, according to

---

8   Heidegger, Martin, *Pensées directrices; Sur la génèse de la métaphysique, de la science et de la technique* (2019, transl. Jean-François Courtine, Françoise Dastur, Marc Launay and Dominique Pradelle, ed. Seuil) p. 322. The translation from French is mine, the French passage is: "La technique n'est ni un « moyen » ni un but, mais plus originellement l'ajointement du domaine de visée et des « buts » qu'il s'autorise pour lui-même. La technique est l'accomplissement anticipé depuis déjà longtemps de l'essence de la « culture » ; celle-ci—encore méconnue—est en son essence « technique » ; raison pour laquelle il demeure dépourvu de sens de se demander quelle est la place de la technique à l'intérieur de la culture

Heidegger, is the *Gestell*, En-framing. To be clear, a proper analysis of the Technique is beyond the scope of our paper, but nevertheless we will attempt to draw some characteristics from Heidegger's and Scürmann's works. Like most of Heideggerian's terms, *Gestell* is hard to properly translate, but En-framing seems quite adequate. Heidegger also characterizes the Technique as *kingdom of doing*, it is in this sense that we should understand the *frame* in En-framing: a closed context of understanding a being according to "what can we do with it". The En-framing as essence of the Technique should be understood here in aletheiological terms i.e., as the mode of revealing proper to this final era of the history of Being: "Technicity is the highest and most encompassing triumph of Occidental metaphysics. In its dissemination throughout 'beings in the whole', technicity is Occidental metaphysics itself."[9]

En-framing as the essence of the Technique refers to the mode that beings reveal to us as such and also the mode of how Being is revealed, hence the characterization alethiological: "And yet the revealing that holds sway throughout modern technology does not unfold into a bringing-forth in the sense of poiesis. The revealing that rules in modern technology is a challenging [Herausfordern], which puts to nature the unreasonable demand that it supply energy that can be extracted and stored as such."[10] That provoking (or challenging as the translator chooses to translate Heraufordem) is the proper way to understand the En-framing, as nature and beings in it are provoked under specific frames (albeit different, with none reigning supreme, hence the Technique is in a sense anarchic). The only criteria so to speak of these frames are realisability and calculability i.e., concrete control for manipulation and mobilization of nature under this scope. All of nature is meant to stand-reserve and be mobilized for its energy: "Enframing is the gathering together that belongs to that setting-upon which sets upon man and puts him in position to reveal the real, in the mode of ordering, as standing-reserve. As the one who is challenged forth in this way, man stands within the essential realm of Enframing. He can never take up a relationship to it only subsequently. Thus, the question as to how we are to arrive at a relationship to the essence of technology, asked in this way, always comes too late. But never too late

---

moderne! The original title is *Leitgedanken zur Entstehung der Metqphysik, der neuzeitlichen Wissenschaft und der modernen Technik.*

9   Heidegger, Martin, *Mindfulness* (2008, trans. Parvis Emad and Thomas Kalary, ed. Continuum) p. 133. The term Technicity, used in this citation is the translator's choice on the original Heideggerian term: "Technik", the one that I prefer to translate as Technique.

10   Heidegger, Martin, *The Question Concerning Technology and Other Essays* (1977 in the English translation by William Lovitt, editions Garland Publishing), ch. The Question Concerning Technology, p. 14.

comes the question as to whether we actually experience ourselves as the ones whose activities everywhere, public and private, are challenged forth by Enframing. Above all, never too late comes the question as to whether and how we actually admit ourselves into that wherein Enframing itself comes to presence.".[11] Here it is clear that the Technique constitutes the real as the standing-reserve and there is a need for theory in order to mobilize and manipulate that very real, that is science: "In order to make clear what the name "real" means in the statement "Science is the theory of the real," let us simply consider the word itself. The real [das Wirkliche] brings to fulfillment the realm of working [des Wirkenden], of that which works [wirkt]. What does it mean "to work?"[12] There is a need for science in the Technique, because the real needs to be manipulable i.e., to work. This "to work" should be considered, as the rest of Heidegger's analysis of the Technique to his major influence on it i.e. Jünger and the latter's work Der Arbeiter.[13] There Jünger points out that the Technique is to ensure the Worker's mobilization of the world and nature, so "to work" means to be able to provide energy-for whatever purpose in whatever frame of understanding that the En-framing provides as the aletheiological principle of the Technique.

The En-framing here is very consistent with most understandings of science, as science provides a theoretical context of usage for every being in its scopes and that is the reason why both Heidegger and later on Scürmann treat science under that light i.e., as a way to calculate beings in their proper domains of usage. In the context of the four cited propositions above about thinking, obviously a simple calculation cannot really be considered thought. So it is quite true that under that light, science doesn't think and that thinking itself is a dubious possibility in the Technique under its essence as En-framing seeing as man is thrown into it directly and does not form a relation towards it afterwards: "But Enframing does not simply endanger man in his relationship to himself and to everything that is. As a destining, it banishes man into that kind of revealing which is an ordering. Where this ordering holds sway, it drives out every other possibility of revealing. Above all, Enframing conceals that revealing which, in the sense of poiesis, lets what presences come forth into appearance. As compared with that other revealing, the setting-

---

11   Heidegger, Martin, *The Question Concerning Technology and Other Essays* (1977 in the English translation by William Lovitt, ed. Garland Publishing), ch. The Question Concerning Technology, p. 24.

12   Heidegger, Martin, *The Question Concerning Technology and Other Essays* (1977 in the English translation by William Lovitt, ed. Garland Publishing), ch. Science and Reflection, p. 159.

13   Junger, Ernst, *Der Arbeiter Herrschaft und Gestalt—The Worker Dominion and Form* (1981, transl. Bogdean Costea and Laurence P. Hemming, ed. Clet-Kotta, bilingual edition).

upon those challenges forth thrusts man into a relation to that which is, that is at once antithetical and rigorously ordered. Where Enframing holds sway, regulating and securing of the standing-reserve mark all revealing. They no longer even let their own fundamental characteristic appear, namely, this revealing as such.".[14] Scientific revealing, as the theory of the real, is also marked and in a privileged way at that, at least according to Heidegger (and according to Scürmann). That is the sense of Heidegger's phrase: "Science does not think."[15]

This privileged place of science in the Technique is most apparent in Heidegger's text: "Modern physics is the herald of Enframing, a herald whose origin is still unknown."[16] When Heidegger speaks of science, as many in his times, he has in mind modern Physics. Then a question would arise: "why is this paper, a criticism on the Heideggerian position of science, focused on mathematics?" The answer to that, is that modern Physics, according to Heidegger, is mathematical in nature, in the sense of calculable: "Modern science's way of representing pursues and entraps nature as a calculable coherence of forces. Modern physics is not experimental physics because it applies apparatus to the questioning of nature. Rather the reverse is true. Because physics, indeed already as pure theory, sets nature up to exhibit itself as a coherence of forces calculable in advance, it therefore orders its experiments precisely for the purpose of asking whether and how nature reports itself when set up in this way."[17] Hence mathematics are only a tool in his eyes for Physics. The aim of this paper is to show, in an immanent way no less, that Gödel's theorems of incompleteness are prime examples of thinking in the Heideggerian sense and hence showcase that there are ways that science thinks and thinks most radically concerning the Technique.

While that principle of En-framing is not a concrete *pros hen* in the Aristotelian sense, it is a principle of an epoch of Being. Scürmann's ambiguous characterization of the Technique here is very helping: "the principle of anarchy". The above citations have made clear at least two most important

---

14   Heidegger, Martin, *The Question Concerning Technology and Other Essays* (1977 English translation by William Lovitt, ed. Garland Publishing), ch. The Question Concerning Technology, p. 27.

15   Heidegger, Martin, *What is called Thinking?* (1968 English translation by Fred D. Wieck and J.Glenn Gray, editions Harper & Row, Publishers) p. 8.

16   Heidegger, Martin, *The Question Concerning Technology and Other Essays* (1977 English translation by William Lovitt, ed. Garland Publishing), ch. The Question Concerning Technology, p. 22.

17   Heidegger, Martin, *The Question Concerning Technology and Other Essays*, 1977 in the English translation by William Lovitt, ed. Garland Publishing), ch. The Question Concerning Technology, p. 21.

points about the Technique: 1. that it is the end in the sense of τέλος of Occidental Metaphysics and 2. that there is no supreme arche all the while the Technique constitutes itself as a principle of the revealing of Being, hence principle of anarchy. In Scürmann's terminology each arche is an origin, that is a new way of Being revealing itself: "The origin as arche, even critically articulated in epistemology, is still conceived in view of a mediate, genetic production of knowledge. To explain substance and becoming, or to explain our knowledge of them, is always to trace substantial being, becoming, or knowledge to an entity that 'gives' them: forma dat esse, "the form gives being."[18] On the other hand, the originary, in Scürmann's terminology is the Being itself, as pure presence, hence outside any arche and narration of its origin: "Likewise, the 'originary' is the deconstructed principium. A principle governs beyond time. It manifests itself in its effects. But the originary manifests nothing; it is manifestation, the temporal event of manifesting. Understood originarily, an entity is true as it enters into presence. Its manifestation is its truth. In this way, the deconstruction of the 'principle' leads to a differential understanding of truth: the field in which 'there is' truth is the difference between a modality of presence and presencing, or between the given and the giving. This differential, phenomenological understanding of truth precedes all of its causal, metaphysical conceptions. It is also prior—indeed, more originary than—economic arrangements and their description."[19] Beyond the Technique there no new arche as Scürmann argues, only a new originary experience, hence an ontological anarchy. It is through this perspective that science has to offer as thinking in dialog with philosophy and art. Salanskis has already argued about the thinking-as-hermeneutics character of mathematics in his book *L'herméneutique formelle.*[20] Here the point is to also show the trangressive character of science in the example studied here (thinking according to Scürmann and Heidegger is always radically transgressive towards any arche). So far science was seen only under the light of the theory of a pre-given real, this paper's purpose is to show that science and in this case the example chosen, can point towards the limits of the En-framing as a form of revealing i.e., as a form of aletheia.

---

18   Schürmann, Reiner, *Heidegger on Being and Acting: From Principles to Anarchy* (1987 English translation by Christine-Marie Gros in collaboration with the author, ed. Indiana University Press), p. 150.

19   Ibid.

20   Salanskis, Jean-Michel, L'herméneutique *formelle : L'infini, le continu et l'espace,* (2013 edition, Klincksiek).

The two theorems of incompleteness of Gödel

Under the conception of science as the theory of a manipulable and standing reserve real, the two theorems of Gödel seem odd, as mathematical theorems. The reason for their odd character is that they don't provide useful tools in the mathematization/calculabilization of beings and Being, rather they limit any such attempt. We will examine these theorems under the light of the Heideggerian concept of thinking as elaborated so far and under the line of thought of Jean-Michel Salanskis' book *L'herméneutique formelle*. Firstly, these theorems don't say anything about any beings treated by mathematics, but rather something about mathematics themselves and even more so, something negative i.e. they show an impossibility and hence the limits of the "calculable". Secondly, they don't really try to clear an enigma of the world or life. Finally, they don't really show towards a way of acting/doing. Concerning the first negative proposition we cited as what thinking is-not, we don't have "anything" being closed to a frame of usage, but rather a scientific way to show the intrinsic limits of calculative reflection and production (or better yet provocation, to utilize the Heideggerian term Heraufordem).

Before the elaboration on the theorems themselves, a quick briefing of the historical context is necessary and more specifically a brief talk about Hilbert's program. In this program, Hilbert posed some propositions to be proven, where if they were proven true, then mathematics could be considered a machine of pure mechanical calculation. Hilbert's program "calls for a formalization of all of mathematics in axiomatic form, together with a proof that this axiomatization of mathematics is consistent. The consistency proof itself was to be carried out using only what Hilbert called "finitary" methods."[21] Finitary here characterizes a process the can be calculated in a finite amount of time, hence it already shows towards a "doing" or rather a guarantee of realizability. It is important to understand how this finite calculability characterizes the "doability" even in the level of Hilbert's intuition: "Hilbert sees the finite mode of thought as a separate source of a priori knowledge in addition to pure intuition (e.g., of space) and reason, claiming that he has "recognized and characterized the third source of knowledge that accompanies experience and logic."[22]

---

21   Zach, Richard, "Hilbert's Program," *The Stanford Encyclopedia of Philosophy* (Fall 2019 Edition), Edward N. Zalta (ed.), Available at: https://plato.stanford.edu/archives/fall2019/entries/hilbert-program/ [Accessed on 23.04.2023, at. 10:30].

22   Richard's translation of Hilbert is found on: Hilbert, David, 1931b, "Die Grundlegung der elementaren Zahlenlehre", *Mathematische Annalen*, 104: 485–494. Reprinted in Hilbert (1935, 192–195) and Ewald and Sieg (2013, 983–990). English translation in Ewald (1996, 1148–1157).

It is clear that both Hilbert and Heidegger agree on their view on mathematics, as a calculation, but it is for the first that this is the value of mathematics. Hilbert's known demand "we must know, and we will know" is very indicative given the aforementioned context. That was Hilbert's program, but Gödel's theorems brought ruin to this conception and demand (as there will be problems we will never know the answer to, if there is one at all). This ruin is both on the level of the science itself and the intuition of what is and/or should science be.

Concerning the two theorems in question, we will first give their classic forms: the first theorem of incompleteness states that if a system contains arithmetic (actually the theorem holds if a system contains a true sub-system of arithmetic, but this is a detail given the scope of our paper), then that system cannot be both complete and consistent and the second theorem, that if a system contains arithmetic, then if it can pose the proposition signifying its own consistency, it can never prove it i.e. the proposition stating a system's consistency is undecidable in that very system. The proof of the first theorem is based upon Gödel's original idea of "arithmetizing syntax" and then drawing an argument ad absurdum by constructing a proposition that could be considered neither true neither false. That way Gödel constructs a proposition for which no proof or negation could exist in the system. The second theorem is an almost immediate consequence of the first.[23]

In brief we will also mention the historical context of what followed these two theorems, at least two consequences of them that we find very interesting and telling of our point about another character in science (the character that we will argue constitutes true thinking). Firstly, Turing formalization of the Turing machine calculation model and his theorem concerning the problem of halting: this theorem states that given a proposition, then the proposition stating that the first one is undecidable, is itself undecidable (and hence the corresponding machine would never halt and produce an output).[24] This theorem showcases the intrinsic limits of calculability as well from a mathematical standpoint as well. The second important work following Gödel's theorems, is Tarski's work on truth. Tarski shows that for every mathematical (i.e. formal) language, the predicate of truth of its propositions is

---

23   Raatikainen, Panu, *"Gödel's Incompleteness Theorems," The Stanford Encyclopedia of Philosophy* (Summer 2020 Edition), Edward N. Zalta (ed.). Available at: <https://plato.stanford. edu/archives/sum2020/entries/Gödel-incompleteness/> [Accessed on 23.04.2023, at. 10:30].

24   Sipser, Michael, *Introduction To The Theory Of Computation* (2006, Thomson Course Technology).

definable only in it's metalanguage. From there a regression ad infinitum follows.[25] Tarski argues that it would be impossible to consider any spoken language as formalisable, seeing as these languages contain the predicate of their proposition's truth in themselves.

How and why these two theorems could be considered thinking in a Heideggerian sense.

Having outlined these two theorems, their historical context and what followed, we hope to have shown how they showcase a reflection on truth and provability in the context of mathematics. This paper's focal point remains to show that this reflection is properly thinking in a Heideggerian sense all the while being properly mathematical. We search then her for what truly counts as mathematical thinking; hence we will not talk and/or argue about any platonistic position of Gödel[26] as these sorts of positions are rather philosophical and not properly scientific (this distinction will become clearer in terms of manners of thinking later on). We will argue that the arithmetization of syntax is properly mathematical thinking and we will define what that is. Briefly speaking the arithmetization of syntax is a process to attribute a specific (unique) number to a proposition (any more detail would be both redundant as the sources on it are abundant and detrimental because it would

---

25   Tarski, Alfred. 1944 & 1956. "The concept of truth in the languages of the deductive sciences," expanded English translation of Tarski's original 1933 publication titled "Pojęcie prawdy w językach nauk dedukcyjnych." In: *Prace Towarzystwa Naukowego Warszawskiego*. Wydział III: Nauk Matematyczno-Fizycznych. 34. PWN Warszawa.
- 1944. "The Semantic Conception of Truth and the Foundations of Semantics." *Philosophy and Phenomenological Research*, Vol. 4, No. 3 (Mar., 1944), pp. 341-376. Edited by Jan Zygmunt.
- 1956. "The Concept of Truth in Formalized Languages." In: *Logic, Semantics, Metamathematics. Papers from 1923 to 1938* by Alfred Tarski. Ed. by J. H. Woodger. Oxford Clarendon Press, pp. 152–278.
- For further clarification in respect of the French and the German translations of Alfred Tarski's work, please refer to: Gruber Monika. 2016. *Alfred Tarski and the "Concept of Truth in Formalized Languages": A Running Commentary with Consideration of the Polish Original and the German Translation*. Switzerland: Springer. https://doi.org/10.1007/978-3-319-32616-0.

26   The following article elucidates a lot the path of Gödel's mathematical Platonism: Wrigley, W. (2022). "Gödelian Platonism and mathematical intuition." (*European Journal of Philosophy*, 30 (2), 578–600. https://doi.org/10.1111/ejop.12671). Briefly, mathematical Platonism is a position on the nature and being of mathematical objects, notions etc. The common ground of Platonists on mathematics could be summarized in 3 propositions as follows: 1. mathematical objects exist, 2. mathematical objects are abstract, 3. mathematical objects are independent of any intelligence perceiving them (much less creating them). This position was helpful for Gödel to differentiate between "provable" and "true" and hence arrive at his theorems.

derail the line of questioning).[27] The arithmetization of syntax is a sense the translation of Cantor's diagonalization in the context of mathematical logic. It is a methodology to construct arguments ad absurdum in order to show the limits of logic. The finitude of human reasoning and intuition is formalized in this methodology and we consider exactly this "formalizing" character to be what is most truly mathematical as a manner. Gödel's theorems detach "truth" from "provability in mathematics and in a way show that truth is not formalizable in any given system (that contains arithmetic). The arithmetization of syntax is a formal methodology to build formal arguments about the limits of formalizing. This formalizing could also be considered a translation of the term *Gestell* as the being exists only under the specificity of it's usages and that in a mechanical and replicable manner. After all the frame that a being falls in, should be able to treat it in the same way as all other beings "of the same type". Hence no true and open questioning happens about beings, but rather only questioning about how they could be used formalized and framed.

The questioning that we speak of here has a name in philosophy: hermeneutics. Salanskis in his book *L'herméneutique formelle*, characterizes mathematics already from the title: it mathematics that can be considered as formal hermeneutics and by extension all sciences could be considered forms of formal hermeneutics. Before going deeper into Salanskis' work, we first have to mention the hermeneutic circle and argue along with Salanskis that this is thinking according to Heidegger (to be more specific and to use Shcurmann's terms, it is anticipating thinking, a thinking that opens the place for the anticipated thinking to come). The hermeneutic circle is based upon the realization that to even ask a question presupposes some sort of pre-comprehension of the subject in question. This pre-comprehension is internal and has a double function in questioning: firstly, it functions a principle of judgement to every relative answer one reaches (it is the reason an absurd answer can be considered so, when treating a subject that is questioned i.e. unknown) and secondly it gets deeper and more nuanced every time one arrives somewhere with their questioning. This second function of pre-comprehension ensures that no answer is final for any sufficiently deep questioning (i.e. questioning that treats primordial concepts such as space, time, truth, being etc).

---

27   Button, Tim and Walsh, Sean, *Philosophy and Model Theory* (2018, ed. Oxford University Press), pp. 130-131. There the authors explain the process of the arithmetization of syntax in a very clear manner.

According to Salanskis, this process characterizes mathematics and their questioning. Of course, the questions that are asked are not about this kind of triangle or that property of prime numbers, but rather questions concerning space, or sequenciality as a primordial content. The mathematician in contemplating about space arrives in geometry, topology and every other domain treating such questions. In our example, Gödel's theorems advance further from the previous conception of "truth" as "provability" and they do so in a purely formal way. The questioning about truth continued after Gödel and still does to this day and of course preceded Gödel (Hilbert's program, Cauchy's work on the foundation of mathematics, are prime examples but far from being the only ones). This way of considering mathematics in our example, shows that mathematics can be viewed as something much more rich than an organized self-generating corpus of knowledge where the mathematician is nothing but the means. Rather mathematics is the name we give to the collective formal questioning of mathematicians, a questioning that advances and becomes richer precisely because it questions these primordial concepts. This way of considering mathematics also results to a more nuanced conception of scientific progress: progress is not being made via the accumulation of true theorems and proved practical methodologies that give results, but rather progress is only possible in formal questioning (as we pass from system to system, so to speak with the terms of Slaanskis and exactly via this accumulation of systems and hypersystems) and precisely because it is formal i.e. progress is a property that can only apply to formal contents. One could see this in the Technique: an epoch of being, where humans are obsessed with progress, only because Being is taken as En-framing/formalization, but we digress.

We agree with Salanskis that mathematics should be considered as their own form of hermeneutics i.e. the formal hermeneutics. Here formal points to the character of passing from system to system: a mathematical question about space for example, starts from a context of a specific mathematical systematization concerning space and moves either in that very system or passes to another (usually via defining an new system that contains the starting one, or by defining another system altogether). A very clear example here is with geometries: we start with the euclidean geometry, we defined spherical and minkowskian geometries and then moved to the more general system of riemannian geometry. Mathematicians build systems in order to questions systems (another very clear example would be how topology questions geometry with algebraic means). There is a very interesting passage of Salanskis that helps seeing the movement of hermeneutic questioning in it's different ways: "Very roughly, we could say that poetry elucidates from *word* to *word*, philosophy elucidates from *word* to *system* and mathematics elucidate from *system* to *system*."[28] The formal then is found in our case from syntax to syntax, from system to system.

Thus far it has been sufficiently shown that the two theorems in question can be considered thinking in Heideggerian terms, but that only in a formal way i.e. taking the characteristics of thinking according to Heidegger, along with the view of mathematics as their own way of hermeneutics, as Salanskis proposes. The point of this paper is also to indicate "how" these two theorems are thinking, not only "that" they are. Heidegger, repeatedly and in many texts, calls the Technique the end of Occidental metaphysics where: "Most thought-provoking is that we are still not thinking not even yet, although the state of the world is becoming constantly more thought-provoking."[29] That limit character of the Technique demands to be thought, it provokes thinking. In order then to properly think these theorems as mathematical thinking, it is necessary to do so in terms of the Technique as limit epoch of the history of Being, rather than confirming our hypotheses in a purely formal way.

A Heideggerian/Schürmannian interpretation of the theorems of incompleteness

The use (and many times abuse) of Gödel's theorems is known and it would be redundant to try to address it here. On the other hand, we will attempt an interpretation of our own, along the lines of Heidegger and Scürmann, hoping we will not be abusing these two theorems. Our point in this final section of our paper is to show how these theorems show, in a way beyond the Technique as end of the history of metaphysics, in the sense of no more possible arches being possible. That would be a proper reason why they constitute thinking in a Heideggerian and Schürmannian sense, they clear the way.

We characterized the technique so far as *Gestell* (which we translated as is usual by En-framing and we also considered another translation: formalization), we also saw Scürmann's characterization: the principle of anarchy. Both Heidegger and Shcurmann after him, envision another beginning of

---

28   Salanskis, Jean-Michel, L'herméneutique *formelle : L'infini, le continu et l'espace* (2013, ed. Klincksiek), pp. 8-9. The passage is my translation of the following passage: "Très grossièrement, on pourrait dire que la poésie élucide de mot en mot, que la philosophie élucide de mot à système, et que la mathématique élucide de système à système."

29   Heidegger, Martin, *What is called Thinking?* (1968 in the English translation by Fred D. Wieck and J. Glenn Gray, ed. Harper & Row, Publishers) p.4.

thinking, a thinking that would be based in absolute openness, Scürmann has a reason when he speaks of anarchy. They envision a thinking outside principles, that would be what Scürmann names the attended thinking. The characterization of the Technique as principle of anarchy then is very intriguing and purposefully ambiguous. While the Technique is the end of metaphysics it is based upon a principle: the *Gestell*, the En-framing. On the other hand, that principle is a no- principle as it it derives Being from beings, the beings become a la carte according to possible usages. Hence the Technique is indeed the principle of anarchy, but a principle, nonetheless. To use the Heideggerian image, the Technique is like Janus, with two faces, one looking back to metaphysics and economies of presence based on principles and the other towards the other beginning and to an economy of pure presence, without any principles. Here the concept of system is central to understand the Technique as an epoch of Being. Systems are necessary frames for beings to exist, in a way, in the Technique nothing exists unless it's in one or more systems (this would be a reversal of previous epochs where, the being and the phenomenon where the center around which a system was build, here the very being is decided upon the effect of being included in a system or not).

This is exactly where the value of these theorems as attending thinking is found. The undecidability in mathematics is very much a predicate of propositions, but in a much more radical sense, undecidability is the being of truth in mathematical thinking. That is the ground founded by these two theorems, the undecidability as being of truth precisely in the science whose true propositions hold the "most certainty". These theorems prove in a way that mathematics cannot be a system i.e., that formalization is not formalizable (one could also remember Heidegger claiming the essence of the Technique is nothing technical). These two theorems open the Janusian essence of Technique in a formal way.

To reformulate our point in terms of intuition, as the terms is used in mathematical circles, we would like to appeal to the term counter intuitive. A counter-intuitive result destroys and rebuilds all the intuition of mathematics whether that of a single person or the mathematics community as it is. Gödel's theorems did exactly that, on the largest scale possible. Also, it is important to show that every time such an important counter-intuitive result comes to light, new domains open in mathematics enriching it radically. The hermeneutic character is most strongly shown in these cases. The previous formalization is nullified in favor of a new one and the ground is reformed by the uncanny result (we use the term uncanny to translate the term Unheimlich). The term *Unheimlich* is very interesting here as it shows an uprooting, and it is precisely because of this uprooting that a new rooting is possible. This process of uprooting-rerooting is not formalizable and that will always be outside of the scope of formalization. One could see this dipole scheme in Scürmann's book *Broken Hegemonies*[30] with birth-death. Scürmann's scheme is at the same time more deep and more extended as it applies everywhere and every scale.

Here we only talk about these theorems under the light of the formal and it's limits. Whenever a limit is posed its "outside" is posed as well and in a way the theorems of incompleteness on thinking upon the formality of truth and of provability they point towards the fact (in a negative way) that outside any possible formal is formalizing and thinking. The thinking found in these two theorems is an uncanny thinking that becomes a pathway to the uncanny of modern mathematics and their results.

Conclusion

The theorems of incompleteness are true examples of mathematical thinking in our epoch especially, as they indicate the proper way of understanding this kind of thinking: as a formal way to repeatedly surpass the formalization by surpassing every formal along the way and ultimately as a thinking that goes beyond the principal character of the Technique. It is this thinking and it's possibilities that miss from Heidegger's thought, although that's understandable as in his era as well as in ours, science is considered as another tool of manipulation and mobilization of nature and Being. Our position is that there is another character to science, an indispensable character to the way towards the *Ereignis/Enteignis*: the self-destructing openness of the formal against itself. Our position is not based on a simplistic conception like "abolish the formal", but rather we hope to point to an attitude towards it. This attitude is to always distrust formal and always be open to it's own possibility of self-destruction (the term destruction here is meant keep the connotation of the Heideggerian *Destruktion*). In science, these results and theorems are relatively common, and they help to build that attitude. Science as formalization saves us from any static formalism. It is in this manner that sciences cause fissures and breaks in the false unity that is the Technique, as it poses as a principle which tries to unify beings under it. It is these fissures and breaks that allow the open multiple to show itself, even though for but a brief moment.

---

30   Schürmann, Reiner, *Broken Hegemonies* (2003, English translation by Lilly Reginald, ed. Indiana University Press).

As an end note, this paper's purpose is to trace "the Salvation that grows from the danger" in science and more specifically in the heart of what is considered by Heidegger, not exactly science, but rather what gives science its essence i.e., mathematics. This expression "what saves" is taken from a verse of Hölderlin,[31] that Heidegger always refers to, especially when writing about the Technique: "To save" is to fetch something home into its essence, in order to bring the essence for the first time into its genuine appearing. If the essence of technology, Enframing, is the extreme danger, and if there is truth in Hölderlin's words, then the rule of Enframing cannot exhaust itself solely in blocking all lighting-up of every revealing, all appearing of truth. Rather, precisely the essence of technology must harbor in itself the growth of the saving power. But in that case, might not an adequate look into what Enframing is as a destining of revealing bring into appearance the saving power in its arising?"[32] Exactly this saving power and in science no less, is what this paper attempt to bring to light, via the example of Gödel's incompleteness theorems.

Bibliography

Ambrozy, Marián, *Heidegger's View and Approach to Science and its Similarities and Differences Before and After the "Turn"*, published on Φιλοσοφια vol.22 2021

Button, Tim and Walsh, Sean, *Philosophy and Model Theory*, 2018, ed. Oxford University Press.

Gruber, Monika. 2016. *Alfred Tarski and the "Concept of Truth in Formalized Languages": A Running Commentary with Consideration of the Polish Original and the German Translation.* Switzerland: Springer. https://doi.org/10.1007/978-3-319-32616-0.

Heidegger, Martin, *What is Called Thinking?*, 1968, transl. Fred D. Wieck and J. Glenn Gray, ed. Harper & Row, Publishers.

Heidegger, Martin, *The Question Concerning Technology and Other Essays,* 1977 transl. William Lovitt, ed. Garland Publishing.

Heidegger, Martin, *Pensées directrices; Sur la génèse de la métaphysique, de la science et de la technique,* 2019, transl. Jean-François Courtine, Frnaçoise Dastur, Marc Launay and Dominique Pradelle, ed. Seuil.

---

31   Hölderlin, Friedrich, *Selected Poems* (1996, English translation by David Constantine, editions Bloodaxe Books), Ch. Patmos, p. 54. The verse in question is: "Where there is danger some / Salvation grows there too." and it is taken from the hymn Patmos.

32   Heidegger, Martin, *The Question Concerning Technology and Other Essays* (1977 in the English translation by William Lovitt, ed. Garland Publishing), ch. The Question Concerning Technology, p. 28.

Heidegger, Martin, *Mindfulness*, 2008, trans. Parvis Emad and Thomas Kalary, ed. Continuum.

Heidegger, Martin, *What is a thing?*, 1967 transl. W. B. Barton, Jr. and Vera Deutsch, ed. Gateway Editions.

Hölderlin, Friedrich, *Selected Poems*, 1996, English translation by David Constantine, editions Bloodaxe Books.

Junger, Ernst, Der *Arbeiter Herrschaft und Gestalt—The Worker Dominion and Form*, 1981, transl. Bogdean Costea and Laurence P. Hemming, ed. Clet-Kotta, bilingual edition.

Raatikainen, Panu, "Gödel's Incompleteness Theorems," *The Stanford Encyclopedia of Philosophy* (Summer 2020 Edition), Edward N. Zalta (ed.), URL = <https://plato.stanford.edu/archives/sum2020/entries/Gödel-incompleteness/>.

Richard, Zach, "Hilbert's Program," *The Stanford Encyclopedia of Philosophy* (Fall 2019 Edition), Edward N. Zalta (ed.), URL = <https://plato.stanford.edu/archives/fall2019/entries/hilbert-program/>.

Salanskis, Jean-Michel, *L'herméneutique formelle : L'infini, le continu et l'espace* (2013, ed. Klincksiek)

Schürmann, Reiner, *Heidegger on Being and Acting: From Principles to Anarchy* (1987 English translation by Christine-Marie Gros in collaboration with the author, ed. Indiana University Press.

Schürmann, Reiner, *Broken Hegemonies*, 2003, English translation by Lilly Reginald, ed. Indiana University Press.

Sipser, Michael, *Introduction To The Theory Of Computation*, 2006, Thomson Course Technology.

Tarski, Alfred. 1944 & 1956. "The concept of truth in the languages of the deductive sciences," expanded English translation of Tarski's 1933. Pojęcie prawdy w językach nauk dedukcyjnych. In: *Prace Towarzystwa Naukowego Warszawskiego*. Wydział III: Nauk Matematyczno-Fizycznych. 34. PWN Warszawa.

- 1944. "The Semantic Conception of Truth and the Foundations of Semantics." *Philosophy and Phenomenological Research*, Vol. 4, No. 3 (Mar., 1944), pp. 341-376. Edited by Jan Zygmunt.

- 1956. "The Concept of Truth in Formalized Languages." In: *Logic, Semantics, Metamathematics. Papers from 1923 to 1938* by Alfred Tarski. Ed. by J. H. Woodger. Oxford Clarendon Press, pp. 152–278.

Wrigley, W. (2022). "Gödelian Platonism and mathematical intuition." *European Journal of Philosophy*, 30(2), 578–600. https://doi.org/10.1111/ejop.12671.

ABOUT THE AUTHOR

MYRON A. VOURAKIS holds a Masters degree in History of Philosophy, Metaphysics and Phenomenology (2020-2021) from the University of Sorbonne (Paris 4). He also holds a Bachelors in Mathematics (specialized in pure Mathematics) (2013-2019) from the University of Athens and half a Masters (first year of Masters, in France it's considered a M1) from the University of Paris (old Paris 7—Diderot) in History and Philosophy of Science. Also, he has been awarded a scholarship in 2017 for Erasmus in Paris Sorbonne, Paris 6—Pierre et Marie Curie.

LinkedIn: https://www.linkedin.com/in/myron-vourakis-47965b240
Email: myronyourakis@gmail.com

Artemis Papachristou

God Did Not Die, He Was Transformed into Big Data

The title is a re-phrase from an interview with G. Agamben with the title *"God didn't die, he was transformed into money"*—An interview with Giorgio Agamben—Peppe Savà https://libcom.org/library/god-didnt-die-he-was-transformed-money-interview-giorgio-agamben-peppe-savà

Philosophy and Praxis: the necessary Societal Cybernetics

As we have seen through multiple views starting with the Renaissance philosophers, *Nature* and *Culture* are two discrete but complementary systems regarding the human's existence on Earth. They act cybernetically, one feeding each other in a constant loop, always reconsidering the place of humans on Earth. Inside the one created by humans, namely *culture,* there are also two other systems that we could say that appear more opposing to one another than complementing one another. This is the eternal battle between *theory* and *practice.* Humans, through the dualistic Cartesian anthropocentrism, saw themselves as something special and discreet from nature, "a kingdom within a kingdom" as B. Spinoza mentioned while criticizing this view. B. Spinoza insists that the creation of purpose and meaning in human life is only a creation of their imagination. He states that he personally does not attribute "beauty or ugliness, or order or confusion to nature" and he insists that these distinctions are illusions and creations of the human mind and imagination.[1]

The order of mind vs the order of hands

Thus, we could say that through their anthropocentrism, humans created two conceptual "kingdoms": the one of the minds (theory and philosophy) and the other of the hands (creative gesture). Philosophy is an abstraction; a compression of reality and design can be seen as a manipulation of reality. Heidegger, expressed in his "Thinking, Building, Dwelling", includes the making as a complementary and necessary condition to the thinking and the inhabiting process of humans on Earth. All of them act cybernetically, in harmony, and make us contemplate, search, and eternally reconsider our place on Earth and in life in general. After confronting the complex world, humans

---

1   Spinoza, Baruch. *Correspondence* to Oldenburg, 20.xi.1665: 32.

create new mental habits to weave and curate the concrete world with classifications, introducing abstractions that they try to make logically consistent. A clear example of the main human theoretical endeavors to "make sense of the world is the invention of classification systems. "Men prefer order to confusion" as Spinoza said. These classifications are drawn from empirical observation of their environment and are tested through the design of tools and then inform our understanding of the world, adding cybernetically to what is considered true until that moment. We create fictions and factions (fact + fictions) that are creations based on facts that feed the reality back while creating new facts and new fictions etc. The importance of design and practice after the theoretical trials can be seen in the philosophy of F. Bacon where he analyses, in his New Organum, how the hand and mind act cybernetically with the help of the creation of instruments in order to add to our comprehension of the world.2 The philosopher Leonardo Da Vinci distinguished this separation between theory and practice more clearly and insisted on the importance of invention and so did Adam Smith. The latter specifically considers that the makers were the ones who added to the general improvements instead of the philosophers or men of speculation "whose trade it is not to do anything, but to observe everything". 3

Design as conatus and Conatus as ego

We could agree that design is part of human's distinct animality: *Design is the most human thing about us- design is what makes the human* as claimed in the famous book *"Are We Human? Notes on an Archeology of Design"*. In the same book it is also mentioned that *"Design always presents itself as serving the human, but its real ambition is to redesign the human"* showing not only the importance of creating things to understand the human nature but also the notion of design that includes the ego which always tries to go beyond the limits of that nature. But even in the gesture of creation, inside the *construction* (or more accurately in the Greek gesture of ποιείν-κατασκευάζειν) and in what we more generally call

---

2   "Neither the naked hand nor the understanding left to itself can affect much. It is by instruments and helps that the work is done, which are as much wanted for the understanding as for the hand. And as the instruments of the hand either give motion or guide it. So, the instruments of the mind supply either suggestions for the understanding or cautious." Narrator, Aphorisms: Book One: II Bacon, Francis. 1620. *Novum Organum.*

3   "Many improvements have been made by the ingenuity of the makers of the machines, when to make them became the business of a peculiar trade; and some by that of those who are called philosophers or men of speculation, whose trade it is not to do anything, but to observe everything; and who, upon that account, are often capable of combining together the powers of the most distant and dissimilar objects." Smith, Adam. 1776. *An Inquiry into the Nature and Causes of the Wealth of Nations*, p.11.

design, hides the arbitrariness of the human mind. This is where the anthropocentric narrative of *giving sense* and *purpose* is constructed and where Spinoza's view on human illusion is in a way certified. P. Valery, in his text on Leonardo da Vinci, shows that this narration of continuity is actually something completely arbitrary, a creation of our minds:

> "The wonder is that we sometimes receive an impression of accuracy and consistency from human constructions made of an agglomeration of seemingly incompatible elements, as though the mind that arranged them had recognized their secret affinities. But the wonder passes all bounds when we perceive that the author, in the vast majority of cases, is himself unable to give an account of the paths he followed, and that he wields a power whose motive forces he does not know."[4]

The "make sense" notion is nothing more than *"psychological postulate of continuity"*, a need to give a narrative on a thing and see it as a whole. This necessary attribute of continuity and meaning is the one that feeds our *conatus*, referring to the Spinozian version of conatus as *the effort by which each thing tries to stay in existence, and that effort is the actual essence of the thing.*[5]

The *Conatus* can be found in physics in the concept of inertia, but it can also be biologically found in the attribute of the nerves to still maintain some of their "livelihood" for some time even after the death of the organism. It is an interesting biological phenomenon that if seen philosophically, is in a way a physical expression of the Spinozian conatus aspect included in living things.

But aren't all living creatures, including humans, constantly working against entropy from the moment they are being brought into life? *Conatus* in the Spinozian term then, is involuntary, if we see it as the necessary and constant survival work against entropy. When the term applies to human animals, it also includes existential angst, the search for purpose in life.

A contemporary reading of Spinoza can cancel his claim that there is no purpose in life, but it could emphasize at the same time his view, that the need for giving purpose is a distinct characteristic of human nature (even if it is a creation of their imagination).

---

4   Valéry, Paul, Malcolm Cowley, and James R. Lawler. *Collected Works of Paul Valery, Volume 8: Leonardo, Poe, Mallarme.* Princeton University Press, 1972. http://www.jstor.org/stable/j.ctt13x17tt.

5   Spinoza, Benedict (de), *Ethics, III: The Affects.*

Design can be seen as conatus in a double way:

- conatus = working against entropy + the effort to stay in existence ---> trying to find purpose and meaning in order to have the will to stay in existence ---> creation of things (design) in order to search for this meaning

And as:

- creation of things in order to make our existence extended and thus somehow be immortal.

This can be translated literally through the scientific effort to extend the length of human life expectancy but also metaphorically, in the will of creators (either scientists or artists) to become legendary and *live forever through their creations*.

At this point, I would like to use the Spinoza's anti-anthropocentric view to show how anthropocentric humans are:

Another attribute that can be seen as certain and standard in human nature is their eternal will to doubt even if they arrive at some conclusions, for them to evolve further. G. Vico clearly states that natural human aspect by talking about the "natural curiosity which is the daughter of ignorance and the mother of knowledge"[6] but also before him, F. Bacon, implies the importance of doubting by mentioning the inertia that dogmatic sciences introduce—meaning that they prevent the creation of useful works by their absolute opinions they carry as concrete truths.[7] Even B. Spinoza, who had anti-anthropocentric opinions, mentions in his *Ethics* that "all men are born ignorant of the causes of things", and that "all men want to seek their own advantage and are conscious of wanting this.[8]

We could say that this specific nature of curiosity can also be seen as a form of the Spinozian *conatus*. The need for existence is connected to the need for giving meaning and purpose and this purpose can be seen as the one that

---

6   "...exercise that natural curiosity which is the daughter of ignorance and the mother of knowledge, and which, opening the mind of man, gives birth to wonder, ..." Vico, Giambattista. *New science*, p. 106.

7   In Aphorism LXXXV, in *Novum Organum*, Francis Bacon: "So that, if the truth must be spoken, when the rational and dogmatical sciences began the discovery of useful works came to an end. ..." and in Aphorism XI, "As the sciences which we now have do not help us in finding out new works, so neither does the logic which we now have help us in finding out new sciences."

8   Please see: *Ethics*, Benedict (de) Spinoza.

humans strive for. That means that the notion of trying to somehow live—stay as much as they can in life—can be seen as the purpose of living per se so that to live means that you "have to strive for immortality".

Philosophy as a design process

An interesting view on the philosophy-praxis polarity is the opinion of Reza Negarestani that philosophy is part of the design space. He refuses to consider philosophy as a separate discipline and believes that it is itself a design process. For him, evolution can be considered a design gesture, and we humans, while being part of it in the way that Plato refers to as *Methexis,* have some agency to the narrative. He claims that through this participation we can create different forms of design by introducing different constraints and parameters. We might take each current condition for granted and be entrenched in it in a way we don't have a choice, but at the same time we are also able to change the narrative with the appropriate conceptual gestures. This is the power of this distinct human animality called *speculation*: humans, by using their philosophical and imaginative skills to apply various concepts and ideas, they manage to "rewind the tape" and change the narrative of existing but also future conditions. R. Negarestani concludes that the philosophy that acts as a design space "opens the gates to reconfigure parameters of participation and *methexis*" in a way that allows us to think differently and radically. We can then claim that by this design gesture we can thus change the conditions of our participation and *methexis*.[9]

Conatus as the Invisible Hand

Adam Smith's *Invisible Hand* is stated within his economic analysis of society and while describing the means and need for production. The connection of the term with capitalism is clear. We could go further by saying that this non-stop effort for evolution and immortality mentioned above, makes humans move for the *"better"* and we can thus make a clear connection between this and the *Conatus* by seeing the contemporary version of both in capitalism. The extreme version of ego and the notion of eternally evolve to achieve more, cannot be seen anywhere else better than in the creation of capitalism. In capitalism—even if the search for meaning is absent and the creation of meaningless things is part of its game—the rule is the non-stop movement of the wheels, the eternal competition, and mainly the constant strives to evolve and become the better version of oneself. All this with profit always

---

9   Please see: Sheltering Places, Season 4, Episode 1 (Feb 2, 2021).

as a parallel goal. We are of course speaking from the moment of the inevitable upcoming collapse of the game and from the dawn of one of its effects: anthropogenic climate change. It is inside this exact collapse that we can think of *Conatus* as a paradox. The same force that moves "the wheel" and strives for eternal existence, is the same that causes self-destruction.

Conatus as a paradox: conatus as a self-cancelling force

Another characteristic of the human mind is that it is able to take the hypothetical seriously. By predicting the changes that we create in the climate, we can calculate the time of the destruction of the habitable conditions and thus the probable time of our extinction. In the book, *Are we human?* it is eloquently stated that "The human might be the only species to have systematically designed its own extinction and seems to be getting close to accomplishing the goal". In the age of climate crisis and apparent climate change, the relationship of humans and nature, as we knew it until recently, is now totally reconsidered. Today, both theorists and designers call themselves *Speculators* and *Futurists*. The reflection on the *future*, that appears sooner than we expected, is accelerated through the need for finding a solution for the climate emergency and the new threat of extinction. There have been moments when theorists developed concepts and then, there have been design efforts expressing the theories of some philosophers materially. Today, reality changes so quickly, that this relationship is inverted, and technology is in some way ahead of our concepts.

This non-stop effort for the *better* is the same one that guides us in the destruction of ourselves. It is guiding us to self-destruction by the extreme effort of self-maintenance. There is this paradox included in the contemporary *Conatus* of humanity: that this greediness to *go further and better* is the same reason for the inevitable stop and the destruction of our home, Earth and thus ourselves.

But the societal need for *Conatus* found the solution! Humans have always imagined versions and ways to *live forever*. This striving for immortality can be seen in the scientific efforts to freeze human bodies but mostly in our egoistic effort to make our consciousness live eternally, beyond human extinction. Artificial Intelligence is of course tangible proof of that wish. Apart from seeing AI as just an effort to understand more about our human nature we cannot forget that it is a tool to extend the life of this human nature, a mechanism to extend our *Conatus*. Both efforts cannot be but anthropocentric efforts. An already existing creation that, with some use of additional AI, can act as an *Automata* after our extinction but also and can be seen as a parallel layer of our collective consciousness, is *Big Data.*

Big Data as the contemporary collective Conatus of humanity

One of the (maybe involuntary) cultural creations of humans is Big Data. By 2025, IDC (International Data Group) predicts there will be 163 zettabytes of data.[10] Big Data philosophy "encompasses unstructured, semi-structured and structured data, however, the main focus is on unstructured data."[11] There have been a lot of efforts to curate and organize data (for example Map Reduce using a parallel processing model) but it is certain that there is still a great amount of unorganized information. Critical data studies investigate the side effects of this second layer of chaotic human information. Being a version of a collective intelligence, Big Data already has a positive version finding its best example implemented through Taiwan's government with its version of digital democracy, digital activists, and its free open-source software movement.[11]

Big Data can be seen as an extension to the attempt of communicating and proving humans' existence in the Universe, going further from the creation and release of the Pioneer plaques in space in 1972-3. It is a result of human creation, beyond what can be called human. It can potentially be seen as something that accumulates all the consciousness and essences and reflects the minds, thoughts and ideas of all humans who register in it. It has the potential to include all the possible know-hows (thus also the processes of making) and in general *all the knowledge in the world.* This could be the platform that can potentially act as an *Automaton* and realize the anthropocentric dream of avoiding death and leaving human memory eternally in the Universe.

Distinct AI can be an edited and curated version of personalized storage of memory and consciousness, whereas Big Data can be seen as the *raw* version of humanity: a platform that is the amalgam of human knowledge and consciousness—the Spinozian "that men's minds differ as much as their palates do".[12] It includes all uncrated humanity in its arbitrariness and entropic form. Entropy in physics reflects disorder and the biggest value of it is equal to the complete disorder of everything and the *end of life.* The interesting thing about the entropic condition of the biggest part of Big Data is that it is the

---

10   Please refer to Wikipedia's link on Big Data: https://en.wikipedia.org/wiki/Big_data.

11   Please see: "How Taiwan's Unlikely Digital Minister Hacked the Pandemic" by Andrew Leonard in WIRED. Available at: </https://www.wired.com/story/how-taiwans-unlikely-digital-minister-hacked-the-pandemic/>[Accessed on 23.04.2023, at. 09:10].

12   *Ethics,* Benedict (de) Spinoza.

one that includes all these narratives about human life on Earth. In our narrative, it is the one that—even entropic—can reflect the dream of the eternal *Conatus*, thus *immortality*. Thus, we have another paradox here: the complete entropy that normally in physics equals the end of life, in this concept of *Big Data as Conatus* the complete entropy is the continuation of life (by "life" here meaning the reflected and stored memory of the totality of human consciousness, knowledge and creation). The next time we like that healthy recipe post on Instagram or send that funny cat video to our Facebook friends, we unconsciously contribute to the amalgamation of the Internet of things that will reflect humankind in the post-human future. Isn't our Facebook profile photo or our carefully curated Instagram posts proof of vanity and a personal will to have our memory forever alive, a personal *Conatus*? We unconsciously contribute to the collective *Conatus* through *Big Data*.

The Spinozian way of Big Data and the Internet of things could be seen as an extension of Nature. Spinoza said that *"God has no kingdom over men except through those who have sovereignty."*[13] Today sovereignty hides mainly in the Cloud, in the planetary scale computation, as B. Bratton analyses.[14] Thus God did not die...he was just transformed into Big Data, where (s)he is worshipped through the Internet of things and receives our prayers through our touch screens.

> The paper was initially prepared as a part of the research done for the New Centre for Research and Practice: *Machines before the Machines: A prehistory of Cybernetics, under the tutelage of* **Brunella Antomarini**

Bibliography

Smith, Adam. 1776. *An Inquiry into the Nature and Causes of the Wealth of Nations.*

Leonard, Andrew. 2020. "How Taiwan's Unlikely Digital Minister Hacked the Pandemic in WIRED". Avaialble at: </https://www.wired.com/story/how-taiwans-unlikely-digital-minister-hacked-the-pandemic/> [Accessed on 23.04.2023, at. 09:10].

Colomina, Beatriz Mark, Wigley and Istanbul Tasarım Bienali. 2016. *Are We Human?: Notes on an Archaeology of Design.* Zürich Switzerland: Lars Muller.

Spinoza, Benedict de. 1677. *Ethics.*

---

13   Op cit.
14   *The Stack*, Benjamin H. Bratton

Spinoza, Benedict de. 1665. *Correspondence to Oldenburg.*

Bratton, Benjamin H. 2016. *The Stack: On Software and Sovereignty.* Cambridge Massachusetts: MIT Press. http://site.ebrary.com/id/11206783.

Bacon, Francis. 1620. *The New organon.*

Vico, Giambattista 1725. *The New Science.*

Agamben, Giorgio—"God didn't die, he was transformed into money"—An interview with Giorgio Agamben—*Peppe Savà.* Avaialble at: </https://libcom.org/article/god-didnt-die-he-was-transformed-money-intervie w-giorgio-agamben-peppe-sava/>[Accessed on 23.04.2023, at. 09:20].

Heidegger, Martin. 2001. *Poetry Language Thought* 1St Perennical Classics ed. New York: Perennical Classics.

Heidegger, Martin. 1971. *Building, Dwelling, Thinking, in Poetry, Language, Thought* (translated by Albert Hofstadter), 1971.

Valéry, Paul James R Lawler Malcolm Cowley and Jackson Mathews. 2015. *The Collected Works of Paul Valery. Volume 8 Leonardo Poe Mallarme.* Princeton New Jersey: Princeton University Press.

Big Data on Wikipedia: https://en.wikipedia.org/wiki/Big_data.

Sheltering Places, Season 4, Episode 1 (Feb 2, 2021): https://www.youtube.com/live/V1SsE88Y5QI?feature=share.

ABOUT THE AUTHOR

ARTEMIS PAPACHRISTOU is an architect of theoretical and physical spaces, based in London. She studied architecture in Greece at the University of Thessaly and continued her studies in philosophy at the New Centre for Research and Practice. She also holds a MA in Situated Practice from the Bartlett School of Architecture, UCL, where she was a Teaching Assistant in 2020-2022. She has worked, exhibited, and gave talks in Europe and the USA (ex. *Amphibious Habitats Arch. Exhibition* in Malaga, Spain, *Alien Processes* Conference in the New School in NYC among others). Artemis currently works as an architect in London and contributes to the &&& (Triple Ampersand) Journal.

LinkedIn: https://uk.linkedin.com/in/artemis-papachristou-33229057
Email: llll.artemis.papachristou@gmail.com

Alma Dema & Risvan Tërshalla

The Inherent Connection between Folklore and Culture (The Case "E madhe gjëma e mëkatit, Tat Tanushi i Bubutimës")

Abstract: *Réne Wellek and Austin Warren explained the nature and necessity of the writer's reliance on mythology (folklore): "Saying the writer needs myth is a sign of [the] need he feels to join the society, to find his place in it." The following paper follows Wellek and Warren's point of view to analyse the inherent connection between folklore and culture in "The Great Horror of Sin, Tat Tanushi of Bubutima", written by Mitrush Kuteli in 1972. William Bascom in 1954 claimed that the functions of folklore are to amuse, to validate culture, to educate, and to maintain conformity. Considering these functions, the paper has made an effort to search for and find them. Methods used include textual analysis, close reading, close observation, ethnographic method, narrow focus, and wide focus. The work found the application of William Bascom's four functions in Mitrush Kuteli's work.*

Keywords: Mitrush Kuteli, William Bascom, functions, folklore, education, cultural validation, education.

Introduction

Mitrush Kuteli (1907-1967), pseudonym of Dhimitër Pasko, known in Romanian as Dimitrie Pascu, was born in Pogradec on the banks of Lake Ohrid on 13 September 1907, attended a foreign-language school in Greece (a Romanian commercial college in Thessaloniki), and later moved to Bucharest, where he studied economics and graduated in 1934 with a dissertation on the banking systems of the Balkans. It was also in Bucharest that Kuteli began publishing the collections of short stories for which he is best known.

His first book, "Netë shqipëtare" (Albanian nights), published in Bucharest 1938, was a compilation of eight tales on village life in and around his native Pogradec. Romanian culture, still under the spell of national poet Mihai Eminescu, had left its impact on Kuteli and the many Albanian writers and intellectuals living there in the early decades of the twentieth century. Kuteli set the standard for the short story in southern Albania by attaining a higher level of literary sophistication.

He derived many elements for his tales from the Tosk Albanian oral literature he had heard as a child, using them to create crystalline motifs of village life and a lively narrative style. Kuteli's syntax and lexicon are elaborate, and his diction is often compelling. The peasant themes and the mixture of folksy humour and old-fashioned adventure made his tales popular with broad sections of the reading public during the Second World War and thereafter.

Kuteli died of a heart attack in Tirana on 4 May 1967, bereft of the honour and recognition due to the man who had made the short story a popular genre in Albania and who, had politics not interfered, might otherwise have been the leading prose writer of the fifties.

According to Shatro, Bavjola (2016) Mitrush Kuteli willingly acquiesced by producing noted translations of recognized Soviet authors such as Maxim Gorky, Aleksey Tolstoy, Konstantin Paustovsky, Aleksandr Aleksandrovich Fadeyev, and Nikolay Ostrovsky. Aside from these writers recommended by Soviet cultural and political advisors, Kuteli also managed to publish some translations of his favourite nineteenth century Russian authors: Nikolay Gogol, Ivan Turgenev, Ivan Krylov, and Mikhail Saltykov-Shchedrin.

Due to this vocation and his systematic research and studies, folkloric components predominate in Kuteli's creative work (1972; 174). He deals with possible and impossible facts, the usual and the unusual, the real and the fictional, the fantastic and the artistic, and the inherent and the illusory.

He obtains folkloric subjects in two ways: as a displacement of an existing initial form with its physical opposite and as a suspended form that separates the soul from the body that through metamorphosis is reunited after an almost circular journey with new experiences, acquisitions, symbols, and eternal messages. All these segments seek and reveal the human being in his dimensions in the world "of in here" and "of in there".

This research originates from a religious belief and the language ideology based on autochthonous culture. Therefore, sometimes, the fantastic is not felt or touched as a whole even though it is acquired as a multitude of existences and occurrences and as reversible horizontal transformations, as happens in "Night in the Month of May", "*Lugetërs*[1] of Our Village", and "Uprising for *Lugat*".

---

1   Thus, according to Donat Kurti, it is believed that the lugati is the soul of a bad person who, after being buried, returns to the earth in any other form, which is why it is said "He

Mitrush Kuteli's literary work makes him one of the most important authors of Albanian literature and culture. In the *Literary Works of Mitrush Kuteli*, Sali Bashota (2007; 3-5) asserts the essence of his art is the story, where his prose has managed to create high values in Albanian literature, precisely with poetic language and the functionalization of the literary narrative.

Thus, in Kuteli's story "Autumn of Jeladin Bey", (1972; 174) Maro of Kovi (Kovi's wife) pours a bunch of curses on Beu that he wanted to dishonour her without even knowing his daughter. These curses and the way they flow are typical of folk conversations:

> Poo on a stick! Istanbul's son of a donkey, Balderdash! May God make you mad! You dishonoured me, so let God take your eyes out! You ruined my life, so may you die blind! May the wolf rend your bowels! May you be roasted alive on a spit! May you be lost and never heard of again! May you be buried alive; may you be burnt alive…

Indeed, such signs of an oral discourse that opens up to interdiscursive and intertextual play in the text reflect the relationship of the writer to the oral world. For Kutel, orality as a text and as ethnology, thus also as a ritual, is not only knowledge and passion, but also direct experience, an experience felt in the use of the ethnic-folkloric syntax used in the example above.

In his prose, the dimension of orality as an experience in almost all cases comes to the fore, and this form of expression should be sought in Kuteli's experience and passion for the literary-folkloric tradition and the creativity that originates from it. It must be said that this particular passion does not rise as an authorial artistic goal over the preliminary oral creation and the living material from the life of the ethnos.

Thus, in the story "The Third Autumn Night", the magical ritual is mainly given as a presentation of the character, while "Lugetërt of Our Village" (1938; 295) presents a series of stories related to a theme, with a type of character and a type of equivalent situations that are all related to a *lugat*, a symbolic figure of Albanian folk creativity. The whole basis of the narration and the situations is popular, where the oral intertext constitutes the text itself. In "Lugetërit of our village" (1938; 295):

> Last year we had as strong lugat Shabani's Shaqo and, another year that was also lugat and this year Cutes's Mero. This monk Mero fell and died there, both from some ailment

---

changes his mind as a lugat.…" Lugati is probably to have an evil spirit because it causes a lot of damage. It annoys the livestock, beats it, overturns the barrels, drops the water, spills the cow's milk, etc. Kurti, Donat, O. F. M, *Prralla Kombtare, Mbledhë prej gojës së popullit*, BLÊ I, Botimi i Dytë, A. Gjergj Fishta, Shkodër 1942, 259-260.

because it had been written to him. As long as she was alive the village had said that he would have raised lugat. And indeed, as soon as he died, he fell and rose again.

In this context, the creative world of popular creation is built by overthrowing the world of reality. In popular creation, the narrative has no Saxon character. At its centre is not a hero but a character. His character is inimitable. The folk creation (fairy tale) does not deal with grandiose themes; rather it is a manifestation of ancient forms, consciousness, and subconsciousness.

According to Vladimir Propp, (2004; 27), folk creation (fairy tale) has a meaning. Kuteli has chosen not to tell fairy tales or legends but to play the role of mediator between what he knows (heard) and what he tells. As he says himself, he does not narrate the event but talks about the event, a position that allows Kuteli to identify the folklore in the representative culture and reinforce the culture in it.

In the introduction to "The Great Horror of Sin, Tat Tanushi of Bubutima", Kuteli (2011; 12) says "we are writing it on the epistle as we have heard it..." One cannot but prove that, in any case, Tat Tanushi is not identified with the features of a hero but of a character. However, he cannot be imitated and has not been imitated; the whole fable of the novel deals with a simple theme with a grand style, preserving the meaning of the representative culture and acting both in the consciousness and in the subconscious of the reader who also takes the role of the character.

According to Aurel Plasari, (1995, 34) Kuteli's narratives embody a grotesque realism that speaks to readers with a universal language but also have a large-scale use of the processes of folk stories, with local colours, turned into art by Kuteli; they also bring the reader the special Albanian "brand". His special style and method constitute an innovation in narrative prose and mark the birth of modern Albanian prose. Today, he is considered one of the masters of the Albanian word because he chooses the allegory derived from the fairy tale and all folkloric creativity.

This close relationship is felt in "The Big River", "August Night", "Night Month's May", "April Night", "How Did Ago Jakupi Find the Fay of God", "Rina Kateriniza", "The Dead", "Autumn of Jeladin Bey", etc., but the paper brings to light the connection between folklore and culture in "The Great Horror of Sin, Tat Tanushi of Bubutima".

In this short story, the fantastic takes on a very wide scope. The work we are dealing with belongs to a literary genre that knows no boundaries, no time and no space. The role of the characters and the exchange of their temperaments become the bearers of the fantastic, of the impossible, which, emerging and born as an ethnic-folkloric layer, reaches biblical, extraordinary proportions, coming from the divine.

Kuteli, introducing the concept of the fantastic, shows an extraordinary creative ability to "perform magic" with the concept of time and space. Both of these concepts are aligned as constituent elements of the textual structure and also of the worldview of the characters concerning life and death. The time-space relativity creates a broad background, simultaneously renewing models of the oral tradition and bringing models of the tradition of Albanian literature.

Kuteli not only found his place in the fairy tale, legend, myth, and anecdotes but also left his indisputable mark on it, managing to find a permanent thread between the folklore and culture of his country.

To these long-standing connections, Kuteli gave his original viscosity, letting us understand that his was more than an artistic and literary vocation, more than passion and natural talent. He was called and chosen by the autochthonous vocation of ancient and early Albanian roots. This call is felt in most of his stories, such as "Babalja", "The Beauty of the Sea", "The Rich Man Who Was Very Poor", "Uprising for Lugat", "The Lugetërit Our Village" and especially in "The Great Horror of Sin, Tat Tanushi of Bubutima".

The functions of folklore

Folklorist William Bascom (1965) identifies four functions of folklore that also work in the family folk group. He asserts that folklore serves to amuse, validate culture, educate, and maintain conformity. Folklore lets people escape from repressions imposed upon them by society. Folklore validates culture, justifying its rituals and institutions to those who perform and observe them. Folklore is a pedagogic device which reinforces morals and values and develops wit.

For Hamiti, Sabri (2009; 361-363) "The Great Horror of Sin, Tat Tanushi of Bubutima" is a painful story about human love. Tat Tanushi of Bubutima in Illyria is a learned and pious man who falls in love with Kalia from Galilee. His powerful love for her begins to rival his love for God, so Tat Tanushi falls into sin. Referring first to Hamiti, we can begin to perceive the knots that connect Tat Tanushi with ethnic Albanian culture (Illyria).

This perception, which, however, initially has a subjective character, in the depth of perception turns into a judgment and takes an inherent form. According to Kuteli, all the content of his well-known short story is derived from two legends heard in the villages of Pogradec and the surroundings of the Dry Mountain, which is reflected and created in its playful waters.

Legends, according to Malinowski, Bronislaw (1926:24), are believed to be true and contain important factual information.

To measure the authentic connection that folklore creates with (native) culture, Bascom (1954; vol. 67: 335) states that the time(s) and place(s) where the legends are told, the identity of the narrator, the composition of the audience, the factor of private ownership, the style of recitation, the participation of the audience, the attitudes of the people, and even the functions are to a considerable extent unique or distinctive in the various categories that are recognized. Therefore, it is rightly said that the unique *"identity card"* that "The Great Horror of Sin, Tat Tanushi of Bubutima" has acquired must be sought and found in its connection with folklore.

The short story starts like this:

> In the early days, a priest named Tanush lived in the bay of the East Church. He evangelized in the village of Illyria, the parish of Apollonia, which is at the mouth of the old Aouses (the ancient name of Vjosa). The name of the village is Bubutimë, after the noise made by the sea. We warn the readers not to look for this ancient village in the place where it was founded because earthquakes and wars have destroyed it and today the place is covered by a dense forest (p. 13).

Does The Great Horror of Sin, Tat Tanushi of Bubutima have the gift of entertaining?

Literature has proven the ability to offer us new experiences at safe distances. It allows us to experience a range of feelings, perhaps unknown before, such as melancholy, triumph, conflict, intrigue, betrayal, loyalty, death, birth, discovery, and almost anything else that people can experience. We, as readers, often unwittingly and unconsciously adopt and even become fond of artificial memories.

This way of perceiving and feeling becomes a source of calmness and amusement, just as it becomes a challenge to know and meet each—other.

Todorov, Tzvetan (2015:41), in "Introduction to Fantastic Literature", defines three conditions to build a dynamic relationship between the reader and the pleasure that the text can give him: a) the text must force the reader to consider the world of the characters as a world of living men, and for the events shown he may hesitate (oscillate) between a natural explanation and a supernatural explanation; b) hesitation must be experienced by a character; so the role of the reader is entrusted to him, a character, and at the same time, hesitation appears and becomes one of the themes of the work; in the case of a naive reader, the real reader identifies with the character; and c) the reader is asked to maintain a certain attitude towards the text: he will reject both the allegorical interpretation and the "poetic" interpretation.

Entertainment is, for Bascom, too, one of the functions of folklore and an important one. He (1954; vol. 67; 343) developed this concept but it cannot be accepted as a complete answer because it is clear that beneath a considerable amount of humour lies a deeper meaning. The same applies to the concepts of fantasy and creative imagination.

The fact that the storyteller (narrator, in our case) in some societies is expected to modify a known legend by introducing new elements or giving a romantic twist to the fable carries in itself a fundamental importance for the study of the dynamics and aesthetics of folklore, but one might ask why the narrator chooses to introduce specific elements.

The short story studied here is honest and open to its reader from the title on because it indicates the kind of humour and fun it is meant to convey, the kind of fun we will encounter. Grammatical inversion emphasizes the obvious aestheticism but raises curiosity and the desire to prove it.

We accepted since the beginning that "The Great Horror of Sin, Tat Tanushi of Bubutima", is a short story with emphasized fantastic characteristics, and in this way we justified its connection with the autochthonous Albanian culture (Illyria) and in this context following the series judging by Todorov, T. (2015:108), it is good for us to define the three main functions of the fantastic: to cause special effects on the reader, such as fear, horror, or curiosity (this as a cause of the constituent aestheticism); to serve the narration, which keeps the interest in the development of the intrigue events in tempo; and to allow the description of a fantastic universe.

Tat Tanushi, first of all, causes admiration for the way he loves and cares about his girlfriend, an admiration and love that is somehow attributed to Albanian men. This kind of attribution, which is rare in Albanian literature, comes as the narrator's desire to raise it to a moral and ethical norm:

> Kalia looked at him with a smile and waited.
> - I want to tell you, Noemi, that I love you so much...
> She laughed and hit his chest with her small fists.
> - Tan, you've told me this a thousand times.
> Then suddenly she stopped laughing.
> - And the more times you tell me, the more I will listen to you.
> He continued as if he hadn't heard it at all:
> - ... and there is nothing on earth, or in heaven, or the waters that I love as much as you... (20-21).

This kind of entertainment leads to the fascination giving to the reader the character's role, turning him into an eyewitness of what happens, and it is clear what is hidden. Kuteli, for Plasari, (1995: 52) is a fantastic writer because for him the investigation of the fantastic world is fruitful not only to discover the sociological parameters of literary genres but also to check the meeting points between writing and reading, something which, in our case, the presence of the reader makes a character.

Aren't we amazed at all the turns of events, the platonic love, and the unparalleled adoration that we encounter? Are we not amused and delighted when we feel the rare tenderness and depth with which young people fall in love? And don't we get upset and saddened when Noemi dies before bearing fruit, and aren't we left speechless by Tata's despair? Are we not fascinated by the dynamic, artistic, and fantastic refraction that Kuteli makes of the biblical myth, the approach and distance that allows us to be a character too?

All this wonderful structure of Albanian letters sometimes hides and sometimes highlights the moral and ethical attitude of the author to fascinate us with; according to Calvino, Italo (2015; 64), the ambiguous and allegorical conception of the fantastic supports the dominant idea of the structure of the legend because the fantastic hides the author's moralistic attitude towards reality; even at first glance it may not be discernible.

In this sense, according to Uçi, Alfred (2001:108), Kuteli invents stories with ghosts and *lugetër*, with grotesque hyperbolizations, so it cannot be seen and evaluated in any other way than as an enrichment of the aesthetic concept of reality in art and the diversity of the literary creativity of the nation.

What kind of cultural connection is established with the folkloric stratifications in "The Great Horror of Sin: Tat Tanushi of Bubutima"?

The researcher Xhiku, Ali (2004; 227) suggests approaching the topic in this manner. It would be naive to think that Kuteli wanted to bring the romantic worship of folklore to Albanian literature. Therefore, it would not seem convincing at all if it were reasoned only in this way since Kuteli's views on folklore and the multiplicity of features of his narratives (stories) are reminiscent of the views and practices of romantic creators.

Reading his work unique these days in the Albanian literary field, but also referring to the criticism and considering the numerous translations and studies of the best world authors, Kuteli remained the detector of a rare calibre of the treasure of indigenous folk creativity. This does not make him feel compelled by any literary or non-literary circumstances but because he feels that the popular fountain offers rest for his tired soul and offers models of getting away from everyday problems and troubles, the therapy used in his artistic creativity.

However, Kuteli would not have been able to become the carrier, a brave intermediator, if he had not known well and qualitatively the raw material, of his beloved homeland. He wouldn't have had the success he continues to have if he hadn't known well the troubles, worries, sorrows, disappointments, joys, and achievements of his people that are poured into songs, dances, tales, myths, and legends.

So, Kuteli knew and used the folklore of his people only with the full knowledge of his culture, and he acted as Bascom describes.

Folkloric layers that constitute the seed of his creativity as a special artistic type produce meaningful layers of reception of the message in the work. *Tat Tanushi* is a love novel, not in the first sense of the word but in the semantic-stylistic connections it creates to materialize this unique human feeling:

- **The presence of epithets:** her *beautiful* eyes became two *dark* holes, *thin* lips, *sunken* pit, and *hard* nipples; yellow... *Black* angel, the *stern* river of wrath, (p. 25)
- **The presence of comparisons:** your caresses are sweeter than wine... your teats are like two gazelle birds. Your hair is like a herd of goats grazing in Galaad. (p. 31) like a flower fades and like a dream goes man and flies (p. 25). Her thin lip was red like pomegranate juice (p. 19)
- **The presence of hyperboles:** it smelled of death as the smell of old graves when they are opened. (p. 25)
- **The presence of magical numerology:** three years passed like this and in these three years... you turned forty years old... (p. 30) ... faithful from seven villages around to hear him (p. 17)
- ... in the Seventh Synod of the Church (p. 18)
- **The presence of the laconic:** I don't know what I want to say, but even those who told me the story [were] shocked at this point when they talked about her beauty. (p. 19)
- **The presence of the antithesis:** a white dove and a black dove, they fell madly in love (p. 17)
- ... poison and joy altogether (p. 25)

- **Rhetorical question:** Why my God, why? What did I do to you that you follow me with your hatred? (p. 26) What joy of life remains unmixed with bitterness? What glory rests above and unmoved? (p. 24).

According to Bascom, the second function of folklore plays an important role in the evaluation of culture, in justifying its rituals and institutions to those who perform and respect them. With justification, we do not seek to be involved in Tata's sin of the flesh or to defend him; we simply try to remain within the Albanian culture and what remains outside of it.

The bringing of Kalia from Galilee in Judea justifies the action of many young Albanians (Illyrians) who had the obligation to take the bride to the captured mountains because they were the same blood; they were all cousins. This action of Tat Tanushi seems to also be defended by Kuteli (2011; 16) when he says: "What apart from this? As far as I know, dear readers, love is neither white, nor black, nor any other colour, but only love and nothing else. It is like the wind; it blows where it wants, and we hear its whisper".

The moral values we learn from the inherent connection between folklore and culture.

Stories and legends, for Malinowski, Bronislaw (1926; 18-24), reside in the lives of the natives, in what they call ethnicity. They are not on paper. When it happens that a researcher puts them on paper, he feels unable to evoke the atmosphere in which they flourish, giving us only a part of the mutilated reality. Malinowski also (1926; 19) admits that the myth (legend) cannot be explained but serves as "an order, a statute and often a practical guide" for magic, ceremony, ritual, and social structure.

Myth (legend) fulfils a necessary function in primitive culture: it expresses, enhances, and codifies belief; defends and enforces morality; guarantees the efficacy of the ritual; and contains practical rules for the guidance of man. Thus, myth is a vital component of human civilization; it is not an idle tale, but a hard-working active force; it is not an intellectual explanation or an artistic image but a pragmatic map of primitive faith and moral wisdom, which Kuteli has done best.

Kuteli, omniscient about what he had to convey in this legend, paints the entire atmosphere of the conception of the story, equipping it with necessary details to give the participant the right to observe without depriving us of a single moment of aesthetic pleasure. It skilfully uses the reference as an open form of intertextuality (Piégay-Gros, N. 2011; 68) as an absent relationship sending us to the original text without naming it.

On the other hand, by giving us the right of the character in addition to the reader, it has created that other form of intertextuality which is the literary allusion (Ibid; 75), so we can understand with revealed words what the author wants to say in a crosswise way. So, seeking to verify the thesis raised at the beginning, we will try to outline the already embedded knowledge on morality and ethics: morality and ethics are not the same because morality refers to the values of good, right, and truth, while ethics is about codifying these values and simplifying them, so people understand when an action leads to moral values.

Returning briefly to the fable of *the long narrative* (a term borrowed from Gjika. Kastriot), we would synthesize that the protagonist of the novel, Tat Tanushi, is an Orthodox priest who is allowed to marry Noemi, whom he had taken from Galilee in Judea, and for this reason, her name changed into Kalie.

The two were very much in love, but Kalie according to the biblical interpretation of the concept of biological reproduction, "could not tie trees—wasn't able to have children". As soon as the reader grows fond of the two lovers, the reader is informed of Kalie's illness, which has a karmic spiritual origin. Her illness will not only push events further but will also test Tat Tanushi's love and patience after her subsequent death.

The subjectivization of her description even in this state shows that even the disease does not differentiate them.

Tat Tanushi's courage to express his feelings through his haunting hyperbolizing as a centre of the universe pushes him towards blasphemy, including uncertainty in the physical and metaphysical concepts. A haunted, disappointed, desperate, repentant sinner seeks the grace of God, which is denied three times in a row, and not only that: he is cursed with immortality.

This is where Tat Tanushi's downfall begins, leaving the village where he has evangelized and the flock he has shepherded and fleeing, seeking nowhere. The years pass and become centuries; he falls into the waters and does drown, enters the fire and does not burn, goes through wars and is not killed, because the eternal feminine has bound him to the ground with strong chains and the time for **catharsis** has not come.

This proximity reminds us that the relationship between myth and ritual has often been discussed, and not enough has been said about the relationship of myth to the prevailing worldview and religion. The relationship of values expressed in narratives to actual behaviour and sanctions is another important topic. I cannot but believe, states Hallowell, Alfred Irwing (1947; 548), that the surface has not been "scratched" and that much valuable material which will deepen our understanding of culture remains to be clarified by those of us who systematically study oral accounts in all their aspects of society.

We have accepted up to this moment of our discussion that "The Great Horror of Sin, Tat Tanushi of Bubutima", preserves and even deepens a sometimes visible and sometimes hidden connection with authentic Albanian culture, embodied in its folklore layers. Seeking to prove the third function of folklore according to Bascom, we can state that beyond the typical atmosphere, the essence of stylistic figuration, the ritual of burying the dead, and the representative individual with Illyrian character and temperament, we cannot say that the behaviour and the spiritual, human, and religious activity of Tat Tanushi refer to the values of *good*, *right* and *true*.

It is easily understood that Tat Tanushi deliberately and consciously goes against the functional religious laws and canons. Beyond the fact that he does not accept the loss of her love, he does not accept death or even more so the resurrection, opening the grave to see his dead wife, carving frescoes with her face and image, and he commits the sin of the flesh inside the church and continues to ask for God's grace.

The principle of good can be treated subjectively, but right and truth cannot, so the behaviour and experience of Tat Tanushi, if it is not right, is not true either, and if it is not true, it is not right either. By the same logic, we would also follow the codification of these values and their simplification for people, which is highly unlikely to happen.

To fully understand knowledge and its role in human life, we must have more knowledge about the specific functions of each of these forms in different societies, and by this, we mean that the novel, even though it is built on legendary folklore layers, does not remain the specific and isolated case with features of Albanian culture only.

The indisputable moral value of this whole event, both specific and deep, which we learn from Tat Tanushi's wanderings to find death and the grace of God, is that love is a universal and eternal feeling. The only thing that will be able to save us is love.

Compatibility with cultural behaviour patterns
Following Bascom's line of discussion, folklore fulfils the pleasure of maintaining conformity, to accept patterns of behaviour, and to spread a pleasure of particular importance, though often overlooked. The conformity with

cultural patterns of behaviour which are also related to validation and education about the connections of culture deserves to be distinguished from them. More than serving to validate or justify institutions, beliefs, and attitudes, some forms of folklore seem to be important tools to exert social influence and control.

As an institution of a special category in Albanian popular beliefs, in its canons, in the unwritten and collectively implemented laws, adultery is punished. Although we can easily justify Tat Tanushi's action with the fact that his current wife had died, in these canons, a period of mourning is clearly and strictly defined. Therefore, *the long narrative* (Gjika, K.—Seminary of Pristina 2017), in this case, does not maintain the required compatibility that is observed in folklore.

Folklore is also used to express social approval of those who conform; some forms such as "praise names" and songs weave praises specifically for this purpose. In many societies, folklore is used to control or influence the activities of others from the moment the first lullaby is sung to them. Folklore can also become an internal control of behaviour, as noted in the works of Opler, Moris Edward (1938: xii), and the statements of Raum, Otto Fridrich (1930; xi) on the proverbs of the Chaga people. Their intrinsic value to the Chaga lies in two qualities: they are a legacy of their ancestors including tribal experience, and they serve as instruments both for self-control and for the control of others.

In the case of our discussion, Tat Tanushi is a priest, and his human behaviour and activity is determined from the beginning. He can never oppose or bypass it. His main principle is self-control and only if he realizes this can he control, guide, and lead others. Tata insults the grace of God and being aware of it, asks to have it again, not respecting the religious heritage or the experience of his previous teachers.

Conclusions

Finnish folklore researcher Honko, Lauri (2006; 45) points out that the biggest difference between oral and literary storytelling is that the literary author, even if he draws on tradition, does not let the elements of tradition determine the solution to the fable or form, while the oral (folk) singer is limited by tradition and by the horizon of the audience's reception.

This paper tried to highlight the inherent connection between folklore and the culture which produces it, embodied in "The Great Horror of Sin, Tat Tanushi of Bubutima". From the beginning, we defined the type and subtype of the long narrative and the level of the folkloric layer which gave us the right to investigate it according to Bascom's folklore functions. It was highlighted that the novel had prominent folkloric features and elements as well as uniqueness as a genuine artistic and literary work.

Although it is accepted both by the author and by us, that the fable is built on two legends heard in the Pogradec area, the extraordinary style of Mitrush Kuteli, his vocation for art and culture, and his love for Albanian language, customs, and traditions, is undeniable. He aspired to thread the connection between the Albanian culture and the folklore that comes from it.

"The Great Horror of Sin, Tat Tanushi of Bubutima" amuses and fascinates like any other folklore that rises above the local culture, proves, and deepens the connection with culture and folklore, and tries to maintain the compatibility between heritage and its processing as dictated by the formula of self-control and control of others. As for the way and strength of education, the novel preserves its uniqueness as a literary type of fantastic literature.

References

Bashota. Sali. 2007. "Vepra letrare e Mitrsuh Kutelit," *Bibliotetra*, Viti 4, Nr. 2, Nëntor 2007, Prishtinë.

Calvino. Italo. 2015. "Mbi përrallën", *Pika pa sipërfaqe*, Tiranë.

Dushi, Arbnora. 1947. "Folkloristikë—koncepte modern", *Dukagjini*, 2006, Pejë.

Hallowell, Alfred Irwing, 1947. "Myth, Culture and Personality," *American Anthropologist*, 49,

Hamiti, Sabri. 2009. "Letërsia moderne shqipe", UET Press. Tiranë.

Kurti. Donat, At O. F. M, 1942. "Prralla Kombtare, Mbledhë prej gojës së popullit", BLÊ I, Botimi i Dytë, A. Gjergj Fishta, Shkodër.

Kuteli. Mitrush. 1938. "Netë Shqiptare," *Naim Frashëri*, Tiranë.

Kuteli. Mitrush. 1972. "Tregimi të zgjedhura," *Naim Frashëri*, Tiranë.

Malinowski, Bronislaw. 1926. *Myth in Primitive Psychology*, New York.

Opler, Moris Edward. 1938. "Myths and Tales of the Jicarilla Apache Indians." *Memoirs of the American Folklore Society*, 31 (1938).

Piégay-Gros. N. 2011. Nathalie, *Poetika e intertekstualitetit*, Parnas, Prishtinë.

Plasari, Aurel. 1995. "Kuteli midis të gjallëve dhe të vdekurve", *Apolonia*, Tiranë.

Propp, Vladimir. 2004. "Morfologjia e përrallës, përktheu nga origjinali Agron Tufa, "Shtëpia e Librit dhe e Komunikimit & Aleph", Tiranë.

Raum Otto Friedrich and International African Institute. 1940. *Chaga Childhood; a Description of Indigenous Education in an East African Tribe.* London: Pub. for the International Institute of African languages & cultures by the Oxford University Press.

Shatro, Bavjola. 2016. *Between(s) and Beyond(s) in Contemporary Albanian Literature.* Cambridge Scholars Publishing. p. 44.

Todorov. Tzvetan. 2015. "Hyrje në letërsinë fantastike", *Pika pa sipërfaqe,* Tiranë.

Uçi, Alfred, 2001. *Estetika e groteskut: Grotesku në letërsinë shqipe,* v. IV, Mësonjëtorja, Tiranë.

William R. Bascom. 1954. "Four Functions of Folklore Author(s)" *The Journal of American Folklore,* Vol. 67, No. 266 (Oct.—Dec., 1954).

Xhiku, Ali. 2004. *Letërsia shqipe si polifoni,* Dituria, Tiranë.

ABOUT THE AUTHORS

DR. ALMA DEMA is a senior Lecture of Comparative Literature and Cultural Anthropology at the Department of Literature, Faculty of Education, Aleksander Moisiu University of Durres in Albania. Her professional interests range from anthropology, comparative literature, cultural studies. Some of her papers and articles have been published in scientific journals, such as Science Arena Publication Specialty Journal of Humanities and Cultural Science and International journal of science, Mondo Italo—Albanese Italy, Interdisciplinary Journal of Research and Development, Albania, Haemus, Rumania, Context, North Macedonia, etc. She has published two monographs A treatise of some of Albanian Anthropological Attributes, in Riga, Republic of Latvia 2019, and Traces of ethnological thought in fairy tales' field, 2018, Duures, Albania. She has also referred her papers in national and international conferences and congresses as: State University of Pushkin, Leningrad: Continuous Education for Sustainable Development, Lifelong Learning, Russia, Central Connecticut State University, in the conference "International Journal of Arts & Sciences", Siena, Italy, International conference: "Languages, Cultures, Ethnos. The Formation of the Linguistic World-Image, Philological and Methodical Aspects", Russia, Children of the Future, international conference hosted by University of Cambridge, England.

Email: demaalma@gmail.com
ORCID: 0000-0002-2691-1262

DR. RISVAN TËRSHALLA is a senior lecturer at the Department of Sociology at "Aleksandër Moisiu" University, Durres. He holds a Bachelor's degree from the University of Tirana, Faculty of Social Sciences. From the same university, he has earned Master's Degree and Doctor Degree in Philosophy and Political Philosophy. His papers and articles have been published in scientific journals, such as Science Arena Publication Specialty Journal of Humanities and Cultural Science and International journal of science, Interdisciplinary Journal of Research and Development, Albania, Haemus, Rumania. He is a member of Albanian Institute of Sociology. The topics in his papers take a wide range from The liberalization of visas; spiritual or political necessity to The impossibility of adapting to the social as one of the individualism's resources, from The ethics in the ancient Albanian laws to The individualism concept in postmodern context, from Professional ethics as a necessity in university curricula to Human right and the "problem" of sexual orientation in the context of international migration. His professional interests range from moral philosophy, communication and human rights.

LinkedIn: https://www.linkedin.com/in/risvan-tershalla-8466a0228/
Email: risvantershalla@gmail.com

Eriola Qafzezi

Hindered With(in) Hedges:
Exploring on Hedging as Stylistic Devices Employed by Detective Writers: The Case of Agatha Christie in Translation into Albanian

Abstract: *The current paper has explored the use of hedging as a stylistic device employed in literary writing, more specifically in detective novel. Hedging refers to those expressions that make statements more indeterminate, inexact or reduce the strength of assertion on the behalf of the writer. At times, they are considered a device to gain reader's acceptance of knowledge claims and reduce levels of criticism, contributing to politeness and interaction in communicative purposes. At other times, they allow writers to express uncertainty about the level of truthfulness or trustworthiness of their statements. This paper presents the results of a qualitative study by having examined the latter use of hedging devices, as means of expressing vagueness, confusion, lack of certainty and withholding information intentionally to distort the readers in search of the thread that connects events and characters. The study has brought relevant literature review, outlining main contributions that recognize the different types of hedging and the purposes for which they are employed by the writer. The practical part of the study has exemplified cases of the use of a multiplicity of hedges in detective writing. To fulfill such purposes, we have selected Agatha Christie as a representative of detective writers, since her novels are a perfect example of hedging and enigmas that engage readers to solve the puzzles that are intentionally and masterfully intertwined by the author through complicated plot but simplicity of language. We were thus involved in comparative translation study, and we tried to find out who gained an edge on hedges, writer, translator, or both. Having observed hedging devices and their types, we found out that they were still preserved in the Albanian translation.*

Keywords: hedges, detective, translation, communication, intention.

Introduction

The present study aims to contribute in the field of discourse analysis of literary texts, more specifically of the detective novel, by uncovering the underlying nuances of meaning of the narrator's stance towards characters and events through exploring motivations of linguistic choices in language use and results on the process of communication. The study of linguistic discourse, together with unraveling of intentional use of linguistic devices from the author contributes to deeper understanding of literature. Furthermore, comparison and juxtaposition of author's choices with translator's choices would help us reflect on the significance and intentionality of use and exploitation of such devices from both author and translator and draw further conclusions on the process of translation and its purposes, and a reconsideration of the notion of debatable notions such as 'equivalence' and 'faithfulness'. Our approach in the current paper is to provide a qualitative analysis of hedges as a pragma-stylistic choice of the detective writer towards choices made by the translator. To fulfill such aim, we are going to bring some literature review about hedges and purposes of employing them in order to create a theoretical background that will be supported with examples in the practical part of the paper. Examples will be juxtaposed both in the original and translation. It is hoped that through such a discourse analysis process, both about the original and its translation, will explore meanings produced by specific choices in language use and effect that such choices have on readers and their involvement in the process of sense-making and character individualization while interacting with detective novels (as produced in the original vs in translation). Due to space limitations, the study will not enter into quantitative analysis, which, in itself, would yield important results about the statistical use of hedging in detective novels and their translations, but such a thing is outside the scope of the current paper.

1. Literature review on hedges as stylistic devices

The aim of this section is to bring to the foreground aims of using different types of hedging in literature and other types of writing. The use of hedging as a linguistic and stylistic device has different purposes among which we can mention politeness, respect, caution and, in the case of detective novels, creation of vagueness up to the point of withholding and hindering information and obscuring the facts, in order to (mis)guide readers until the revelation of the mysterious veil cast on purpose by the author and/or the narrator. The word 'hedging' was coined by George Lakoff in his article *Hedges: A Study in Meaning Criteria and the Logic of Fuzzy Concepts*. In examining different degrees of truth, Lakoff states that logicians assume that sentences of natural languages are true, false or 'nonsense', and such a thought, for lack of a sensible alternative, has also been shared by most contemporary linguists, especially those delved into formal semantics. However, as Lakoff asserts, such an assumption can be proved wrong by students of language, particularly psychologists and linguist philosophers, who are quite aware that natural language concepts have vague boundaries and fuzzy edges, therefore, natural language sentences are often neither true, not false, nor nonsensical, but rather true *to a certain extent and false to a certain extent, true in certain respects and false in other respects* (Lakoff, 1973: 458). The purpose of discussing fuzzy logic, as maintained by Lakoff, is to show that we need not turn to despair when faced with vagueness and fuzziness. The latter can be studied seriously within formal semantics and give rise to all sorts of interesting questions. We support Lakoff's approach that some of the most interesting questions are raised by the study of words whose meaning *implicitly* involves fuzziness—words whose job is to make things fuzzier or less fuzzy (Lakoff, 1973: 471).

The list provided by Lakoff starts with hedges: he analyzes *sort of* as a deintensifier juxtaposed to the intensifier *very*, in that it takes values that are close to true and makes them false while uniformly raising values in the low to mid-range of the scale, leaving the very low range of the scale constant. Some other hedges mentioned by Lakoff are *kind of, loosely speaking, more or less, roughly, pretty much, relatively, somewhat, rather, mostly, technically, strictly speaking, essentially, in essence, basically, principally, particularly, par excellence, largely, for the most part, especially, exceptionally, quintessentially, literally, often, almost, typical, typically, as it were, in a sense, in one sense, in a real sense, in an important sense, in a way, in a manner of speaking, details aside, so to say, virtually, all but technically, practically, nominally, actually, really, -like, -ish, pseudo-, crypto-*, etc. (the complete list of examples an reasoning can be found in Lakoff, 1973: 472-508). But hedges, as Lakoff emphasizes, can reveal a great deal more about meaning, rather than just degrees of category membership distinctions, such as revealing assumptions or presuppositions that negate the literal meaning. Such a realization would invite us to rethink the value of connotations and other pragmatic aspects of meaning, mostly considered as irrelevant to the assignment of truth values since truthfulness is considered to involve only literal or denotative meaning. This, as Lakoff rightly puts it, would indicate that semantics cannot be considered independent of pragmatics, but the two are inextricably related together (Lakoff, 1973: 474). Yet, as Lakoff himself consents, hedges have barely begun to be studied, and he has discussed only a handful (Lakoff, 1973: 483). Therefore, he raises some interesting questions that deserve merit of study such as: Do hedges interact with performatives? Are there hedges in lexical items? What are the primitive fuzzy concepts in natural language? What are the possible types of membership functions? Lakoff concludes as follows: the logic of fuzzy concepts can be studied seriously; in natural language, truth is a matter of degree, not an absolute; fuzzy concepts have internal structure; semantics is not independent on pragmatics; algebraic functions play a role in the semantics of certain hedges; perceptual finiteness depends on an underlying continuum of values; the logic of hedges requires serious semantic analysis for all predicates; *hedges show that formal semantics is the right approach to the logic of natural language and that axiomatic theories will be inadequate (*raised as a claim, but if proved a correct guess, he states, then we will have learned something very deep and very important about natural languages and how they differ from artificial languages); and, in addition to degrees of truth, degrees of nonsense are needed to account for certain hedges (Lakoff, 1973: 491-494).

Following Lakoff's purpose in the above-mentioned article to get the study of fuzzy propositional logics off the ground in the hope that others would carry it further, we continue our section of literature review with other representatives that have further attempted to formalize the study of hedges even within taxonomies of classification and types of hedges. Since the early 1970s the concept of hedge has evolved, especially since it has been adapted by pragmatics and discourse analysis. Together with Lakoff's original use of the term for expressions that modify the category membership of a predicate or noun phrase, the idea of hedged performatives was widened by including also modifiers of the speaker's commitment to the truth-value of a whole proposition. For instance, Prince et al. (1982) distinguish between fuzziness within the propositional content (approximators) and fuzziness in the relationship between the propositional content and the speaker's commitment to the truth of the proposition conveyed (shields). It is relevant here to mention the approach of Vande Kopple towards hedging as interactive elements that modify the truth-value of a proposition and act as bridge between the factual interpretation of the writer and the descriptive knowledge (W. Vande Kopple,1985, cited in J. M. Hasan, 2018: 101). The examination of hedging has also been enriched from contributions through the dimension of pragmatic aspect of communication and social interaction, such as politeness strategies (Brown & Levinson, 1987), mitigation of one's commitment to truth (Markkanen & Schröder, 1997), and increased chances of ratification (Hübler. 1983). From the end of the 19080s attention has been devoted to the use of hedges from cross-cultural perspective, analyzing the phenomenon of hedging in academic texts, such as Ventola & Mauranen (1996), Clyne (1991), Kreutz & Harres (1997), Vassileva (1997), Schmied (2010), Serholt (2012), Dheskali (2018), Shafqat A. et al. (2019), etc. who have observed cultural and gender differences in the use of hedges, drawing interesting conclusions from their studies, most of them contributing to the general conceptualization and awareness of hedging as a culturally determined phenomenon from the pragmatic point of view.

Our purpose in this paper is to also provide a taxonomy of hedging devices, which will also servo to complement the comparative outlook on the use of hedging in English and in Albanian. However, we are quite aware from the start that such a taxonomy cannot yet be all-inclusive since current research is still contributing to a more well-rounded understanding of the phenomenon and what it entails. To provide such a taxonomy we refer to Salager-Meyer (1994) who believes that there are two purposes for using hedging devices: making issues fuzzy (to lower chances criticism faced when the author presents materials explicitly) and enhancing precision of claims (by using hedging devices, careful researchers present their strongest claims) (Salager-Meyer, 1994: 151). We discover thus another area in which hedges are frequently used—research and reporting data deriving from research. In another highly interesting and relevant research, Salager-Meyer acknowledged hedges as linguistic resources that convey fundamental characteristics of science of doubt and skepticism and considers three views of hedges: strategies that minimize threat and signal distance and avoid absolute statements, strategies that reflect level of certainty of knowledge, and strategies of politeness in social interactions and negotiations between writers and editors (Salager-Meyer, 2017: 127-143). She enriches her study with examination of frequency of hedges with reference to genre and rhetorical sections of scientific papers. The taxonomy of hedges introduced in her paper is also quite relevant to the aims of our study and for anyone, even students as Salager-Meyer asserts, to become aware of hedges as neglected language forms. Her taxonomy represents the most widely used hedging categories, (as she herself hedges) at least in scientific English.

1	*Modal auxiliary verbs*			may, might, can, could, would, should		
2	*Modal lexical verbs*			to seem, to appear (epistemic verbs), to believe, to assume, to suggest, to estimate, to tend, to think, to argue, to indicate, to propose, to speculate		
3	*Adjectival, adverbial and nominal modal phrases:*			*Probability adjectives*	*Nouns*	*Adverbs*
				possible, probable, un/likely	assumption, claim, possibility, estimate, suggestion	perhaps, possibly, probably, practically, likely, presumably, virtually, apparently
4	*Approximators of degree, quantity, frequency and time*			approximately, roughly, about, often, occasionally, generally, usually, somewhat, somehow, a lot of		
5	*Introductory phrases*			I believe, to our knowledge, it is our view that, we feel that		
6	*'If clauses*			if true, if anything		
7	*Compound hedges*			*a modal auxiliary combined with a lexical verb with a hedging content*	*a lexical verb followed by a hedging adverb or adjective where the adverb (or adjective) reinforces the hedge already inherent in the lexical verb*	
	Double hedges	*Treble hedges*	*Quadruple hedges*			
	it may suggest that; it seems likely that; it would indicate that; this probably indicates	it seems reasonable to assume that	it would seem somewhat unlikely that; it may appear somewhat speculative that	it would appear	it seems reasonable/probable	

Table 1. Taxonomy of hedging categories in scientific English language (Salager-Meyer, 2017).

Such a taxonomy is quite helpful in analyzing different types of genres and examining the frequency of each type of hedges and draw assumptions on reasons and intentions of usage. Apart from the use of hedges in academic or scientific writing, the use of hedging in literature also deserves due attention. M. Toolan, in *Language in Literature* includes several activities and tasks for students, among other things, to reflect on presupposition and to distinguish presupposition from assertion and entailment, describing different types of presupposition triggers and juxtaposing irony, humor and modality with presupposition and hedging devices (M. Toolan, 2010: 214-243). Such useful activities raise our awareness about what language users explicitly state and what they fail to say or what they imply through intentional use of hedges, in literature as well as in academic writing. Following the same line of thought, G. Leech in *Language in Literature, Style and Foregrounding,* while analyzing pragmatic principles in Shaw's *You Never Can Tell* draws our attention to the frequent use of hedges in conversation, and, particularly, in refusing conversational rights and the way they contribute to conversational (im)politeness (G.

Leech, 2013: 130-131). Therefore, we can relate utilization of hedges to the larger phenomenon of communicative and commentative potentials of any language. It is quite interesting to explore manipulative stretches of language, frequently found in detective fiction, in order to investigate on the role linguistic and stylistic devices have on the reader and the intentional 'games' that author or narrator 'play'. As Alexander maintains, explicitly *manipulative stretches of narrative text are frequently found in detective fiction, a stylistic sub-genre which delights in consciously and unequivocally playing manipulative 'games' with its readers* (M. Alexander, 2009: 13). We consider this correlation between hedging devices and detective fiction to be of particular relevance for our study, especially through the lens of a comparative study, it would be interesting to discover what happens with hedges as we cross linguistic and cultural boundaries.

2. The engulfing world of Agatha Christie

This paper intends to contribute to a pragma-stylistic approach to analysis of detective novels, since hedging devices can frequently be encountered in such a genre. The detective genre does still need some thorough attention and formal study as it seems to be one of the frequently read types of fiction, but, still, one of the neglected ones as far as formal study is concerned. Pragmastylistics, a branch of stylistics, applies ideas and concepts from linguistic pragmatics to the analysis of literary texts and their interpretation (Black, 2006; Busse et al., 2000, quoted in Safaa K. Merzah, Nawal F. Abbas, 2020 :120). It is concerned with the extent to which pragmatics contributes to the study of literature, it looks at the usefulness of pragmatic theories to the interpretation of literary texts. Pragmastylistics, in consonance with Black (2006), is concerned with showing the extent to which pragmatics contributes to the study of literature; it looks at the usefulness of pragmatic theories to the interpretation of literary texts (S. K. Merzah, N. F. Abbas, 2022: 333). Hickey (1993: 584) differentiates among stylistics, pragmatics and pragmastylistics by raising the following questions: Linguists ask: *"What do you say or what aspects of language are used?"*; stylisticians ask: *"How do you say what you say?"*; pragmatists ask: *"What do you do with what you say?"*; and pragma-stylisticians ask: *"How do you do, what do you do?* (Hickey 1993, quoted in Safaa K. Merzah, Nawal F. Abbas, 2020: 120). Viewing Agatha Christie's novels from a pragma-stylistic perspective, we raise the question: How does the writer do, what she does? How is it possible that, through a magnificently simple language, quite a complicated plot is threaded? How is the reader involved and manipulated, through interaction with the writer/narrator? We think that Christie, through continuously frequent and intentional use of hedges, clues and red herrings, intends for readers to be in the dark, creates suspense and elevates the essence of mystery. At other times, some of the clues, for example, can also be retrieved in the way hedges are used to reveal the way characters act or the way the narrator feels about them, finalized with revelation of the murderer.

Agatha Christie established many of the elements which she continued to employ for fifty years: a country setting, a formulaic structure in which all is not what it seems, and a detective who keeps clues to himself, making a startling revelation of guilt and innocence in a final meeting of all the characters (Wigginton 1997, in P. Zhang, 2001: 139). The novels of Agatha Christie are constantly involving readers and raising levels of interaction with readers through heightened caution and curiosity simultaneously. The readers are left guessing the killer, most of the times misguided and taken aback, as the real identity of the murderer is revealed by the narrator. Due to space limitations, we have focused only on one novel from Agatha Christie—*And Then There Were None*. There are ten people on an island and we are left to guess who is the killer; paradoxically, it has to be one of the ten characters. The idea of the island, or enclosed circle, on the margins of civilization, being cut off from the world so that society has no means of knowing what happens to the victims and thus there is no hope for them to be saved is frequently employed in literature, especially in Agatha Christie's detective fiction. This is the very reason why Wargrave chooses an island; there, he can become the murderer he could not be while in the civilized world (Laurent, 2022:113). It is fascinating to analyze the novel from the stylistic perspective since for Agatha Christie the psychology of the murderer is quite important and it also provides a lead or clue to the identity of the murderer, thus, getting into the characters' minds and collecting clues from traces of conversation, we are also getting closer to revelation of mystery. A careful search of the language of conversation from the original novel has led us to identify examples from all types of hedges in the original novel and we have compared their types and use in the Albanian variant. We are not involved in statistical analysis of hedges in both languages; our aim is to provide a qualitative approach to the use of hedging in English vs in Albanian and draw conclusions on the decision-making process the translator is involved and whether intentions of the original detective writer have been preserved.

3. Comparative approach on the use of hedges in translation of detective novels: the case of Agatha Christie

According to the reader-response theory with reference to translation studies, the position of the translator involved in 'meaning construction' has multiple implications for translators. Being in the role of the reader in the first place, the translator is the one who (re)constructs the meaning of the original for himself/herself and also for the target readers. This task involves the translator intimately in the understanding process before the actual translation stage begins. It also acknowledges translator's responsibility in the construction of the meaning of the source text into the target language, to such a degree that Diaz-Diocaretz calls the translator a "co-producer" of the source text (H. Ghazala, 2011:111). It is our interest to observe the attitude of the translator towards use of hedges in the original, thus, in this part of our study we bring several examples to illustrate the various types of hedges as in the taxonomy presented in *Table 1,* juxtaposed to their translation in the Albanian variant of the novel.

'Nobody *could* have clambered down here, I suppose?' (p. 138)	*Një mendje më thotë* që s'ka mundësi të jetë ngjitur njeri këtu? (p. 93)

Table 2. Modal auxiliary verbs

But it *appears* to me, reviewing the whole business, that one particular person is sufficiently clearly indicated. (p. 186)	Por duke e rikëqyrur gjithë këtë histori, *në sytë e mi* është një person i caktuar mbi të cilin bien qartazi dyshimet. (p. 128)
We *seemed* to have much in common. (p. 19)	*...dukej* që kishim shumë gjëra të përbashkëta. (p. 11)
Tell me, Miss Claythorne, did she *appear* to be troubled by a sense of guilt or a feeling of remorse for her attitude in the matter? (p. 213)	Më thoni diçka zonjusha Klejthorn, a u *duk* ndopak e shqetësuar nga një ndjenjë faji ose brenge për qëndrimin e saj në atë histori? (p. 147)

Table 3 Modal lexical verbs

No one hiding – no *possible* hiding-place. (p. 147)	As edhe një vend i fshehtë, asnjë vend ku *mund* të fshiheshe. (p. 99)
He'd got one or two *unlikely* convictions out of them. (p. 47)	Kështu kishte ndodhur që iu pati shkulur nja dy dënime *që s'të bindnin dhe aq fort.* (p. 31)
'Seems to me its owner is the most *likely* person to know that. (p. 221)	Për mendimin tim, pronari i tij është njeriu *që duhet ta dijë më mirë se kushdo tjetër.* (p. 153)
'Is there any *possibility* other than suicide?' (p. 87)	Thua të ekzistojë ndonjë *mundësi* tjetër përveç vetëvrasjes? (p. 59)
'When did I lay *claims* to being an honest man? No, indeed, I never said that.' (p. 262)	E kur *qenkam hequr* si njeri i ndershëm? Jo, vërtet, kurrë s'e kam thënë atë gjë. (p. 180)
Wife murder is *perfectly* possible – almost natural, let's say! (p. 168)	Të vrasësh gruan është *krejtësisht* e mundshme, le të themi edhe e natyrshme. (p.114)

Table 4. Adjectival, adverbial and nominal modal phrases

'Just now we had a *somewhat* disturbing experience. (p. 70)	Sapo përjetuam një përvojë --- shqetësuese. (p. 46)
He said, showing his teeth in a *somewhat* mirthless smile (p. 153).	Duke zbardhur dhëmbët në një buzëqeshje --- të trishtë, ai tha. (p. 103)
Everything – *somehow* – was a little queer. (p. 43)	Diçka nuk shkonte ashtu siç duhej. (p. 28)
And doctors overwork and have *a lot of* strain.' (p. 182)	Po kështu doktorët punojnë shumë dhe --- nën tension. (p. 125)

Table 5. Approximators of degree, quantity, frequency, and time

I have no knowledge whatsoever of the woman's state of health.' (p. 108)	*Nuk kam as idenë më të vogël* lidhur me gjendjen shëndetësore të asaj gruaje. (p. 72)
And out of his knowledge concerning us, he has made certain definite accusations. (p. 74)	Dhe *njohuritë e tij* rreth nesh, e kanë shtyrë të bëjë disa akuza të caktuara. (p. 48)

Table 6. Introductory phrases

After all, people don't like a Coroner's Inquest, even *if* the Coroner did acquit me of all blame! (p. 14)	Tekefundit njerëzve nuk ua ka qejfi dikë që është bërë objekt hetimi i gjykatës, madje edhe *atëherë kur* është shpallur e pafajshme nga të gjitha akuzat! (p. 7)
I presume they would be lethal *if* a sufficiently large dose were given. (p. 217)	Ma merr mendja që bëhen diçka vdekjeprurëse *në qoftë se* merren në sasi të konsiderueshme. (p. 150)

Table 7. 'If' clauses

That may have been a false statement, made so that Rogers *should appear* to be in the same position as ourselves. (p. 168)	Kjo mund të jetë një deklaratë e rreme, e bërë me synimin që Roxhersi --- të jetë në të njëjtën situatë si puna jonë (p. 114)
I *must appear* to be the next victim. (p. 311)	Unë *duhet të hiqesha si* viktima e radhës. (p. 215)
He *would* swear *definitely* that there had been eight china figures upon the dining-table when he laid the table for lunch. (p. 177)	Ishte *gati* të betohej --- se kur kish shtruar darkën në tryezë kishin pas qenë tetë figurina porcelani. (p. 121)
His head was crushed in by a heavy marble clock that it *seems reasonable* to *suppose* fell on him from the window above. (p. 298)	Dikush ia hapi kokën me një bllok të rëndë mermeri, i cili, *po të arsyetojmë*, u lëshua mbi të nga një prej dritareve. (p. 205)
But it appears to me, reviewing the whole business, that one particular person is *sufficiently clearly indicated*. (p. 186)	Por duke e rikëqyrur gjithë këtë histori, në sytë e mi është një person i caktuar *mbi të cilin bien qartazi dyshimet*. (p. 128)
Or he *might possibly pretend* to be mortally wounded himself, might drag himself groaning to her door. (p. 254)	Ose edhe *mund të pretendonte* se ai vetë ishte plagosur për vdekje, duke u hequr osh te dera e saj me rënkime. (p. 175)

Table 8. Compound hedges

As the several examples selected to illustrate the diversity of categories of hedges found in the original and its Albanian variant show, there is generally a tendency on the behalf of the translator to preserve hedges, which shows that the translator is close to the original intentions of the writer. The category or subcategory of hedges may not have always been preserved, but, the intention of the writer/narrator is transmitted clearly. We also observe a tendency towards explicitation in Albanian.

Conclusions

We conclude the paper by recalling Lakoff's approach that natural languages are reflective, thus, as users of language we are not only saying things, but we are also constantly reflecting on the status of what we say or write. Hedges constitute an important interactive strategy in communicative situations, be they academic writing, scientific discourse, or literary discourse, among many others. We cannot consider hedges as purely linguistic devices merely to convey fuzziness or vagueness, they are used for a variety of purposes and intentions from the writers, and, as such, they should also be faithfully brought in translation (faithfulness here refers to intentionality of author for using hedging devices primarily). The comparative study has revealed that Agatha Christie has frequently employed hedging devices to withhold information, create vagueness and also individualize characters' and narrators' attitude. Such a purpose has been faithfully recreated through use of hedging even by the translator. The latter may have employed another category of hedging, as exemplified in the paper, following the proposed taxonomy; yet, intentionality behind the use of hedging devices has been preserved. Such an affirmation is reinforced through the strategy of compensation on the behalf of the translator. To conclude, we restate the reciprocal inter-relationship among linguistics, semantics, stylistics and pragmatics, as proved by the current study. This study can be further extended in the future by adapting a quantitative approach and extracting statistical data on the use of hedges and their specific types in the original and then in its translation. The comparison after the quantitative study, together with the qualitative approach in the current study, will yield important results and reflections on the natures of both English and Albanian language as well as the specific genres within the literary polysystem in each country.

References

Alexander, M. 2009. *Rhetorical Structure and Reader Manipulation in Agatha Christie's 'Murder on the Orient Express'.* In miscellanea: A Journal of English and American studies 39 (2009): pp. 13-27.

Ghazala, H. 2011. *Cognitive Stylistics and the Translator.* Sayyab Books, London, UK.

Hasan, J. M. 2018. *A Stylistic Study of Hedging in Agatha Christie's 'The Murder of Roger Ackroyd'.* In *Journal of Basra Research for Human Sciences. No. 2, Vol. 43,* 100-113.

Lakoff. G. 1973. *Hedges: A Study in Meaning Criteria and the Logic of Fuzzy Concepts.* In *Journal of Philosophical Logic 2* (1973) 458-508. D. Reidel Publishing Company, Dordrecht-Holland.

Laurent, É. 2022. *Enclosure in Agatha Christie's Works.* Humanities and Social Sciences. HAL Id: dumas-03575249.

Leech, G. 2013. *Language in Literature, Style and Foregrounding.* Routledge. New York. USA.

Merzah, S. K., Abbas, N. F. 2020. *Deception in Flynn's Psychological Thriller 'Gone Girl' (2012): A Pragma-Stylistic Analysis*. In *European Journal of Literature, Language and Linguistics Studies—Volume 3, Issue 4*, 118-147.

Merzah, S. K., Abbas, N. F. 2020. *Vagueness and Withholding Information in Christie's (1926) Detective Fiction 'The Murder of Roger Ackroyd': A Pragma-Stylistic Study*. In *Arab World English Journal (AWEJ) Volume 11. Number 3*, 331-348.

Prince, E, F., Frader, J. & C. Bosk. 1982. *On Hedging in Physician-Physician Discourse*. In Di Pietro, R. J. (ed.) *Linguistics and the Profession*. Norwood, N. J.: Ablex, 83-97.

Salager-Meyer, F. 1994. *Hedges and Textual Communicative Function in Medical Written English Discourse*. In *English for Specific Purposes,13 (2)*, 149-170.

Salager-Meyer, F. 2017. *I Think That Perhaps You Should: A Study of Hedges in Written Scientific Discourse*. In *The Journal of TESOL France*, 127-143.

Toolan, M. 2013. *Language in Literature, An Introduction to Stylistics*. Routledge. New York. USA.

Zhang, P. 2001. *A Discourse Stylistic Approach to the Critics of Christie's Works*, In Comparative Literature: East & West, 3:1, 134-154.

Primary works

Muçi, V. (transl.) 2019. *Dhe nuk Mbeti më Askush*. Dituria. Tiranë.

Christie, A. 1939. *And then There Were None*. HarperCollins Publisher. London.

ABOUT THE AUTHORS

ERIOLA QAFZEZI, Ph.D. is a full-time lecturer in the Department of Foreign Languages at the Faculty of Education and Philology at Fan S. Noli University, Korça, Albania, where she has been teaching since the year 2005. From 2001 to 2005 she completed Bachelor Studies graduating as a Teacher of English as a Foreign Language, to be followed by achievement of Master of Science Degree in Linguistics, Translation Studies, completed in 2011, and Doctor of Science Degree in Linguistics, Translation Studies in 2014. She currently teaches Translation, Text Analysis, Theory of Translation, Text Typology and Translation, and ESP. Dr. Qafzezi's research interests relate to translation, linguistics, discourse studies, media studies, technology and education, online teaching and learning, etc. As part of her ongoing research, E. Qafzezi has published several papers that focus on the interrelationship of language and culture, translation of children's literature, intertextuality, media discourse, online teaching, and learning, etc.

Emails: eriola_bonja@yahoo.com & eqafzezi@unkorce.edu.al

A Book Review

Venera Russo on Will Durant's
*The Story of Philosophy: The Lives
and Opinions of the Greater
Philosophers [1926]*, Simon &
Schuster Paperbacks (2005)

Durant's "Story of Philosophy" is developed in eleven chapters, many of them are each dedicated to a single philosopher, plus an introduction and a preface. The time span covered goes from Plato to Durant's contemporaneity (around 1920). Many important figures and currents are missing, for instance the Scolastica, Hegel and Marx. This has been the source of a severe criticism against the book, till the point that Durant himself, pushed by his publishers, feels the urge to justify his choices in a preface to the second edition, titled "Apologia pro libro suo." In this latter one, Durant convincingly stresses his aim of humanizing (i.e. popularizing) knowledge in a time in which "[h]uman knowledge had become too great for the human mind." (p.9) and technical registers have turned the sciences into domains inaccessible for the average educated reader.

I am inclined to praise this choice, as well as I agree on the fact that common access to the language of knowledge is a matter of democracy, without which a priesthood or specialists would rule the world. The clear parallelism is with Plato, who, along with the technical works for his Academia, did not disdain writing dialogues for the general public.

I will add just one more consideration on the matter, which Durant does not mention but that is probably implied in the word "story" in the title of the book.

A story is not a history, there is something personal in it and the implication of a subjective point of view. Durant attempts to give his personal narration of the western philosophical tradition. He dedicates tens of pages to Kant and not even a line to Saint Augustin. His aim is not exhaustion, as well expressed in the note to the reader ("this book is not a complete history of philosophy", p. 21), but a personal communication with the reader, with which he is able to establish a friendly relation from the very first pages. From this perspective, I find all the stylistic and content-related choices perfectly fitting the main *intentio auctoris*.

The book opens with an introduction that goes straight to the matter of the "uses of philosophy". Durant talks of the delight of a wisdom that opposes itself to the everyday chaos and inevitable decay of things, that passes on the certainties, following the lure of the unknown.

Since the first chapter, Durant makes clear his stylistic inclination for pure narration. The figure of Socrates is outlined in a powerful way, with an abundance of details and reporting several pages of Plato's Apology.

Also, the description of Plato himself is full of personal items like physical appearance and the passionate temper. Of Plato Durant catches all the very human contradictions: Despising poets and being a poet himself, criticizing the priests but preaching about morality.

The thought of Plato is explored in a threefold way: Politics, Psychology, Ethics. All the items are tied up, for the state is the result of the men belonging to a community, consequently a man or a woman that is educated with a good balance between physical training and smoothing disciplines like music and science, in the background of a reassuring religion, is the better candidate to realize that he owes a lot to the other members of the community. This latter one is a condition necessary for the "democratic aristocracy" envisaged by Plato to take place. Whoever passes the hard tests to be ruler conducts a stainless life and is entirely committed to the sake of the State. Only if every class -producers, auxiliaries, and guardians- has and does "what is one's own", there could be a just state.

The figure of Aristotle is outlined by its rivalry, even incompatibility, with his master, for "geniuses accord with one another harmoniously as dynamite with fire" (p.70). While Plato focused on mathematics and pure philosophy, Aristotle turned to biology and natural sciences. Poetry versus precise terminology, myth versus encyclopedia are the opposite poles where the two geniuses' thoughts dwelled. Aristotle stands out in the history of philosophy for the systematization of his inquiry that moves from biology to aesthetics, passing through psychology, and, despite his many errors, poses the basis for modern science.

At this point, Durant's Story jumps straight to Francis Bacon, overlooking all the philosophical production of the Middle Age. This choice, an easily criticizable one, is clearly justified in a few lines in the last page of the chapter dedicated to Aristotle: a thousand years of "darkness" followed Aristotelian thought before the "resurrection of philosophy." The omission of Augustine and Aquinas, not to mention the Jewish and Middle Eastern contributions is maybe the major controversial aspect of this book. Still, let us use the word "controversial" rather than drawback. As a point of fact, though this omission could disappoint many experienced readers, it has to be borne in mind that the major aim of this book is divulgative if not even genuinely pedagogical, as already mentioned. The idea that Medieval philosophy is close to theology to the extent of being deprived of its genuinity is massively spread till nowadays (see Copleston, 1972, Introduction). The reader could feel discontented but surely not astonished about Durant's omission. The main point is: Is this exclusion justified by the main "intentio" of the author? I would tend to answer affirmatively. The goal of philosophical divulgation is reached by Durant, in my view, in three ways: First, selecting what is most relevant; secondly, picking up the philosophical questions that are still concerning the common reader of nowadays; thirdly, narrating in a compelling way. One could wonder how St. Augustine could fit these requirements and judge in his own way the appropriateness of Durant's jump from Aristotle to Bacon.

A quite different issue is the implicit consideration of theology as an imperfect imitation of philosophy. But, here again, we are talking of a stance that is widely shared with which one could disagree or not.

After a few, powerful, pages, on Stoicism and Epicureanism in the historical background of Rome, Durant offers to the reader an interesting table of "philosophic affiliations" that tracks the history of philosophy from Parmenides to Croce and Santayana. Though somehow simplistic, for some links should have been clarified, like the one between Hegel and Schopenhauer, the scheme is a fascinating synthetic overview of the Western philosophical tradition through its excellent minds.

Francis Bacon is greeted as the voice that announced the resurrection of thought after the dark centuries dominated by dogmas and idols.

Bacon represents the perfect combination of knowledge and action. Philosopher in his inner self and statesman during his life, he melted wisdom and strategy in such a fruitful amalgam to build the basis of what will afterwards be the English pragmatism. It is with Bacon, according to Durant, that modernity starts to appear with its main issues of domination of nature, reflection on the method of inquiry and systematization of science.

Baruch Spinoza's thought is depicted as massively influenced by the philosopher's Jewish origins and education. The excommunication he underwent due to his ideas, marked his life and mind deeply. The entire life of Spinoza is courageous and solitary standing for his ideas of unity. Unity of God and Nature, of mind and body, and unity among religions. He incarnates the true philosophical model of the "wisdom lover" and conducted a life according to his philosophical creed. Durant considers Spinoza as one of the most influential philosophers of all time. Personally, I think he is correct, especially if we think that a treatise on human emotions by the well-known neuroscientist A. Damasio (2003) is inspired by Spinoza's thought (the French version of the book is even translated as Spinoza avait raison!).

Skipping Hobbes and Pascal, Durant focuses on the French Enlightenment and the destruction of the feudal system, through the brilliant and powerful voices of Rousseau and, above all, of Voltaire.

Durant chooses to treat Kant and German idealism in the same chapter, dedicating the most part of it to Kant himself, with a minor note on Hegel, and references to Locke, Rousseau, Hume, Berkeley, and once more Voltaire, in relation to their historical importance for the background in which the Kantian system took place.

Kant is depicted as a short and timid man who never left his homeland and that yet, unexpectedly, caused a revolution with his Critique of Pure Reason. Two goals were the basis of Kant's thought: to save religion from reason and at the same time to spare science. He pursued his aims by postulating a priori knowledge that is not determined by the senses, picturing the mind as an organ that makes order in the chaos of the sensible world, yet without the possibility of knowing the reality in itself, but only through phenomenal interactions. Science got spared, though limited in the phenomenal world. In the Critique of Practical Reason faith was assured a safe place in absolute ethics, independent from both the phenomenal world and theoretical reasoning but derived from the inner self by intuition. Religion so conceived has lost its ruling power over the external world and has submitted itself to morality.

About Hegel, Durant reports a series of indirect accusations that could be questionable, like those ones of obscurity and eccentricity. He makes, nevertheless, a very brief but powerful portrait of the great philosopher of the oppositions, whose life, ironically enough, was marked by many contradictions.

It is very probable that Durant takes a precise stance, according to which his Story makes justice in the diatribe between Hegel and Schopenhauer. The contemporaries praised the former and almost discarded the latter. On the contrary, Durant dedicates a few pages, though intense in their brevity, to Hegel, but an entire chapter to Schopenhauer.

Schopenhauer is introduced as one of the sons of the disillusionment of his age: Europe was in chaos and the myth of reason had questioned the existence of God so strongly that there was no shelter left for the most part of European intelligentsia. In addition, some biographical events added more gloom in an already dusk scenario, and he developed his concept of Will in the context of a solitary and suspicious, even paranoid, life. The very nature of mind has to be inquired, according to Schopenhauer, not in the surface of rational thought but in the inner instinct of striving for life. The Will is the vital force about which men are only half conscious, and that gives unity to consciousness. The Will is the very essence of reality, where individuality is only an illusion and only life through species exists. Human life is thus on the sway of desires driven by the Will, where suffering alternates with brief moments of fulfillment of a desire soon replaced by a new desire that causes new pain or, even worse, by an intolerable sense of boredom. Only philosophy, as objective knowledge of the Will, could lead a man out of the vicious cycle and give him some rest. Also, Arts are able to sublimate the Will, as well as religions are disciplines that contrast it, especially Buddhism and Hinduism.

Before taking a leap towards his own contemporaneity, Durant makes just two stops by the evolutionist Spencer and the solitary thinker Nietzsche, plus a short introductory paragraph on Comte and Darwin.

Spencer is greeted as the philosopher that suggested applying the theory of evolution to every field of studies. Lacking formal education and more interested in reality than in books, he was a keen observer and was incredibly talented at picking up and classifying information from his own everyday environment. His speculation starts from the awareness that the real nature of both mind and matter is unknowable, thus Philosophy should turn to what can be known and take its place as the discipline unifying the results of the sciences under the leading principle of evolution. This insight reaches its peak of cogency within the discipline of sociology, which Spencer massively contributes to raising to a scientific level.

According to Durant, Nietzsche's thought has a great debt towards Darwin, no matter if Nietzsche used to refute and even despise those who most influenced him, and so he did with Darwin. Christian by family education, he firmly rejected Christianity in his adulthood. Weakly by nature, he praised war and the domination of the strongest. In his vision, in the struggle for life what matters is not sympathy or faith, but strength and power. He made poetry of philosophy with the *So Spoke Zarathustra*, where he finally defined his Superman (Übermensch) in lines of inspired intensity. In Nietzsche's conception only strength is moral, and society is necessary not to breed the masses but to produce a few exceptional individuals. Among them, there was Nietzsche himself, a romantic genius who paid with madness his eccentric and solitary profondeur.

In chapter X, Durant sketches the European philosophical scenario of his own contemporaneity through three thinkers: Bergson, Croce, and Russell.

Bergson is introduced as the bishop of anti-materialism and anti-mechanism. His insight of time as duration and accumulation defies determinism and opens a view on human nature characterized by aeternal change and unforeseeability. Man is essentially action and creativity and cannot be reduced to the laws of physics and biology, which are conceived as repetition. Evolution is not to be considered as a mechanical selection through the adaptation to the environment, but a creative growth. In the same token, the real way to knowledge is not intellect but intuition, the direct feeling of life in which we are merged.

Benedetto Croce is sketched as a man involved in politics without being a real politician, for he came to despise the public affairs and all their absurdities. His main interests were mind and ideas. According to Croce, reality could not be really known if not in the form that it takes in our minds, hence philosophy was reducible to logic. It is interesting to note that Durant sees in Croce a massive reminiscence of Scholasticism, despite his declared anticlericalism and agnosticism! At the same rate, the lack of pragmatism and the obscurity of his terminology unveil the influence of Hegel upon his system. Croce drives all his religious force towards beauty and Art, that he sees as the result of a powerful inward imagination.

Russell is the last European philosopher examined. According to Durant, his thought, and maybe his inward life, had two phases. In the first one, he worshiped mathematics in an almost religious way and, not surprisingly, he claimed that philosophy had to have the same a priori truths than mathematics. Then the First World War broke out, and Russell revealed his courageous love for humanity by stepping into public affairs denouncing the absurdity of war. He paid for his pacifism with the loss of his chair at Cambridge. Thus, the cold mathematician turned into a committed socialist who believed that private property was at the origin of wars and that only through dialogue and sharing humanity could avoid bloody conflicts.

Chapter XI depicts Durant's contemporary scenario in America picking up the following triad of philosophers: Santayana, James, Dewey.

According to Durant, there are two Americas in relation to philosophical thought, arts, and literature. The first one is strictly tied to European tradition, arts, and manners, whereas the second one is much more direct and task oriented. Santayana belongs to the first America.

He had Spanish origins and he retired to Europe in his old years, till his death in Rome.

His starting point is that idealism is right, though useless: We perceive the world by our senses, there is no other way to knowledge, no matter our skepticism. Either our senses deceive us or they do not, we still live in the reality they convey to us, in a kind of "animal faith". Reason is not an enemy to Instinct, on the contrary it is the conscious state of our instinctive nature, the sublimation of humanity. By the same token, religion is not truth but a poetic myth that lures us with its beauty, and that fills us with a melancholic sense of nostalgia.

William James is introduced by Durant as one of the philosophers that best interpreted American sensibility and attitudes. His pragmatism begins from some psychological arguments: Mental states are not chains of thoughts but a flux that reflects the world in a very effective way. There is no Noumenon, nor soul or Absolute to long for, only this flux. Truths are related to human needs; they are convenient formulations that have successful results in practice. If an idea helps us lead a better life, it is convenient to believe in that idea. James was hostile to all the obscurities that had poisoned philosophy through certain formulations in metaphysics and epistemology and tried to turn towards the real world of things and action.

Durant claims that Dewey represents a case in which philosophy ceases to deal with unsolvable problems and attempts to create a path for human elevation. He did it through his reflections on education and democracy. His stance was naturalistic, as a point of fact, he claimed that the mind must be understood in biological terms. Thought arises in specific situations and in a cultural milieu, in order to solve problems by formulating and testing hypotheses. Since the social environment has the power to train instincts, it is reasonable to think that education could play a pivotal role in ameliorating human nature.

Durant's (selected) Story of Philosophy ends here. Some final considerations on our part will try to make a general evaluation of the book.

Throughout the volume, it is quite clear that the author's main aim is to report the thoughts of the most eminent philosophers through their personalities. They are not just thinkers, but characters of a story, the story of philosophy. Or, better, the "humanized" story of philosophy. In this perspective the exclusion of Marx or Kierkegaard are questionable but not wrong, for a narrator has unlimited liberty in plot development and character selection. Not the accusation of oversimplification could stand, for a narrator chooses his target audience and acts accordingly.

And yet, some stylistic items remind us of the most used handbook organization scheme. It is true that Durant picks up only some philosophers, but he analyzes them in a systematic way (i.e., Politics, Ethics, Psychology), with the exception of the secondary notes and the introductory paragraphs with reference to minor "characters" of the "Story." Is this a contradiction? Maybe it is, and it is the only relevant drawback that I see in this book. As a point of fact, Durant could have pushed his stylistic choices further, sparing the reader from this slightly fastidious sensation of reading a simplified manual. However, this is the best way Durant envisages to popularize philosophy among the general public. The main point is: Did he succeed in his aim? Did he give a compelling, if not at all exhaustive, account of the Western Philosophical tradition?

For the most part he did, though with picks of mastery in some chapters, like those about Socrates and Aristotle, and a few disappointing results in others, like the almost tedious paragraphs dedicated to the analysis of Voltaire's works, which is excessively detailed in my opinion. Nevertheless, for every philosopher, Durant was able to outline a profoundly human character that pops out of the page like in the most enjoyable narrative. A wise and stylistically well fitted use of quotations embellishes each chapter. Even some criticism is done in the shape of an enjoyable friendly conversation with the reader. This latter one navigates easily in a domain, the history of philosophy, that tends to be hostile to the less educated mind. This is a major merit that I do attribute to Durant, since we have to keep in mind that in 1926, when the book was first released, there was a scarcity of friendly handbooks on philosophy, which are abundantly available nowadays. Durant is a pioneer, in this respect. And a captivating narrator.

References

Plato. *Apology of Socrates* [between 399 and 387 BCE]

Copleston, Frederick C. *A History of Medieval Philosophy*. University of Notre Dame Press, 1972.

Damasio, Antonio. *Looking for Spinoza: Joy, Sorrow, and the Feeling Brain*. Harcourt, 2003.

ABOUT THE AUTHOR

VENERA RUSSO holds a PhD degree in Philosophy from Sofia University "St. Kliment Ohridiski". Dr. Russo is a teacher and a researcher interested in Philosophy of Language, Linguistics, and Second Language Acquisition. She studied Linguistics and Modern Languages at the University of Palermo and specialized in E-Learning at the University of Florence and in Media Education and Communication at the University of Padua.

Publications:

Russo, Venera. "The Phenomenology of Women. On Female Discourse in Julia Kristeva and Simone De Beauvoir's Works". *In Statu Nascendi—Journal of Political Philosophy and International Relations Vol.* 5, no. 2 (2022): 109-124.

Russo, Venera. "The Phenomenology of Women. On Female Discourse in Julia Kristeva and Simone De Beauvoir's Works". *In Statu Nascendi—Journal of Political Philosophy and International Relations* Vol. 3, no. 1 (2020): 115-125.

Russo, Venera. "Cross-language Relation. The implication of Relativity in Translation and Vice versa" *In Statu Nascendi—Journal of Political Philosophy and International Relations* Vol. 3, no. 1 (2020): 127-136.

LinkedIn:
http://linkedin.com/in/venerarusso
E-mail: russovenera@gmail.com

Part II:
Politics, Economy, And Theory Of International Relations

Piotr Pietrzak

Approaching Regional Conflicts through the Prism of Ontology *in statu nascendi*— the New Compartmentalization of the IR Theory

This publication is dedicated to my students, whom I want to encourage to adopt more ontological modes of thinking to untangle the modern world's complexity.

"Each one of you my young friends, will find in your life your own Westerplatte. A task, you must assume and complete. Some battle which is impossible not to fight. Some duty, some obligation, from which [you] simply cannot escape, and from which it is impossible to desert. A certain order of truths and values you are obliged to maintain and defend." **—by John Paul II**

Abstract: *This study suggests a new way of approaching contemporary conflict by embracing much stronger ontological roots in our literature on the subject that might reinvigorate the pursuit of the truth about international relations to make it easier for IR scholarship to reach traditionally uncharted and neglected territories of science. Specifically, it puts forward the ontology in statu nascendi to deal with a modern conflict of global or regional importance in a more approachable manner, for this new compartmentalization and a supplement to the existent IR theory was explicitly designed to embrace a more systematic, interdisciplinary, and contemplative mode of IR-related deliberations that hopes to convey the central meaning of the given research area by breaching the division between the main conceptual, methodological, and analytical differences between what appears to be a collection of rival approaches, theories, and traditions that should be better integrated within IR theory. It essentially postulates building empirical bridges of mutual understanding instead of walls of division to approach our research area more constructively.*

Keywords: new compartmentalization of IR theory, supplementing existent IR theory, ontology *in statu nascendi*, candidate for a new ontology, ontology merging, ontology integration.

Introduction

Why would we go to such lengths to put forward a new compartmentalization of IR theory only to approach an ongoing conflict? To start with, there is a hope that this could actually help us to do a better job explaining various dimensions related to the modern security dilemmas, geopolitics, and geoeconomics of any given conflict in a more approachable manner than traditional methods. Still, the paradox of the situation is that this goal cannot be attained in the first place without digging deeper into IR theory itself and supplementing it with various philosophical debates that result in a more robust compartmentalization than could be used under such circumstances. I argue in this case that only by reformulating and re-compartmentalizing existent theory will we be able to offer a custom-made practical solution to seemingly unresolvable conflicts. This, in turn, could bring us closer to reaching a reasonable conclusion and termination of hostilities between the conflicting sides. Countries don't go to war for no reason. Any conflict sees an escalation of preexisting tensions, differences between two or more parties triggered by certain circumstances. The existence of those disagreements and those circumstances preexist actual fighting on the ground. Every mediator will tell us that in many cases, it is easier to prevent a war than to force parties engaged in an ongoing confrontation to end it, for once the war machine kicks off, it can get out of control very quickly because there are many parties that benefit from ongoing confrontation—especially if they decide to labor under the misconception that they are winning.

Even if a conflict starts as a one-dimensional confrontation between two parties, after a time, it very often deteriorates into a vicious circle of violence that inadvertently starts producing more negative consequences for more and more people, including those in neighboring counties and distant places, even other continents. The best ad hoc example here is the confrontation between Russia and Ukraine that escalated in 2022, producing skyrocketing inflation in Europe, the United States, Russia, and even such distant places as China, Bangladesh, Indonesia, Yemen, Nigeria, and Tunisia. This occurred because these countries rely heavily on the wheat imports and other agricultural commodities produced in Russia and Ukraine, and the agriculture-related inflation skyrocketed once it became clear that the traditional route for commercial vessels used by both countries to export their produce through the Black Sea had been severely destabilized by this conflict. Despite this issue having been temporarily solved by the UN-struck deal in 2022, the deal has an expiration date, and the markets are still likely to react negatively to any deterioration of the situation in the region. This in turn is likely to produce broader negative economic consequences, and the end consumer is likely to be overcharged for any actual and supposed transport-related price hikes resulting during this temporary solution.[1]

Naturally, the longer such a conflict lasts, the longer it is likely to produce even more harmful and inherently uncontrollable spillovers that can further destabilize the world's sociopolitical situation and affect the least privileged. That is why the ever-changing realities on the ground require us to adopt a new, more holistic rigor of thinking to comprehend the modern multidimensional challenge in a more approachable manner. I argue in this paper that we must embrace an ontological mode of thinking to deal with these challenges if we hope to find a workable long-term solution to resolve local conflicts and prevent them from escalating into regional problems of global importance. Otherwise, if we cherry-pick one or two IR approaches to our investigations, we will end up with an incomplete synthesis or an ill-calibrated recommendation.

In essence, an ontologist is a truth seeker by default, for he or she can never settle for the more straightforward or approachable answers that only touch the surface of the problem. He or she is always inclined to be excited about digging deeper and deeper to uncover the hidden truth about any given phenomenon with clarity, integrity, and an open-minded attitude. "Ontology deals with questions concerning what entities exist or can be said to exist, and how such entities can be grouped, related within a hierarchy, and subdivided according to similarities and differences (Mccarthy 2018, p. 76-77; Griswold 2001, p. 237, 233-239)."

Ontology in the field of International Relations is used to describe the social reality at hand and to describe the actors, their interactions, and the structure of those interactions. IR theory itself also accounts for a semi-scientific and semi-philosophical compartmentalization that needs a little recalibration to permit our scholars to take full advantage of all of its plasticity to approach the local agents located in a specific time structure from a different, more mature perspective with a more significant likelihood of rediscovering more pluralistic sets of their fundamental properties, characteristics, agency, relationships, functions, events, instances, axioms, and possible future superstructures that could be used to supplement our static tradition with more liquid paradigms, experimental theories, and diversified approaches in a more

---

[1]   For more information in this respect, please also see Lotanna Emediegwu. 2022. "How Is the War in Ukraine Affecting Global Food Prices? - *Economics Observatory*." Available at </https://www.economicsobservatory.com/how-is-the-war-in-ukraine-affecting-global-food-prices/> [Accessed on 03.07.2023].

hyperbolic, liquid, and flexible way that should contribute to an everlasting endeavor to develop a more approachable landscape of awareness that will edify and incorporate those elusive or vague concepts that are still essentially forming, emerging, adjusting, and coming to reality.

We have witnessed several outbreaks and escalations of local and regional conflicts of global importance since 1991. This is particularly true of the conflict in **Afghanistan**, the ISAF forces' withdrawal from this country in 2021, and the consequent **Taliban takeover** that resulted in a massive deterioration of the situation of the local population in this country. The same is true for the recent civil war in Ethiopia fought in the **Tigray region** between the Ethiopian federal government and Eritrea[2] on one side and the Tigray People's Liberation Front on the other. The good news is that the sides involved in this conflict decided to accept the terms and conditions of the African Union's peace mission and the Ethiopia-Tigray peace agreement signed in Pretoria in November 2022, so there is some hope for a deescalation of the situation on the ground. Still, this conflict has pushed the whole of northern **Ethiopia** further to the brink of a humanitarian disaster of massive proportions.

The instability in the region may have also encouraged other regional players to resort to violence to attain their political goals and objectives. Indeed, just a week ago (on 25 April 2023), Western diplomats and nationals have been evacuated from **Sudan** after the situation in Khartoum further escalated into an open confrontation between two strongmen fighting for control of the capital: **Gen. Abdel-Fattah Burhan** (de facto ruler of Sudan: the head of the military junta that took over the power in the country in 2019) and **Gen. Mohammed Hamdan Dagalo**, the head of the Rapid Support Forces.[3] According to the Armed Conflict Location & Event Data Project (ACLED), there were at least 1,800 casualties reported in Sudan between 15 April and 19 April 2023 in the fight between the Sudanese Armed Forces (SAF) and paramilitary Rapid Support Forces (RSF).

---

2   To understand the **Tigray conflict (2020-2022),** one must look closer at Ethiopia-Eritrea relations: The very fact that Eritrea is a party to the dispute, the fact that President Isaias Afwerki has been heavily engaged in Ethiopian internal politics. In April 2023, Eritrean troops were still located in Tigray region, which suggests that the full resolution of this conflict is not fully attained.

3   The recent visit of **Russian Foreign Minister Sergei Lavrov** to the country suggests that this is not just a local conflict but a major geopolitical confrontation in the making. Russia, the US, Saudi Arabia, the United Arab Emirates, and other powers are surely battling for influence in this important country.

By today's assessment, the situation in the **North Caucasus** is slightly more predictable, but still no one knows how long the Russia-brokered peace agreement[4] will last, and we also don't know if those developments will end the hostilities in the Armenia-Azerbaijan borderland, or if they will be merely a short peaceful interlude that will ultimately lead to the next phase of the Nagorno-Karabakh conflict in the decades to come.[5]

The political situations in **Syria,**[6] **Lebanon, Egypt, Yemen,** and **Libya** are still unpredictable because of the way the Arab Spring unfolded in these countries and triggered either prolonged political instability that cemented the rule of the local despot, a civil war situation that evolved into a local proxy war of regional importance, or some combination of these negative developments. The radicals are further radicalizing because of the drone attacks that resulted in the killings of **Ayman al Zawahiri** of al-Qaeda, and **Abu Bakr al-Baghdadi** of ISIS, which have not stopped their followers from continuing their deadly strategies. On the contrary, some of their supporters just got stronger incentive to continue their jihads. Indeed, the scope and scale of their organizations' global outreach have been seriously undermined, for their presence in Syria, Iraq, Afghanistan, and Pakistan is much weaker than just five years ago. Still, both **al-Qaeda** and **ISIS** continue to exercise a considerable influence in other areas of their regional operations in the Middle East.

---

4   Paradoxically, as much as Russia is clearly interested in destabilizing the situation in Eastern Europe, it assumed a different role when it comes to the situation in North Caucasus; the 2020 Nagorno-Karabakh ceasefire agreement that ended the Second Nagorno-Karabakh War was signed thanks to Russian intervention. It was signed on 9 November by the President of Azerbaijan Ilham Aliyev, the Prime Minister of Armenia Nikol Pashinyan, and the President of Russia Vladimir Putin.

5   In this respect, my strong recommendation is to look at this conflict from the perspective of *The Conflict Resolution Beyond the International Relations Paradigm Evolving Designs as a Transformative Practice in Nagorno-Karabakh and Syria* (2017), by Philip Gamaghelyan. It guides us through a vast collection of contemporary conflict resolution strategies and urges us to adopt much more reliable, refined, and unbiased conflict resolution terminology (particularly in the context of Syria and Nagorno-Karabakh). It accurately portrays some of the most important trends in the most recent conflict resolution-related debates and recommends a selection of very useful literature published by leading scholars in the field. Gamaghelyan also suggests that the over-reliance of conflict resolution practice on the binary frames of classic IR theories is widespread, meaning that overcoming this issue may not be as easy as one may think. As he explains, there are a number of standard practices of international conflict resolution that unintentionally create a counter-productive marginalization across a broad range of issues. For more information, please refer to Pietrzak, Piotr. 2021. "Book Review: Philip Gamaghelyan. Conflict Resolution Beyond the International Relations Paradigm Evolving Designs as a Transformative Practice in Nagorno-Karabakh and Syria"(2017). *In Statu Nascendi 2021: Journal of Political Philosophy and International Relations 4.2.* (pp. 141-148).

6   Please refer to a series of my recent publications related to the Syrian conflict (2011-).

They are still capable of jeopardizing global stability and putting the lives of innocent civilians at risk in many other places around the world.

Meanwhile, **Boko Haram** fighters still terrorize the civilian populations of **Nigeria, Cameron, Mail,** and **Niger**, and given a chance, the members of this organization can cause considerable damage to the way the global architecture of power operates, for their *modus operandi* is driven by a different type of hatred that is deeper than those projected by jihadism, radical Wahhabism, or sectarianism. It appeals to those who blame the West for its imperialist past, its white entitlement, its racist policies, its xenophobic attitudes towards the colonized populations at large, the inappropriateness of certain aspects of the pro-Western education system, the ruthlessness of uncontrollable capitalism, its lack of cultural sensitivity, and so on.

We should also notice spiking tensions between **China** and **Taiwan** over a visit by **US House of Representatives Speaker Nancy Pelosi** in 2022 and various low-intensity escalations caused by China's "Little Blue Man"—the maritime militias—asserting this country's claims in the South China Sea. Finally, as I have already mentioned, **Russia's escalation of the conflict in Ukraine** has evolved into a full-blown protracted confrontation that has only confirmed what we feared for a very long time—that Russia is completely uninterested in playing by the rules of the UN-based security system.

Approaching local and regional conflicts through the prism of IR theory

The Fourth IR Debate in this respect suggests that if we embrace positivist attitudes and hope to conduct successful research in the fields of international relations and conflict management, we will have to religiously comply with various relatively static, positive, conventional, hypothesis-driven methodological requirements to turn such efforts into an all-encompassing scientific process of knowledge creation. This is understandable and rational, for when the domestic-foreign policy distinctions and the boundaries between disciplines seem clearly defined, we can make an educated guess that, indeed, IR scholars would be inclined to do their very best to frame their scientific observations in the most impartial, objective, calibrated, and clear manner, without any hidden agenda.

In the meantime, post-positivist thinkers tend to be somewhat skeptical about trusting in the idea of the existence of knowledge that can exist in some sort of purified manner. They call into doubt the idea of fully trusting the researcher's intentions or following some semi-rationalist wisdom guaranteeing some "universally and unequivocally accepted" standards or ways of doing things. On the contrary, they argue that scientists can no longer take anything for granted, for knowledge as we know it accounts for a collection of temporarily accepted assumptions and paradigms that cannot be seen as absolute in the post-positivist period. From their perspective, it is no longer possible to embrace the traditional rigorous process of observation and careful analysis of all obtainable and verifiable facts and figures, for they cannot be obtained in the first place. So, if we cannot rely on undeniable facts, our data accounts for merely illusionary, easily dismissible starting points or a collection of inherited bias and prejudice. Naturally, the risk here is that even if we try to approach any ongoing confrontations from a broader, more mature perspective, we will have to wait a long time to collect all possible information and clear our doubts. At the same time, relying on guesses, assumptions, and unverifiable knowledge is not an option in the long run. Still, the bottom line is that under some circumstances, we should be able to proceed if we clearly acknowledge the metaontological limitations of our research and refrain from suggesting that our observations are in some way scientific until at least we gain access to more variables and more verifiable facts and figures, especially when it comes to conflict management.

Naturally, even under such circumstances, we can find a way to tackle such issues. For instance, Italian political scientist Giovanni Sartori famously claimed that the man who realizes the limitations of not having a thermometer should still be able to say a great deal about the weather and temperature simply by relying on slightly more vague sets of observations; merely by stating that it is hot and cold, warmer and cooler, we can describe the reality at hand. This is an essential step of measuring variables logically before finding a relationship between them, and this spirit of thinking can also be adopted in conflict management. It is our responsibility to use all methods at our disposal to describe the social reality at hand in the most approachable manner.

We can also strengthen our research in this respect by relying on all available historical, statistical, macroeconomic, and geoeconomic data to increase the likelihood of successfully approaching modern conflicts and, by extension, helping to find the best possible way to resolve them. Subsequently, depending on the main objectives of our research, we can always try to supplement these endeavors with the theoretical achievements of other sub-disciplines of political science such as geopolitics, international law, political economy, political methodology, behavioral studies, comparative politics, political institutions, public policy, and political theory to attain a better overall result. We have an ample collection of very diversified IR approaches, theories, and paradigms at our disposal ready to be deployed in our investigations of the problem at hand, so we can use our disadvantageous initial setting to our advantage by eliminating the mistakes in our thinking by borrowing from the brains of the best IR thinkers in the history of mankind and by using all of the potential benefit that realism/traditionalism, liberalism, constructivism, rationalism, postcolonialism, poststructuralism, feminism, neo-Marxism, and the English School offer if we treat each and every one of these schools in an equal manner. Doing so with dedication, professionalism, and an open mind should help us to get to the bottom of any problem at hand.

Conceptualizing any ongoing confrontation can be challenging due to its constantly changing nature. The use of a highly diversified set of IR approaches in such settings can't guarantee success; it can only increase its probability. It still requires adopting a certain skill in embracing the right proportion of the existent schools, approaches, theories, and paradigms, which can be challenging, especially to young adepts of IR theory. In this respect, I need to admit that one of the most important lessons I learned during my early research relating to the events in Syria (2011-) is that approaching such a complicated conflict from a more holistic perspective could be as challenging as climbing Mount Everest. Indeed, I encountered several conceptual challenges, for the Syrian conflict accounts for a very particular occurrence in modern warfare history that resembles a chameleon (that can change its skin coloration depending on its environment). On some levels, this conflict can be compared to the Spanish Civil War (1936–1939) or the Lebanese Civil War (1975-1990), for there are many vested interests that steer the behaviors of the forces involved in this conflict zone.

Surely by now we know that the Assad regime managed to preserve its power and influence in this country, but some five years ago the situation was far less predictable, for there were eight or nine active sides in this conflict: the regime, the moderate rebels, the jihadist/radicalized groups from al Nusra Front, ISIS, the Kurds, Hezbollah, various Shia and Sunni militias, Turkish, Russian, and American mercenaries, and so on and so forth. Back in 2014, 2015, or 2017 this conflict could be compared to the largely fragmented Italian peninsula of the early Renaissance where each principality and city-state was engaged in a *bellum omnium contra omnes* (war of everyone against everyone).

Naturally, in the dream world, given that it was invented exactly for such purposes, IR theory should allow us to overcome these difficulties and approach even such a diverse conflict zone with relative ease. However, even taking considerable time to familiarize ourselves with the leading theories, schools of thought, and concepts within our tradition again does not guarantee the success of such endeavors. Investing our time and effort to properly comprehend IR theory does not guarantee that we will automatically approach modern conflict in an acceptable manner or that we will become conflict management specialists. Even if we were able to fully comprehend the complexity of any given conflict, we would ultimately face several issues with the way the IR theory is structured and its individual approaches as compartmentalized. On the contrary, by approaching this ever-changing war zone through such a prism one may actually expose such a project to further methodological difficulties related to the way our discipline has been compartmentalized in the first place, for IR theory itself entered a slippery slope of a metaphoric state of *homo homini lupus est* in which each school of thought has no choice but to act hostile out of fear of marginalization.

The nature of the controversy

Approaching today's local and regional conflicts of global importance tends to be very challenging simply because their nature is constantly evolving. Those conflicts are not just traditional confrontations between two standing armies ready to clash at the whims of their leaders. At one point or another, those conflicts are slowly but surely deteriorating, becoming increasingly complex, multidimensional, and highly multilayered confrontations or proxy wars in which numerous vested interests steer the behaviors of both sides involved in this conflict zone and their allies.

Naturally, the pluralism and low degree of integration, internal complexity, and fragmentation do not help our discipline: Robert Keohane[7] suggests that IR theory says more and more about less and less. This trend towards increasingly specialized and narrow areas of study, with scholars becoming more focused on specific subfields and topics within the broader field of international relations, started a long time ago. It is, therefore, necessary to do our utmost to avoid misconstrued characterizations, flawed methodology, and biased narratives, and the best way to do so is to follow the example of Hans Morgenthau, whom I regard as one of the most significant sources of inspiration to my intellectual endeavors for the last fifteen years; this is mostly thanks to his inspiring commitment to seek truth in the realm of international relations. This endeavor has served as my guiding principle for this research,

---

7   The statement that "IR theory says more and more about less and less" is commonly attributed to American political scientist Robert Keohane. Still, this opinion is shared by many IR scholars.

for it postulates doing our utmost to avoid embracing single-dimensional explanations and prioritizing complexity over simplicity. It suggests avoiding well-trodden explanatory paths and entering the most challenging ones in the attempt for self-betterment to meet tomorrow's demands. Why is it so important? In general, the example of this project and many others show that in the modern era, our generation of scholars will be faced with the increasingly more demanding challenge of dealing with vague concepts and will describe ongoing international conflicts that show an inherent propensity to change that requires a systematic inquiry combined with constant methodological adjustments.

However, our discipline also happens to be in the middle of a protracted epistemic and ontological confrontation between various -isms, paradigms, and traditions. Anyone interested in deepening their understanding of the social reality at hand should acknowledge that our pluralism and inherent complexity may also negatively impact our capacity to present credible interpretations of and feasible solutions to ongoing regional conflicts of global importance; we keep insisting on using this theory, even if it happens to be increasingly pluralistic and chaotic at times, for the existent ontological underpinnings of our discipline depend on our ability to cope with this difficulty. This research postulates starting to treat IR theory not as a useful catalog always available for the cherry-picking of the most popular ideas, theories, paradigms, and approaches but in a much more contemplative manner that includes the element of constant change in the circular stream of becoming. In this respect, it is essential to emphasize that it is not a stream of becoming that resists human attempts to impose meaningful order on it. On the contrary, it is a stream that compartmentalizes various new ideas, theories, paradigms, branches of science, approaches, and traditions, a stream that can offer us a certain level of temporary certainty during the uncertain times of fragmented or even liquid reality. This study accounts for a genuine attempt to adopt a far more diverse portfolio of existing interdisciplinary work, approaches, methods, debates, and deliberations, boosted by the resilience of a new political ontology and a hybrid-type study that merges and blends several leading philosophical, political, and IR-related paradigms and approaches into an easily approachable ontology that provides the broader public with the tools to engage in much deeper ontological inquiry into the nature, origin, and genesis of any given concept.

Despite these challenges, the majority of our findings, theories, and traditions are surely worth preserving, even if they require considerable reform in the way we approach theory in general. The challenge ahead is quite consequential, for we are expected to show a far-reaching readiness to satisfy necessary incorporating tendencies, meet the pressure to embrace sound theories and identify poor reasoning, and reject seemingly valid anomalies, and even though it may be unsettling at times, we are still expected to engage in exposing and refuting persuasive fallacies that can cloud our judgment. Adding to the challenge is the need for enthusiasm in acknowledging the need to preserve elements of arbitrariness that are temporarily accepted as leading dogma by our peers and incorporate them into our research, at least until we find a better way of overcoming them in a civilized evolutionary manner without burning conceptual, methodological, or analytical bridges that span various traditions and approaches. Nonetheless, when we question the accepted way of doing things, we are portrayed as immature revolutionary newcomers who show disrespect for the status quo.

The problems that we face today also come from the fact that our discipline exhibits a lack of a broader consensus about the systematic application of IR theory as a consistent unit of in-depth analysis of various conflict-based situations and the nature of the disagreements over the way in which we verify the tangibility and truthfulness of our findings. For instance, according to Robert O. Keohane, given that knowledge is socially constructed, the "scientific success (by extension in IR theory) is not the attainment of an objective truth, but the attainment of a wider agreement on descriptive facts and causal relationships, based on transparent and replicable methods" (Keohane 1998, p. 195). More positivist IR scholars are not comfortable with following such a neopositivist logic, for they are not enthusiastic about accepting doctrines, approaches, theories, or paradigms only because they happen to be more established or they are unquestionable or absolute. Still, we need to recognize that this type if neopositivist reduction is not particularly characteristic to Keohane, for this type of thinking seems to be very characteristic of many neopositivist IR scholars; Keohane has just chosen to be very transparent and straightforward in exposing the current mood and the prevailing opinion regarding what objectivity, clarity, and ideal truth account for in IR theory. We also need to recognize that those positivist attempts to generalize science and make of it a useful forecasting apparatus can be effective only in a limited sense, for, ultimately, they cannot always be right about the future, but they can be useful in identifying certain patterns within international relations and formulating general propositions that would not be applicable to all circumstances. Our social reality at hand is too complex for our theories to be able to predict the behavior of states and individuals within a given structure. Meanwhile, its adventurism in this respect cannot be the only criterium of IR theory effectiveness, for we still have a lot of work to do when it comes to fighting dogma, misinformation, and various forms of bias and prejudice that still exist in our literature.

Surely, there are differences in attitudes towards a constant pursuit of objective truth in the philosophical realm, and settling for the prevailing opinion is more than evident here. As much as overcoming the current status quo may not be easy, this idea is worth pursuing, for such democratization of the scientific criteria of truth is very shaky at its core. It simply does not make sense to accept any idea as truthful only because a large proportion of some members of the academic or any broader community agree with it. This idea is worth pursuing in an evolutionary manner, step by step, for IR theory, along with its respective branches, approaches, theories, and paradigms, would really benefit from a new synthesis that would find a better way to coordinate our most recent discoveries and compartmentalize them in much more approachable manner. There is sense in distilling this know-how from philosophy to apply it to IR theory, for, to paraphrase Karl Jaspers, IR theory must seek better inquiry and verification paths that lie within global reality as it is conceived today in all of its representations. Nevertheless, this is impossible without particular attention to clarity, truth, transparency, respect, and broader attention towards various ontological matters at hand. Naturally, inviting some of the sharpest philosophical minds to our IR-related investigations is not a new idea, for there are several preexisting philosophy-based ontological debates present in IR-related deliberations.

That is why we should see IR theory as a scientific ontology, but it is infused with various philosophical deliberations that date back to antiquity. We just need to recall the work of Hans Morgenthau (1948), Roy Bhaskar (1979), Alexander Wendt (1999), and many others to clearly point out the scope of our influence by the vast collection of philosophical ontologies that have been influencing our way of thinking for decades. But as much as it is my strong conviction that the main elements of these debates remain pertinent to the way our discipline operates today, I am certain the contemporary IR theory can really benefit from more coordinated, frequent, and devoted exposure to the leading philosophical debates of today.

Balancing act

Knowing what we already know about IR theory's strengths and limitations, it is only natural for us to start questioning how we should approach the way IR theory has been compartmentalized, whether we should see it as a scientific ontology or a useful catalogue of functional paradigms and theories, and what it means to be a good IR theorist. In this respect, one may wonder whether it is a matter of sticking to one paradigm, approach, or school of thought and mastering all of its theories or instead taking a holistic approach requiring acquainting or reacquainting oneself with each and every idiosyncrasy of any given tradition. In this respect, a careful ontological thinker would always ask himself the fundamental question of why we would try to build an ontology from scratch or reconceptualize the existing tradition to approach a modern conflict if the IR theory already exists. And the answer would be straightforward, for this subdiscipline, at times, struggles to adjust to the new challenges presented by the inherent and incremental fragmentation, specialization, and professionalization that can be seen within various schools of thought. To fully acknowledge and comprehend the scope of the suggested changes, we first need to specifically imagine the current ontological framing of IR theory and juxtapose it with the desired one.

The best way to explain the status quo in current theory is with the metaphor of a tree. Such an "IR tree" would have several increasingly strong branches (IR approaches and theories such as realism, liberalism, constructivism, rationalism, postcolonialism, poststructuralism, feminism, neo-Marxism, and the English School) that grow in various somewhat uncoordinated ways (Pietrzak, 2021, pp. 43–76, 101–128). In this sense, different scholars from other branches of IR theory would be only remotely familiar with the variety of leaves (paradigms, concepts, ideas), and they would repeatedly use the same leaves. The tree also has cherries (methods and ad hoc generalizations), and instead of everyone collecting various types of cherries from various branches of the tree (which would be desirable), many IR scholars engage in a very selective cherry-picking strategy determined by the strict preferences of their approach. Many IR scholars would eat from one or two branches of this tree throughout their professional careers without exploring the other branches of our tradition (Pietrzak, 2021, pp. 65-68).

This paper also suggests approaching modern conflicts from a slightly different perspective by initiating the process of incremental changes that will ultimately replace the current status quo with a new compartmentalization of our ontological superstructure that will be able to meet the new challenges that the 21st century has brought us. I put forward the idea of the ontology *in statu nascendi* that seeks to bring to the table the most relevant debates and interrelate them with political philosophy to give us a chance to approach this know-how as a new horizon of investigations that aims to be more approachable, more transparent, and more applicable to our descriptions of today's political world. Subsequently, this change to the way we approach theory should produce a considerable improvement in the way we approach contemporary conflicts that have become more elusive, fluid, and unpredictable than ever (Pietrzak, 2021, pp. 129–178).

Research Methodology

This research is supported by a wide array of theoretical foundations, methodologies, interdisciplinary fields of inquiry, and paradigms ranging from various disciplines such as the theory of international relations, international law, geopolitics, conflict resolution strategies, and political philosophy. It aims to provide the reader with a clear and impartial language of analysis capable of embracing a more contemplative, evolutionary manner of investigation that is adjustable to the ever-changing circumstances of the constantly changing situation in the modern conflict zone. It relies heavily on the author's commitment to a systematic collection and analysis of collected data, verifying and synthesizing all the gathered information through verifiable sources, and test-driving the results of this work by relating this debate to the discussions on the scope and scale of the international community's responsibility to bring peace and security back to various local and regional conflict zones of global importance (Pietrzak, 2021a, p. 43-76, Pietrzak, 2021b, 101-154; Tóth 2021).

The main purpose of this paper

This paper is dedicated to everyone interested in expanding their explanatory horizons and challenging their preconceived notions of truth in the realm of international relations. It is designed for use in a wide variety of courses: Global Problems & Global Solutions,[8] On Just War Theory, Human Rights

---

8   **GLOBAL PROBLEMS, GLOBAL SOLUTIONS** aims to provide students with the fundamental tools necessary to understand the post-Cold War global power architecture from theoretical and analytical perspectives. It is addressed to students interested in current affairs, security studies, and leading approaches to violent conflict after 1991. Our primary research area will be approached from geopolitics, security studies, and humanitarian perspectives. During the classes, we try to approach the new world order in statu nascendi from the perspective of various ongoing conflicts and humanitarian emergencies. In just ten weeks of classes, we will examine the roots of competition and cooperation among states by looking at them from the perspective of broader debates launched by Francis Fukuyama in his The End of History, Samuel Huntington's Clash of Civilizations, Zbigniew Brzezinski's The Grand Chessboard, Kenneth Waltz's Balance of Power Theory, Stephen Walt's Balance of Threat Theory, Joseph Nye's Soft Power, and Kissinger's Diplomacy, We will deal with the Putinization of the so-called near abroad, the Zakarian rise of the rest, and the emerging multipolar world in which China's "One Road One Belt" initiative and its more assertive policy in the South China Sea changes the rules of the competition. By the end of March, all students taking this course should be able to independently describe how they perceive the new architecture of global power, explain the

and Humanitarian Studies,[9] On International Relations Theory, Applied Ethics, and Experimental Philosophy. It aspires to provide a valuable new contribution to these rapidly developing research fields.

Literature Review

This research accounts for a natural continuation of my recent publication *On the idea of humanitarian intervention: a new compartmentalization of IR theories,* Ibidem Verlag: Stuttgart, 2021) that launched a systematic inquiry into the nature of the concept of humanitarian intervention, focusing on its primary function of the protection of the endangered civilian populations who find themselves at grave risk of genocide. This publication also includes a recollection of selected historical examples of similar events and the responses to them by the international community, empowered by our modern understanding of the principle of state sovereignty, human rights, and anti-genocide legislation. Applying the *in statu nascendi* ontology that accounts for the latest hybridized compartmentalization of various IR-related theories, the author provides a deep ontological inquiry into the nature, origin, and genesis of the idea of humanitarian intervention and opens a broader debate on the limits of the principle of state sovereignty as well as on the international

---

strengths and the limitations of the UN security-based system, be able to identify the main conflict zones in the world, and apply this know-how to the complexities of the contemporary world of politics.

9   **ON JUST WAR THEORY, HUMAN RIGHTS AND HUMANITARIAN STUDIES** aims to provide students with the fundamental tools to understand the just war theory, human rights, and humanitarian studies. It will introduce students to the historical background of the contemporary just war tradition and familiarize them with leading approaches to ethical/humanitarian analyses of selected regional conflicts of global importance. Our primary research area will be approached from humanitarian perspectives supplemented by selected philosophical approaches. By the end of the semester, all students taking this course should be familiar with the main principles governing jus ad bellum, "the body of international law governing the right of one state to resort to war against another"; jus in bello, "the body of international law regulating the conduct of combatants during the war to minimize unnecessary damage and suffering"; and jus post-bellum, "the body of laws, norms and principles that apply during the transition from war to peace [which] provides relational cohesion to its underlying laws and norms and a basis for assigning responsibility for post-conflict obligations". The students will be able to distinguish between collateral damage that is an unintended consequence of ongoing hostilities and war crimes or acts of genocide. Subsequently, the students will be familiar with the philosophical and ethical underpinnings of the principle of fair treatment of prisoners of war (POWs), the non-combat immunity principle, the principle of last resort, the principle of the right intention, the principle of right authority, the principle of proportionality, the probability of success principle, and the theory related to various exceptions related to those principles during and after the so-called supreme emergencies. Students will be able to independently describe how they perceive the new architecture of global power from a philosophical perspective and explain the strengths and the limitations of the UN security-based system.

community's ignorance of some of the most severe cases of human rights abuses around the world.

It also accounts for a continuation of the paper that was published by *In Statu Nascendi: Journal of Political Philosophy and International Relations* 2019/1, titled "The Syrian Conflict (2011–ongoing): How a Perfectly Winnable Uprising Has Ended Up as a Ferocious Proxy War of Global Importance" and a fulfillment of the next stage of my broader research that relates to finding the best way of describing any ongoing local or regional conflict *in statu nascendi.*

The research is partly influenced by Roy Bhaskar's critical realism that postulates a far-reaching incorporation of ontology into the human sciences. His project distinguishes between the real world and the observable world. It suggests that for science as a body of knowledge and methodology to work or be intelligible, epistemology and ontology need to be separated, and we must distinguish between the transitive and intransitive bodies of knowledge or dimensions (Baskar, 1975, pp. 6-9, Pietrzak 2021, pp. 147-153).

Thanks to exploring some parts of this tradition it became easier for me to differentiate between transitive and intransitive bodies of knowledge, so intransitive choices could be more consistent with a complete preference in IR scholars, which would be concerned with the reasoning underlying choices behind any given approaches that would indicate the individual being that would be inclined to make categorical choices regarding the specific options they prefer (i.e. an individual scholar would always prefer a liberal approach to a realist approach, prefer a realist approach to a liberal approach, or be indifferent to both and adhere to constructivism). In this respect, transitivity would incline the situation with less predetermined choices and would imply a far-reaching unpredictability where the individual scholar would weakly prefer the liberal approach to the realist or would weakly prefer Marxist IR methodology to English school methods but would keep an open mind, and the initial preferences would not affect choices to the extent of those in the complete preferences scenario. The added benefit of this type of investigation would be the unknown direction of their investigations. Each scientist would have to do his own cost-benefit analysis using a variety of criteria and approaches to perform self-determined best choices but embracing a far-reaching interdisciplinary mode of analysis that offers a far-reaching benefit in comparison to the complete or partial (cherry-picking) approach (Baskar 1975, p. 6–9, Baskar 1979).

The other scholar worth our attention in this respect, very instrumental in advocating various ontological deliberations in IR theory, is Alexander

Wendt, who is of the opinion that "a deeper understanding of the nature of existence can help us to better understand and navigate the complex social world in which we live." Wendt's constructivism is one of the most successful IR-related ontologies ever articulated; he proposes that the literature on the subject should adapt to the realities of structuration theory that are a relational solution to the agent-structure problem, conceptualizing agents, and structures as mutually constituted or codetermined entities. According to his *Social Theory of International Politics* (1999), "the way we perceive the world around us shapes the way we interact with it" simply because "the nature of the world is not pre-given or objective, but rather is constructed through social interactions and relationships." In this sense, the study of the nature of existence or being is an essential aspect of understanding how the world works, for there are many factors that impact the way states interact with each other, starting from material factors such as power or resources and ending with the ideas and beliefs that shape their perceptions of the world. Wendt also reminds us that ontology belongs to metaphysics, which scrutinizes the place and the essence of entities that exist in the broader context of similar/different entities in the universe or any other broader structure, and that is exactly what we should aim at (Wendt 1987, Wendt 1999). Elman and Elman (2003, p. 202) suggest that an ontology can plausibly make a universal claim across a broad domain, for it is the study, theory, or science of being and the study of the existence or non-existence of things that deliberates on how things (that exist) relate to each other.

The Responsibility of the Ontologist

At this point, it is high time to start wondering what the responsibility of an ontological thinker in these settings is. Why would we advocate in favor of emphasizing the ontological aspects of any ongoing confrontation in the first place? If I were to explain the nature and the purpose of any ontological inquiry to my four-year-old son, I would probably begin by explaining that it is just like setting off on a fascinating journey. Such a journey leads to the road to discovering the truth about any given object, property, event, process, and relation in every area of social reality, despite the difficulties that one may encounter during the process. In this sense, it is asserted that such an ontologist never settles for the more straightforward or more approachable answer, and he or she is always inclined to be excited about digging deeper and deeper to uncover the hidden truth about the nature of a given phenomenon.

In general, an ontologist's primary responsibility under such circumstances should be to search for the best way of asking relevant questions under any circumstances. He/she should aim to uncover what a given concept, idea, process, or object accounts for. His/her prime motivation should be establishing an explicit, indisputable, and universally agreed-upon definition or explanation of the concepts, trying to determine a set of assumptions about the world, showing all of the properties and the relations between various aspects of the research area, social meanings, and social constructions, investigating any given patterns of interaction that apply to this research, and look into the identity, beliefs, and social contexts of given categories or any subject area he investigates. At times, this would mean digging deeper beyond convenience, beyond what is approachable at first sight, beyond the surface of what is known, and what can be taken for granted. That is why assessing any given local or regional conflict and selecting the best possible response may involve a lot of time and consideration and may be problematic for those without excellent policymaking experience, so the policymaking table is not the place for amateurs. One must be prepared for such a situation; this publication hopes to provide decision-making parties with the necessary training and a handy manual on how to proceed under such difficult circumstances.

The use of ontology in conflict management

Indeed, an ontologist's mode of thinking is applied in IR-related investigations not in some abstract situations, but in real-life situations, when providing an ad hoc assessment of any outbreak of a conflict "in front of our eyes," to advise the decision-makers on how to react under such circumstances. Where human life may be at stake, one has to make an instant decision on what should be done. An ontologist who finds himself in such a situation should make himself aware of his responsibility to respect the situation's urgency. Therefore, one should act and deliberate the fastest one can. However, under such situations when "the clock is ticking very fast," and the deadline is quickly approaching, getting to the bottom of the issue at hand may be tricky without proper experience. That is why assessing any given emergency (mainly) and selecting the best possible response may involve a lot of time and consideration and may be problematic for those without excellent policymaking experience.

Ultimately, a policymaking table is not the place for amateurs, and one must be prepared to provide decision-making parties with a handy solution on how to proceed under such difficult circumstances. This means that we need to be well prepared for any eventuality, any challenge related to describing any ongoing confrontation between various sides both from theoretical and practical perspectives. Ultimately, **Michael Oakeshott** was right to suggest that practice and theory are two distinct modes of human experience that are related but not interchangeable. He claimed that practice involves the use of knowledge in a practical and intuitive way to achieve a desired end while theory involves the systematic and analytical study of knowledge to understand its nature and principles; practice is concerned with doing while theory is concerned with knowing.

A Very Brief Introduction to Philosophical Ontology for the IR Theorist

There are massive differences between philosophical ontology and political/scientific ontology, but ontology *in statu nascendi* hopes to touch upon both to incorporate into this new compartmentalization of IR theory a new horizon of investigations that will offer a more befitting framework capable of bringing all leading paradigms, schools, approaches, and branches of IR theory closer together. This research plans to convey the complexity of all the issues at hand in a much more comprehensive manner and capture them within the process of creation and the process of becoming *in statu nascendi* that will allow us to adjust to the emerging new circumstances of an increasingly complex local, regional, and global environment. The ideas of such philosophers as Socrates, Plato, Sextus Empiricus, René Descartes. Giordano Bruno, Galileo Galilei, Gottfried Wilhelm Leibniz, Arthur Schopenhauer, Immanuel Kant, Georg Wilhelm Friedrich Hegel, Friedrich Nietzsche, Edmund Husserl, Giambattista Vico, Martin Heidegger, Roman Ingarden, Maurice Merleau-Ponty, Emmanuel Levinas, Karl Jaspers, Hans-Georg Gadamer, Cornelius Castoriadis, Zygmunt Bauman, Jacques Derrida and those associated with the the Lwòw-Warsaw School and Frankfurt School can help us strengthen the ontology *in statu nascendi,* for they will add an extra interdisciplinary value to the forthcoming debate that will supplement these endeavors. In the end, its main function is to supplement a new platform of mutual understanding of all existing approaches within our discipline. At this stage, this candidate for a new ontology has already exhibited rather unique and non-standardized characteristics. Most of the above-mentioned thinkers were extremely fascinating and we could surely learn a great deal from their individual projects. What is unique about their projects is the fact that their life's goal was to stay true to their findings, for they treated their ideas as more precious than gold, and some of them were even willing to die for the idea, for the truth, for the integrity of their research. That is why it would be only natural to use some of their incredible ontological findings in IR theory. But it is not a simple operation.

Surely, for some IR theorists, such a maneuver of the stronger incorporation of various philosophical debates into the IR-related debate could be seen as an attempt of "curing the disease by killing the patient," but it is my strong conviction that IR theorists should not fear adopting ontological modes of thinking to their investigations and should not be afraid of philosophy, for at the end of the day one of the forefathers of our discipline, Hans Morgenthau, was playing with continental philosophy like with a doll to look at some IR-related issues from a different perspective. Philosophy is ultimately just a discipline that teaches you how to think in a different, more analytical manner.

In this respect, it is good to acknowledge that being an IR theorist who likes to philosophize is not easy. It is very hard, as a matter of fact. But in this instance, I don't advocate using the work of any given philosopher, or overcrowding your arguments with a vast combination of abstract continental ideas that are not properly "utilized" in IR-theory-related literature. I just advocate embracing a more ontological mode of thinking that acknowledges the need for more interdisciplinary mode of investigation that aspires to change the general landscape of awareness, moving beyond *status quo* and shallow, superficial, and one-dimensional explanations by simply embracing an uncertainty and unpredictability of a self-perpetuating process of continuous attempts to attain a broader clarity and befriending wisdom (Koinē Greek: σοφία sophía). This is exactly why the ontology *in statu nascendi* was coined in the first place, so it would allow us a chance of describing any given conflict from the perspective of all its stages that while pursuing clarity and objective, truthful, and accountable solutions that will help us to build interdisciplinary bridges for understanding some of the most complex matters at hand.

Still, I do understand where my colleagues from IR tradition are coming from and why they are reluctant to supplement their research with Hegelian, Husserlian, or Heideggerian ideas, for they have every reason to find those thinkers very confusing; even those who professionally translate Heidegger from the original German to English complain that some of their thoughts are either not translatable to English or that there are various possible interpretations. So it is perfectly understandable that they don't want to treat continental philosophy as something easily interrelated, clear, or precise, because it is clearly not. But there are some incredible aspects of continental philosophy that could be useful to the IR theorist, and that is why I strongly advocate its broader application to our literature on the subject, for it will allow us to overcome some of the internal conflicts IR theory is still struggling with.

The origin of ontology *in statu nascendi*

Ontology *in statu nascendi* can help us to simultaneously adopt multiple perspectives without synthesizing them or blending them into something new. This compartmentalization allows us to consider various ontologies, epistemologies, and methodologies reach a more mature horizon of investigations and operate as a "working conceptual engine, and not just one cog in the machine." This new compartmentalization of IR theory hopes to convey the complexity of all the issues at hand in a much more comprehensive manner and capture them within the process of creation, the process of becoming—the so-called *in statu nascendi*—that will allow us to adjust to the emerging new circumstances of an increasingly more complex local, regional, and global environment. This can be done thanks to its ability to incorporate the scientific achievements of IR theory and further open up to the various philosophical traditions to attain a new horizon of investigations that will offer a more befitting framework capable of bringing all leading paradigms, schools, and branches of IR theory closer together. The ultimate *ad hoc* goal for the political ontology of *in statu nascendi* is to launch a more comprehensive inquiry into the nature of the contemporary conflict which will emphasize the inherently evolutionary character of every man-made conflict that will be strengthened by a recollection of the selected historical examples of similar events and the international community responses to them from the past; empowered by our modern understanding of the principle of state sovereignty, human rights, and anti-genocide laws and legislation.

The use of ontology *in statu nascendi* in conflict management

Ontology *in statu nascendi* is in the perpetual process of transitioning, forming, and adjusting to the emerging new circumstances of an increasingly more complex local, regional, and global environment at hand, so that is why it it should be useful to those who try to use it to describe an ongoing conflict that also happens to be in a perpetual state of turning into something new, by either escalating or deescalating. In essence, embracing this ontology forces us to multitask and to navigate between different fully diversified approaches that are inherently conflicted. The main reason for this is that our theory tends to be very eclectic and at times confusing, which is why such an endeavor should be reserved only for the most curious scholars, for to reach the peak of our conceptual capabilities, we really must brace ourselves, for we are about to encounter multiple challenges as far as the conceptual, methodological, and analytical levels of our analysis are concerned. This project suggests that we need to put special emphasis on various ontological considerations, but we cannot forget about our tradition and the scientific achievements of each and every approach existent in our tradition. We need to build on this tradition, for it accounts for a great reservoir of studies, methods, and theories that will be supplemented by selected philosophical ontologies. It is a working hypothesis that suggests that only such a holistic approach can account for a qualitative change to investigating various vague concepts. This hybridized mode of studies and investigations hopes to bring more light onto the concept in question and account for a great point of theoretical departure ahead of investigations of various case studies such as the global reaction to both historic and contemporary conflicts.

My main hypothesis in this respect is that most interdepartmental disagreements within our discipline arise because of the lack of proper "communication" between scholars representing various approaches. Naturally, some approaches are much more closely interlinked, such as, for instance, realism and liberalism; despite their internal disagreements, they are closely interrelated in the overall focus and scope of their research agendas. At the same time, other schools of thought may appear somewhat unrelated and are even largely ignored by many IR scholars as they represent far more unorthodox traditions, such as postcolonialism, feminism, poststructuralism, and the IR school of neo-Marxism. Those internal (unresolved) differences do not help while investigating the fluidity, elusiveness, and unpredictability of any ongoing contemporary conflict (especially at its early stages), for they present many conceptual challenges to any contemporary IR researcher who tries to investigate in the most comprehensive manner possible (Pietrzak, 2021, pp. 65–68).

To achieve the desired objectives of broader ontological oversight of the IR theory, it is proposed to adopt ontology *in statu nascendi* that is designed to help the existing IR debates and scholars incorporate a more hybridized interdisciplinary merger of IR theories supplemented by a broader awareness of the leading debates and studies within our discipline, strengthened by various philosophical ontologies that might allow us to "dig deeper" into any concept. This research has no intention of subverting any paradigms, revolutionizing existent IR theory, or reformulating its methodological underpinning. It intends only to offer a supplement and a new way of approaching the literature on the subject. Thanks to the inherent diversity of its methods and approaches and the pluralism of paradigms (taken as a whole), the theory of international relations (IR) with its "security studies component" should be seen as a backbone of this study, which deals with an ongoing conflict and conflict resolution strategies. This tradition presents us with multiple units of analysis applicable to comprehensive investigation. One can argue that IR theory is one of the most sophisticated scientific ontologies ever developed, but, naturally, there is still massive room for improvement. I argue that the best way to strengthen the existing theory is by embracing a more comprehensive ontological shake-up that goes far beyond the English school or constructivist types of deliberations (Pietrzak, 2021, pp. 129–154).

A SWOT analysis of ontology *in statu nascendi*

Strengths

Ontology *in statu nascendi* accounts for new largely hybridized compartmentalization of the IR theory that serves several supplementary roles and supportive-evolutionary functions for each IR approach that ultimately arranges some of the biggest chunks of the IR theory and some interesting discoveries in a more approachable manner by focusing our attention to the analysis of all social structures, preexistent and emerging. Ontology *in statu nascendi*'s biggest strength is the fact that it encourages interdisciplinary discourse and a pursuit of clarity that can change the general landscape of awareness by engaging more respectful attitudes towards other IR scholars and philosophers, for it accounts for a very flexible model that helps to formulate more precise and more relevant questions, so it is easier to approach scholarly texts with ahermeneutical precision, that helps us to look at any idea, concept, process, or pattern through the prism of a multitude of approaches brought to our attention simultaneously.

Weaknesses

The first time I introduced the idea of ontology *in statu nascendi* to a more formal academic gathering was during the public defense of my Ph.D. dissertation on 13 May 2021. Back then it could be seen as a rather experimental candidate for ontology that hoped to supplement IR-related debates[10] with a new hybridised compertmentalization of IR theories and a

---

10   In the context I suggested to try to approach the problem through the prism of various IR approaches: "Realism" (e.g. Hans Morgenthau, Henry Kissinger), "Liberalism" (e.g. Immanuel Kant, John Locke, John Stuart Mill, Hugo Grotius), "the English School" (Hedley Bull, Martin Wight, Charles Manning, Barry Buzan), "Postcolonial Studies" (Edward Saïd, Frantz Fanon, Gayatri Spivak), "Feminism" (Cynthia Enloe, Chandra Talpade Mohanty, Fiona Robinson), "Neo-Marxism" (Antonio Gramsci, Immanuel Wallerstein, and David Harvey), "Constructivism" (James Fearon, Alexander Wendt), "Poststructuralism" (Michel Foucault, Jacques Derrida, Jean Baudrillard, Pierre Bourdieu, Ludwig Wittgenstein).

healthy selection of leading philosophical concepts.[11] The main purpose of this research was to find a better way to deal with various ontological dilemmas related to the idea of humanitarian intervention and its potential application in the Syrian conflict zone (2011-). Back then I postulated that the main characteristics of *in statu nascendi* ontology are its dedication to constant readjustments, interdisciplinarian self-improvement, and inherent pursuit of clarity and truth in the realm of international relations.

I envisioned that inclusiveness would help us to attain the right proportion of existent approaches, theories, and paradigms that exist within IR theory, and supplement this tradition with some of the latest developments the political philosophy that ultimately will allow me to capture the elusiveness of the constantly changing conflict zone such as the one in Syria. That day, I could not envision a better academic gathering that could potentially assess all of the pros and the cons of *in statu nascendi* ontology than the public defense committee composed of two philosophers, two IR theory scholars and one ontologist philosopher, which is what I got. Thanks to the feedback that I received from **Prof. Makariev** (philosopher-humanitarian), **Prof. Grozdanov** (philosopher), **Prof. Kentas** (IR theorist), **Prof. Żukowski** (IR theorist), **and Prof. Dafov** (ontologist-philosopher), who took their time to approach this project in a more critical manner, *in statu nascendi* ontology in 2023 is much stronger than it was in 2021, for they have highlighted a number of potential conceptual issues that I might have previously overlooked:

In this respect, I am particularly grateful to **Prof. Veselin Hristov Dafov**[12], my Ph.D. supervisor, who has remained my academic mentor and a source of academic inspiration ever since. Dafov is an expert in the field of philosophical ontology, and meeting him in 2017 changed the direction of my academic career; without his unyielding patience, mentoring skills, and philosophical counseling skills, I would be still sitting in some Platonic cave

---

11   There was suggested a deep ontological mode of thinking in IR theory, going back to the world's most-renowned philosophical ontology thinkers from the Ancient World, the Middle Ages, and Early Modernity, such as Socrates, Plato, Sextus Einpiricus, Saint Enzelm, and René Descartes. Giordano Bruno, Galileo Galilei, Gottfried Wilhelm Leibniz, Arthur Schopenhauer, Immanuel Kant, Georg Wilhelm Friedrich Hegel, and Friedrich Nietzsche, along with a number of representatives of 20th-century philosophy such as Edmund Husserl, Giambattista Vico, Martin Heidegger, Roman Ingarden, Maurice Merleau-Ponty, Emmanuel Levinas, Karl Jaspers, Hans-Georg Gadamer, Cornelius Castoriadis, Zygmunt Bauman, Jacques Derrida and taking into account various other scientific achievements of the Lwòw- Warsaw School and Frankfurt School.

12   For more information, please see *Prof. Dr. Veselin Dafov's review of Pietrzak's Ph.D. Dissertation, Sofia*, Bulgaria, April 20, 2021. Available at: </https://www.uni-sofia.bg/index.php/bul/content/download/249691/1646163/version/1/file/Dafov.pdf/> [Accessed June 11, 2021].

unconscious of the beauty and importance of various ontological debates and their practical application to the social reality at hand. Thanks to his constant encouragement to search for a uniquely placed conceptual locus between philosophical metaphysics and political theory in an uncharted territory of political ontology, I discovered the beauty of the process of constant becoming, formulation, reformulation, and decomposition of various political concepts and ontologies that led me to reformulation of *in statu nascendi* ontology at least half a dozen of times. Dafov suggested that the main shortcoming of my Ph.D. dissertation and ontology was that it did not pay enough attention to incompleteness in clarifying human subjectivity as political. In this respect, he suggested that the issues of political subjectivity were reduced in this project to thinking of the subjectivity of the political as primarily autonomous and separate in a people or nation, the phenomena of which are, respectively, power and international relations, without considering the subjective nature of the political being as self-creating, which can lead to misunderstandings and omissions. This is a very valuable suggestion that I need to take seriously into account in my future work related to ontology *in statu nascendi*, and any other analysis of various emerging socio-political dilemmas at hand.

I am grateful to **Prof. Plamen Mateev Makariev**[13] of Sofia University for his critical evaluation of my dissertation, for he is an academic who has dealt with similar issues throughout his academic career and is today one of the most recognizable contemporary Bulgarian humanitarian scholars who has dedicated a lot of attention to investigating the unique ethnic model of the Rhodope Mountains in southern Bulgaria. In his review, Makariev suggested that ontology *in statu nascnedi* turned into my dissertation's leitmotif, for it was "entrusted with an extremely large and responsible mission—to serve as a unifying reference framework for the application of competing paradigms." Makariev pointed out that, in theory, "it shows some potential to go beyond our conceptual comfort zone by improving mutual understanding between the representatives of different schools in the theory of international relations, that could potentially help to imagine how some seemingly unrelated things could interact" and that in turn could help us to overcome the one-sidedness of their views, but he suggested that there may be a number of issues related to this ontology's practical application. From his perspective, ontology *in statu nascendi* in 2021 still was quite vague, so he challenged me to

---

13   For more information, please see *Prof. Plamen Makariev's Review of Pietrzak's Ph.D. Dissertation*, Sofia, Bulgaria, March 2, 2021. Available at: </https://www.uni-sofia.bg/index.php/bul/content/download/249695/1646179/version/1/file/Makariev.pdf/>   [Accessed June 11, 2021].

try to present this ontology more convincingly by focusing not on what is expected of it—on this issue in the dissertation enough was written, but what it is—in this sense he suggested trying to differentiate it from the other already available ontologies in the literature on the subject. Hence, it is not hard to imagine how this ontology could potentially contribute to reconciling such diversified positions as realism and liberalism, neo-Marxism, or poststructuralism. I gather that this is a fair observation, for Makariev may have a point when suggesting that expecting that suddenly from the traditionally conflicted IR approaches there would be an endorsement of the idea of launching a more interdisciplinary debate on any given foreign policy challenge, in the spirit of inclusiveness, mutual collaboration, and openness is very naïve at best. But, still, one tends to wonder if there will be a time when all members of our highly diversified tradition may be able to overcome their internal conflicts and come together to try something more productive than taking sides in "the constant war of isms."

Similarly, a considerable portion of **Prof. Giorgios Kentas**[14] review of my dissertation was dedicated to critically evaluating the ontology *in statu nascendi*'s primary purpose. This academic associated with the University of Nicosia suggested that for such an ontology ever to be accepted as a functional compartmentalization of IR theory, it first must be juxtaposed with the ontological developments that already exist and are broadly accepted within the literature on the subject. In this respect, Kentas suggested a need to approach this ontology more systematically by interlinking it with the prolific literature that already exists in the field, particularly the work produced and presented from the 1970s until today. Particularly, there was a need to situate this emerging ontology *in statu nascendi* "in relation" to the scientific developments presented by Alexander Wendt and Roy Bhaskar and further engage in more detailed discussion related to specific nuances related to ontological contributions, debates in the field, and their origins in the philosophy of science and of the social sciences.

According to Kentas' professional opinion, another limitation of my research was that I presented the practical implications of the concept in question (the idea of humanitarian intervention at that time) and coined it as a programmatic statement. Instead, I should have demonstrated more clearly why my analysis of, discussion of, and conclusions based on my empirical

---

14   For more information, please see *Prof. Giorgos Kentas's Review of Pietrzak's Ph.D. Dissertation*, Nicosia, Cyprus, 27 April 2021. Available at: </https://www.uni-sofia.bg/index.php/ bul/content/download/249694/1646175/version/1/file/Kentas.pdf/> [Accessed June 11, 2021].

cases could only be reached through the ontological reconstruction of the main object of my study, as I attempted it, and not otherwise. According to Kentas, I should have presented discussion on the same case studies from other perspectives and shown how my approach differs from them; what it adds in comparison to them.

Subsequently, concerning the practical application of ontology *in statu nascendi*, Kentas suggested that it must first have its main "responsibilities" properly defined if I ever hope for this ontology to be integrated into IR theory's main body. He also suggested that I should have demonstrated my research's innovative features and contribution in my dissertation's early stages instead of situating them in later chapters. Subsequently, during the primary debate, Kentas also recommended incorporating various statistical methods into my future research that could further reinforce this project's central ontological position by adding more context and credibility to my predominantly discourse-based analysis. This would ultimately help me strengthen the conceptual and methodological underpinnings of the new political ontology that I was elaborating.

This was helpful feedback, for many would have told me the project was good enough, and here someone with tons of practical expertise and with a proven track record of mastery of applying various epistemological and meta-ontological insights into his practical analysis of multiple conflict resolution strategies identified a number of issues that shouldn't have been missed in the first place, so there is definitely a reason that Kentas' work is so pertinent to explaining the complex world of international relations, organized violence, regional cooperation in the Eastern Mediterranean, and the particularities of the Cyprus problem. Those critical suggestions have already helped me readjust my attention to theory and practice in my more recent investigations of the social reality at hand. They also helped me understand the importance of delineating what properties, functions, and responsibilities I want ontology *in statu nascendi* to adopt.

I am equally grateful to **Prof. Arkadiusz Żukowski,**[15] the director of the Faculty of Political Science of the University of Warmia and Mazury in Olsztyn, for taking his time to evaluate this project, for he is a man of many interdisciplinary passions ranging from geopolitics to international relations and political science and whose academic interest ranges from the Russian

---

15   For more information, please see *Prof. Dr. hab. Arkadiusz Żukowski's Review of Pietrzak's Ph.D. Dissertation*, Olsztyn, Poland, February 28, 2021. Available at: </https://www.uni-sofia.bg/index.php/bul/content/download/249696/1646183/version/1/file/Zukovski.pdf/> [Accessed June 11, 2021].

Federation's foreign policy to the Kaliningrad Oblast's place in the Kremlin's geostrategic thinking and the varieties of political systems in the world politics. He has spent the last few decades investigating the uniqueness and dynamics of various socio-political dimensions in post-apartheid South Africa. In his review, Żukowski suggested that in the fifth chapter of my dissertation (entitled "The IR-Related Scientific Ontology of /In Statu Nascendi and the Challenge in the General Understanding the Idea of Humanitarian Intervention"), I rightly postulated the need to reframe IR theory within the new boundaries of the ontology of the *in statu nascendi* type of ontological deliberations. In this respect, Żukowski stated that I convincingly made the case that there is a need to adopt a more systematic and interdisciplinary mode of IR research. As this academic stated, I demonstrated enough evidence that using the ontological approach could be very beneficial in this case.

According to Żukowski's assessment, the fifth chapter especially provided a valuable synthesis of the theoretical debate presented in other chapters of this work. He welcomed the supplementation of all the theoretical parts of this research by the recent theoretical findings of **Patrick Thaddeus Jackson, Daniel H. Nexon, John Rawls, Thomas S. Kuhn,** and several leading political philosophers that seem perfectly applicable to this project. This being said, Żukowski, who himself is a prolific author, advised that for ontology *in statu nascendi* to have a chance of succeeding in the highly pluralized world of the IR theory, I should also try to dig deeper into the essence of other leading debates within the literature on the subject, focus on the strengths of this ontology, and try to eliminate its weaknesses, for, as he suggested, this was an ontology still in the early process of emerging and not a completed project. Those were also precious suggestions and words of encouragement, for they have motivated me to approach IR theory in an even more contemplative manner and rethink and strengthen some of my initial hypotheses, assumptions, and ways of doing things. I can only hope that taking such a contemplative route and establishing working relations between international relations theory and various individual philosophical approaches will eventually result in a qualitative change in my future policy-making investigations and inquiries.

I am also very grateful to **Prof. Boris Grozdanov**[16] for his review of my dissertation, for he recognized that there is a clear need for building bridges

---

16   For more information, please see *Assoc. Dr. Boris Grozdanov's Review of Pietrzak's Ph.D. Dissertation*, Sofia, Bulgaria, April 14, 2021. Available at: </https://www.uni-sofia.bg/index. php/bul/content/download/249693/1646171/version/1/file/Grozdanov.pdf/>   [Accessed June 11, 2021].

of mutual understanding between international relations, political science, and philosophy and that political ontology can indeed turn into such a platform for interdisciplinary communication, for it can be borrowed from the field of philosophical metaphysics and reintroduced in a non-philosophical field of science. He agreed with my bold statement that such an interdisciplinary invention could successfully contribute to broadening the debate that will overcome the shallowness of *ad hoc* explanations of the issue in question. Grozdanov suggested that such a strong emphasis on the ontological approach in my dissertation can also be seen in the direction of enriching the space in question, which can allow an ontologist to take a perspective on the topic and ask questions about it aimed at clarification.

In this respect, Grozdanov indicated that the use of an ontological mode of thinking in this project has allowed me to test the results of this interdisciplinary analysis focusing on debates on the scope and extent of the international community's responsibility to contribute to peace and security in contemporary conflict zones such as Syria, Cambodia, the former Yugoslavia, South Sudan, Myanmar, and others. He also suggested that it was original and promising and that it has contributed to developing a new critical analysis and view of the problem. Grozdanov also suggested that I link the results to the problems of systemic constraints, pluralism of discourses, and the unpredictability of the global environment, for it allowed me to retrace the dynamics of the crisis in Syria and critically analyze many models and previous historical examples of humanitarian intervention.

I am very grateful to Grozdanov, for he also challenged me to think about how this research could potentially relate to the possibility of using the metaphysical category "state" (as related to but categorically different from the given and used categories of objects, properties, processes, etc.) for the enrichment of the productive analysis of nature and prospects for conflict development in areas from the given modern perspective. I could consider how it could relate to the possibility of adopting a more quantified approach to the ontological dynamics of the conflict zone with the help of established mathematical apparatus for modeling, including artificial intelligence. Furthermore, Grozdanov also urged me to consider how those new ontological emphases could contribute to future debates concerning humanitarian emergencies.

***

Subsequently, I would like to thank **Dr. Kirril Shields,**[17] a researcher associated with the University of Queensland and the editor-in-chief of *Genocide Studies and Prevention: An International Journal,* for his time reviewing my recent publication *On the Idea of Humanitarian Intervention: A New Compartmentalization of IR Theories* (2021), that accounted for my first academic publication that attempted to introduce the broader academic public to the idea of the ontology *in statu nascendi* in a written form.

In his review, Shields confirms what others have already suggested: from his perspective, the ideas presented in this publication are still works-in-progress, and the applicability of these core ideas remains to be proven. He suggested the book leaves the reader wishing for more evidence of the effectiveness of this new compartmentalization of IR theories. I suppose this was a fair suggestion back in 2021, but lately I have been working quite hard to change this situation.

***

Finally, I would like to thank those six academics and **Dr. Hristo Stoev, Dr. Ognyan Kasabov, and Dr. Georgi Gerdjikov**, for they helped me to evaluate the earlier versions of ontology *in statu nascendi* and showed a lot of dedication taking part in the debate on benefits and disadvantages related to adopting the ontological mode of thinking under various circumstances. I want to reassure you that I take all of your feedback—both large and small—very seriously, for many of your highlighted points hold some weight. I intend to constantly return to your suggestions to reevaluate if they are still valid in the decades to come, and if needed, we will modify ontology *in statu nascendi* to adjust to constantly changing global circumstances because change is a constant feature of our global reality.

Opportunities

As much as elaborating a sound concept that could appeal to the vast majority of fellow researchers is a dream of many scientists, I don't think that the work related to ontology *in statu nascendi* could ever be truly completed, for it is designed to be in a perpetual process of creation, which means embracing a constant process of self-improvement dedicated to academic excellence and clarity. I also want to acknowledge that ontology *in statu nascendi* cannot be

---

17   Please see: Kirril Shields's Book Review: *On the Idea of Humanitarian Intervention: A New Compartmentalization of IR Theories*—Australian Institute of International Affairs. (2022, June 15). Available at: </https://www.internationalaffairs.org.au/australianoutlook/book-review-on-the-idea-of-humanitarian-intervention-a-new-compartmentalization-of-ir-theories/> [Accessed January 11, 2023].

genuinely attributed to or monopolized by one scholar, inventor, or originator.

On the contrary, to the best of my understanding, every serious scholar develops their own ontology *in statu nascnedi* that leads them to more mature scientific discoveries in their fields of interest. My ontology *in statu nascendi* would be different than the ontological mode of thinking adopted by other IR thinkers and political philosophers, for they will ultimately differ from one another, and they should be entitled to develop their own states of becoming, their own processes of onto-epistemo-methodological formation. Each of those compartmentalizations will have its own unique proportion of *in statu nadcendi-ness* that will help it to approach various concepts, processes, and ideas in a very specific manner, some of which would be understood only in hindsight.

Naturally, ontology *in statu nascendi* is also put forward to encourage us to take part in a different type of intellectual journey that is consistent with following one's intellectual curiosity, no matter what. It advocates adopting a more contemplative, evolutionary manner of investigation, perpetual self-improvement, collaboration, flexibility, and openness to different interdisciplinary traditions. It aspires to move our understanding beyond the traditional status quo type of explanations. It is dedicated to overcoming shallow, superficial, and one-dimensional explanations by embracing a self-perpetuating process of continuous attempts to befriend wisdom, which in turn offers a unique intellectual stimulus to accelerate the pace of any given research.

In this sense, ontology *in statu nascendi* (a "candidate" ontology) accounts for a new merger of IR theory and political philosophy that delves deeper into the nature of any given concept because of its evolutionary and contemplative character and thanks to the fact that it closely relates to the idea *of in statu nascendi* that works as a fuel that puts this engine (research) in motion. This is possible if we understand ontology as an evolutionary study of existence and processes of being that coexists with, supplements, and enriches the old traditional study of being, existing, and reality by incorporating various interdisciplinary elements from various schools, traditions, and studies. There are many possible opportunities that ontology *in statu nascendi* can offer us. **It can help us transform international relations theory into a "locus" of interdisciplinary dialogue of all with all that is** based on mutual respect and understanding, pursuit for truth, clarity, academic excellence, and broader accountability and transparency.

Ontology *in statu nascendi* also aims to answer a call for a global IR that decolonizes IR and overcomes Eurocentric/Anglophone bias. For instance, it offers us a chance to incorporate into the mainstream debate such non-Western (rather niche) approaches as the instrumentality of Ubuntu[18] and other African sources of IR Knowledge (Joffrey Doma). Thanks to its inclusiveness, we can also try to incorporate the Egyptian concept of Maat (the principle of order), which informs the world's creation, and how it might be instrumental in understanding African forms of knowledge (Doma 2021, Martin, 2008). Next, we can try to add the **Islamic Umma** and **Sikh Khalsa Panth** and the reconceptualization of universalism and solidarism (Doma 2021, Petito & Hatzopoulos, 2003). Subsequently, we can try to "import" a "non-derivative and non-exceptionalist" global IR through the Sufi philosophy of the 13th century poet **Jalāl ad-Dīn Muhammad Rūmī** (Doma 2021, Deepshika Shahi's (2019)) and engage in a much deeper examination of the Chinese IR exploration of a distinct worldview that draws significantly from ancient Chinese thought and dialectics as well as philosophers such as **Confucius** (Doma 2021, Qin, 2012). Next, we can try to start listening to Latin American voices in international relations studies[19] All of those new initiatives will allow us to establish a new Archimedean point to move the whole discipline forward.

Threats

Naturally, such projects can cause certain controversies, doubts, and reservations, and quite rightly so. The ontology *in statu nascendi* is inclusive, but it is also "respectfully provocative", for, on the one hand, it acknowledges the pluralism of competing ontologies and paradigms. On the other, it postulates a more effective merger of new ontologies and those paradigms with old approaches. It should cause controversies now among all those who are likely to be upset by its impending incorporation into the mainstream of IR theory, for, ultimately, it is designed to be slightly inconvenient for all those IR scholars who are used to the old convenient ways of doing things and don't want to adjust and adapt to something new. Those scholars will likely trigger either a cold or hostile reception to this project. Ontology *in statu nascendi* pokes the "IR bear" by suggesting that specific approaches and paradigms don't go far enough. It suggests that they need to put things into perspective, get out of

---

18   For more information, please see: Joffrey Doma "On African Sources of Knowledge: Studies into the Instrumentality of Ubuntu for IR." Available at: </https://www.e-ir.info/2021/05/03/on-african-sources-of-knowledge-studies-into-the-instrumentality-of-ubuntu-for-ir/> [Accessed on 01/05/2021].

19   Tickner, Arlene B. "Hearing Latin American Voices in International Relations Studies." *International Studies Perspectives* 4, no. 4 (2003): 325-50. Available at: </http://www.jstor.org/stable/44218845/> [Accessed on 20/05/2023].

their comfort zone, and start collaborating to embrace a new ontology, a new ontological way of approaching things in all individual IR approaches. This can be achieved by advocating for the adoption of a scholarship that exhibits an increasingly evolutionary character. Fortunately, an internal inbuilt contingency plan is meant to fix all of the issues this ontology encounters. It offers a chance for self-perfection in the years to come, for even with an imperfect synthesis as in 2021, this contemplative mode of research, combined with the Hegelian dialectic, has pushed this ontology to a new stage of its existence in 2023, and this is possible thanks to its contemplative, inclusive, and receptive mode of operation that is designed to perfect itself in the decades to come.

Ontology *in statu nascendi* used in practice to approach contemporary conflict

The best way to respond to Plamen Makariev, Giorgios Kentas, and Kirril Shields' critical evaluation of ontology *in statu nascendi* is to prove that this theoretical concept can be used in practice. I need to admit that thus far, I have used it to add a new dimension to the analysis of the conflicts in Cyprus, Chechnya, former Yugoslavia, Afghanistan, Nagorno-Karabakh, Iraq, Georgia, Syria, Ukraine, and Ethiopia. I am confident that this framework can benefit any investigation of any contemporary conflict zone.

In my *On the Idea of Humanitarian Intervention* (2021), I researched various ontological dimensions of humanitarian intervention through the prism of the international community's response to one of the most elusive and complicated conflicts in the world; the Syrian conflict (2011–present) started as a popular uprising, evolved into a civil war, and is now a proxy war of all against all. I approached this particular conflict through the prism of the rollercoaster-like and unexpected series of events during and after the Arab Spring in the context of various power struggles in the Middle East. The multitude of political actors involved in those conflicts and the constant change that accompanied them made it impossible to approach them within the framework of existent IR theory compartmentalization, so I coined the term/study project ontology *in statu nascendi* to constrain the critical dimensions within both reformed IR theory and fluid political philosophy within a different horizon of investigations that were captured within liquid global and regional circumstances. Subsequently, I used ontology *in statu nascendi* (to some extent) to investigate the global reaction to the Ghouta chemical attacks of 2013 and the lack of enthusiasm for bringing Bashar al-Assad to justice. Next, after February 2022, I used ontology *in statu nascendi* to provide the reader with "A Comparative Study of Russia's War in Ukraine (2014-, including its 2022 escalation), Russia's aggression in Georgia (2008), and Russia's Military Operations in Syria (2015-)" Finally, I used ontology *in statu nascendi* supported by the IR feminist school of thought to discuss various criminal aspects of the Russian intervention in Ukraine in the paper titled "The Putinization of the Situation of Women and Children during the 2022 Russian Invasion of Ukraine", published *in In Statu Nascendi Vol. 5, No. 2 (2022) Journal of Political Philosophy and International Relations: Special Issue: Gender Equality in Politics and International.*

In each of these, I used ontology *in statu nascendi* to overcome the conceptual limitations of the literature on the subject to reevaluate the object of the analysis to interrelate the results of the investigation with testable and verifiable methods so that the overall conclusion would take into account a variety of opinions, different competing versions of reality, and pluralistic ontological modes of thinking. Ontology *in statu nascendi* redirected these debates to various questions related to various leading ontological components that should define them, such as the requirement of humaneness, the notion of neutrality, the assumption of impartiality, and sovereignty. In this respect, it is again worth emphasizing that ontology *in statu nascendi* proposes initiating the process of incremental changes without postulating the preservation of transitive or intransitive parts of IR theory.

Framing the research in this manner and the use of the ontology *in statu nascendi* to approach the conflict as mentioned above greatly helped during this research, for it allowed me to approach the problem as they arose, going to the root causes and the consequences of various phenomena and the validity of any given theory by inviting every paradigm, school of thought, and tradition to the decision-making table without giving any priority and without bias or prejudice. It relies heavily on the author's commitment to persevere with the problem of employing the evolutionary contemplative process that will lead to great things; it will encourage all approaches and all theorists to work together. It aims to provide a theoretical and meta-ontological underpinning and compartmentalization that constrains debates related to modern conflict with a contemplative, evolutionary manner of investigation adjustable to the ever-changing circumstances that emerge in any given conflict zone. This entails embracing integrity, clarity, and accountability of ontological inquiry and outsourcing it more eagerly to IR theory in a more comprehensive manner by embracing a more contemplative analytical narrative that creates the conditions to get to the bottom of the issue. Subsequently, it offers a perpetual methodological self-improvement mechanism that encourages scientific collaboration, flexibility, and openness to different interdisciplinary traditions. This ontology is strengthened by the recollection of selected historical conflicts and the international community's responses to them, taking into account our modern understanding of the principle of state sovereignty, human rights, and anti-genocide legislation (Albertini & Pietrzak 2022, p. 3–18, Pietrzak 2021, p. 19).

Even if IR theory appears to be driven by a propensity to be politicized, opinionated, or even biased, this can be overcome by our drive to synthesize all the gathered data and to look at it from the broader perspectives present in broader debates. At times, this is a very time-consuming initiative as it requires all the information and the subsequent analysis to be verified and analyzed with verifiable sources. Only after implementing this methodological tactic of proper verification of all initial findings can we interlink, reapply, and provide posterity with a credible and reliable analysis that addresses all of the fundamental causes and the possible effects of a conflict.

Ontology *in statu nascendi* as a mature candidate for a new ontology
The ontology *in statu nascendi* is more mature than ever before and has already started exhibiting rather unique and properly structured characteristics. It can help colleagues deal more effectively with multidimensional structures, fluid environments, and ongoing events that exhibit the characteristics of an ever-changing environment. On a conceptual level, during the investigation part of the research, the use of ontology *in statu nascendi* should help researchers to deal with various unexpected limitations, shortcomings, and concepts that happen to be in a nascent or still vague, not adequately defined stage of becoming. We could postulate that the acquisition of this or any similar ontology will be a sign of maturity in the development of IR theory, for we need a slightly better framework of cooperation to move our discipline forward and equip it to meet the challenges of the 21st century global environment. But this is a relatively passive way of doing things. To achieve the desired effect, it is desirable to investigate the process of building a new ontology from the perspective of the end goal of its inevitable integration into the field of IR theory.

According to H. Sofia Pinto & Nuno J. Mamede (2003), ontology merging and integration are based on a set of operations that must be more thoroughly studied, such as inclusion, polymorphic refinement, and restriction (specialization, etc.). They argue that "ontology building is still more of an art than an engineering task." None of the available methodologies to build ontologies from scratch has been widely accepted. One cost-effective way of building ontologies is by means of reuse. According to Pinto, "It is pretty common practice to reuse some parts of older ontologies to build new ones". This process involves several complex subprocesses: "knowledge acquisition and requirement specification using Natural Language techniques, reverse engineering, knowledge representation translation, [and] technical evaluation." (Pinto 1999).

In this respect, the essence of ontology *in statu nascendi* is that it hopes to evolve into the ontology of dialogue that postulates approaching the regional problems of global importance head-on but flexibly by trying to reach a new horizon of understanding between various parties. Its main feature is following our intellectual curiosity and trying to be as holistic as possible when we approach ongoing conflicts so we don't rely solely on the traditional methodology but supplement it with newly discovered experimental methods when the traditional ones fail to deliver the expected results. Naturally, it may be hard to imagine a hardliner realist scholar working with feminist or Marxist IR practitioners or liberal institutionalists working with constructivists. However, facing challenges head-on is a crucial commonality among successful researchers, but, ultimately, embracing our internal diversity makes our research stronger. This is a necessary precondition for strengthening our discipline.

The spirit of ontology *in statu nascendi* recognizes that it suggests that we can never take anything for granted. Our prime motivation in respect of this study should be to launch an ontological inquiry to improve the way social reality is being described and capture the fragile elusiveness of the potentiality of turning the hostile anarchic global environment into a place that is hospitable for all and not only the strongest players in the global architecture of power. Our main objective should be to start asking relevant questions and try to capture the facts that generally escape the attention of those who rush to easy solutions or straightforward explanations. We must humbly follow our intellectual curiosity whose primary responsibility is to seek clarity, objectivity, and a far-reaching restraint from espousing any shallow explanations of the fascinating global environment around us.

Still, for ontology *in statu nascendi* to successfully evolve into a mature ontology capable of supplementing various conflicting IR traditions, the research area should be able to embrace this ontology and employ it in both theoretical and practical conditions, with various empirical methods, using existing literature as a point of reference, and continuing to test the candidate for ontology until many scholars accept it. As far as this project is concerned, our primary goal should be to broaden a number of preexistent ontological debates in the IR theory that date back to the 1940s and relate them more effectively to contemporary IR debates, for it is my firm conviction that the main elements of these debates remain pertinent to this very day. I am confident that all those preexistent ontological debates in our discipline can be reinforced by interrelating them more holistically within the broader five great IR debates.

The idea of ontology *in statu nascendi* and its possible contribution to the broadening of the understanding of the five great IR debates.
Just a few months ago, in November 2022, I got a chance to implement ontology *in statu nascendi* during a series of lectures offered at Airlangga University in Indonesia, where I was given a fantastic opportunity to pursue my postdoctoral research under the supervision of **Prof. Vinsensio M. A. Dugis** from the Faculty of Social & Political Sciences. From the outset of this fellowship, I was assigned the quite challenging task of explaining to undergraduate students the nature of the great IR debates, and I need to admit that approaching those debates from the prism of ontology *in statu nascendi* made this task much easier than I initially had thought. This research will advance current scholarly debates around three main topics related to the use of ontology *in statu nascendi*, which in this particular instance was particularly valuable, for the great debates account for some of the most sophisticated and interrelated sets of discussions that have taken place in our field in the last 70 or 80 years, so the use of this new compartmentalization has helped to approach those complicated matters and present them to very young adepts of IR theory in a more approachable manner.

Explaining the differences and main assumptions of realism/traditionalism/behaviorism, liberalism/idealism, the English School of IR theory, the postcolonial approaches, neo-Marxism, feminism, constructivism, postconstructivism, or even discussing green IR theory on an individual basis can be challenging, but trying to explain to a bunch of undergraduates the nature of IR theory through the prism of four or five great debates may be very challenging even to more senior IR theoreticians unless, of course, we adopt ontology *in statu nascendi* to the challenge. Ontology *in statu* nascendi is uniquely situated to explain how existent compartmentalization has been attained and how it could potentially be mended.

The first great debate in international relations significantly impacted the development of IR as an academic discipline. It helped shape many of the key debates and themes that continue to impact how we perceive the social reality at hand. It is portrayed in the United States as a starting point for the discipline of international relations. It is understood as a series of debates between realist and idealist scholars that began at the end of the 1920s and persisted throughout the 1930s and 1940s, and, in a way, this debate is still relevant today. On one side of the debate were **the idealists** who believed that international relations could be transformed through the creation of international law, institutions, and norms and emphasized the possibility of a more substantial role for international institutions and international actors capable of far-reaching obedience to the letter of international law and international norms, suggesting that states should be seen as rational actors that can benefit more from economic cooperation and collective action than military conquest, so it is only natural that they would not resort to war and chose the former. They argued that if the perks of mutually beneficial cooperation are spread evenly, it can ensure lasting peace and security.[20]

On one side of the debate were **the realists**, who even back then were very skeptical about the strength and applicability of the international law and international institutions, which, from their perspective, cannot prevent rogue nations from behaving like uncontrollable power maximizers, for there is no one who could act as a global policeman to effectively enforce acceptable behavior of the nation-states. From their perspective, states were the only important actors that mattered in the international system, for they had to learn how to cope with the anarchical nature of international politics that was forcing all political actors to turn to national interest-driven maximizers who first and foremost had to secure their political survival. That is why they had to engage only in the initiatives that would guarantee the expansion or preservation of their power at the expense of other political players, for from their perspective, the only way to ensure stability and peace was through the skillful balance of power and balance of threat. After the Second World War, the realists seemed to win this debate, for many idealists' ideas were perceived as somewhat naïve. Subsequently, this debate shifted towards pursuing the reasons behind the marginalization of liberal and normative thinking in international relations.[21]

The second great debate in international relations was a series of academic discussions between **behavioralists** and **traditionalists** (realists), or between "scientific IR" scholars who sought to refine scientific methods of inquiry in international relations theory and those who insisted on a more

---

20   Please also see: Benneyworth, I. 2011, May 20. The 'Great Debates' in international relations theory. *E-International Relations*. Available at: </https://www.e-ir.info/2011/05/20/the-'great-debates'-in-international-relations-theory/> [Accessed on 20/05/2023].

21   Please also see: Ashworth, Lucian M. 2002. "Did the realist-idealist great debate really happen? A revisionist history of international relations." *International Relations*, 16(1), 33-51.

historicist/interpretative approach to international relations theory. This debate took place in the 1960s; the scholars started reconceptualizing such categories as state, investigated states' power sources, and followed the sociological suggestions suggesting that individuals and states find themselves in certain structures that force them into more assertive actions to survive. According to behaviorists, traditionalists (realists) are unscientific, and the IR theory of the future should rely on more scientific means of collecting data and analysis that should be more verifiable. They encouraged many IR scholars to seek more objective and universal norms instead of subjective and ideological norms. Behavioralists say that international relations should be seen as a science, so the methodology within the international relations theory should be more scientific. Realists did not seem to be preoccupied with those arguments, but they did accept some of those suggestions related to the ontological underpinnings of the structure of their investigations.

The third great debate in international relations was the inter-paradigm debate in international relations theory between neorealism and neoliberalism in the 1980s and between neorealists and neoliberal institutionalists that persisted over the extent of conflict and cooperation in the international system. Both agreed that the international system is anarchic in its nature, but they disagreed on the way of approaching this issue. If we allow a far-reaching oversimplification of this debate, one could claim that neorealists suggested that, in the international system, states should be predominantly concerned with such issues as survival, security, and power. Neoliberalists suggested focusing on matters related to economic welfare, international politics, economic relations, and civil issues such as environmentalism.[22]

The fourth great debate in international relations emerged in the early 2000s. There are various ways of approaching this debate between positivism and post-positivism. It is suggested that this debate relates to the process of knowledge creation. Those of us who take theory and science for granted would be called positivists while rebellious post-positivists question everything about the world. In this respect, it is argued that the positivist period was relatively static and a time when domestic-foreign policy distinctions and boundaries between disciplines were clearly defined and knowledge could be taken for granted. This is no longer the case because post-positivism began to criticize the pure faith in knowledge of the positivist period. It is

---

22   Please also see: Lake, David. A. 2013. "Theory is dead, long live theory: The end of the Great Debates and the rise of eclecticism in International Relations." *European Journal of International Relations*, 19(3), 567-587.

suggested that the post-positivist period has begun to erase borders between concepts due to the increased transmittance between various concepts and boundaries.[23]

There is another way of approaching this debate from the perspective of critical realism. However, in this respect, it is good to clarify that post-positivism is not homogenous. On the contrary, it is highly diversified, for there is a massive difference between Foucauldian biopolitics and the post-positivist settings that underpin the constructivist approaches in **Gramscian post-hegemony** and the post-positivism related to the **Bordieuan nation of labeling and habitat.** In this respect, I underlined that post-structuralists may seem quite complicated because they have dedicated much effort to knowledge-creation.

Regarding the Foucauldian IR post-positivist settings, knowledge is under the control of power, and the primary goal of critical theory is to reveal the relationship between knowledge and power to demolish status quo explanations and liberate the people. We can also focus in this instance on the debate between **Roy Bhaskar** and **Alexander Wendt**. Bhaskar suggests critical realism triggered a strong demand for incorporating ontology in the human sciences. This ontology is essential within a particular structure. His critical realism in the philosophical approach to understanding science and social science is vital because it opposes forms of a man's empiricism and positivism by viewing science as concerned with identifying causal mechanisms. He presents the idea that all learning comes only from experience and observations from a localized perspective; there is a difference between transitive and inter-transitive bodies of knowledge.

In such a setting, one's choices are consistent with a complete preference of IR theories, so imagine that you're a realist. You will always apply realism if you are liberal. You will always use liberal theories to describe the social reality at hand. Or, if you are a feminist scholar in this respect, you will suggest that theory has more responsibility to bring more female voices to the IR debates. That means that when it comes to the way this issue could be approached, you can sometimes be realist, sometimes you can be liberal, sometimes you can be feminist, and you can mix and match, and that's something different, so such an option would be concerned with the reasoning underlying choices behind any given approaches that would indicate the

---

23   Charoenvattananukul, Peera. "Did the Great Debates Really Take Place?" *E-International Relations*, November 24, 2013. Available at: </https://www.e-ir.info/2013/11/24/did-the-great-debates-really-take-place/> [Accessed on 20/05/2023].

individual being that would be inclined to make definite choices over specific options they prefer.

My recommendation in this respect is to first acquaint yourself with the basic notions related to leading theories and paradigms and then move to the great debates because this is a highly sophisticated thing. The other interpretation of the fourth debate suggests that this debate would be centered around responding to the challenges posed by global terrorism and the threat of weapons of mass destruction. On one side of the debate are the neoconservatives, who argue that the United States should take a more aggressive approach to dealing with these threats, including using military force to remove rogue states and terrorist groups. Neoconservatives believe that military power is necessary to protect national security and spread democracy and freedom around the world. On the other side of the debate are the liberals and constructivists, who argue that the use of military force should be a last resort and that greater emphasis should be placed on diplomacy, cooperation, and the development of international institutions and norms. Liberals and constructivists believe that using force can often be counterproductive and that greater attention should be paid to addressing the root causes of terrorism, such as poverty, inequality, and political repression. The fourth great debate has significantly impacted the study and practice of international relations. It has led to renewed attention to issues of security, terrorism, and global governance. It has also stimulated new research into the relationship between military power, diplomacy, and the promotion of human rights.

The fifth great debate in international relations is the most recent debate that emerged in the 2010s and is centered around how to respond to the challenges posed by global inequality, climate change, and other transnational issues that require collective action. On one side of the debate are the globalists, who argue that the solution to these challenges lies in greater cooperation and integration among nations and the development of a more robust system of global governance. Globalists believe that international institutions, such as the United Nations and the International Monetary Fund, should be strengthened and given more authority to address global issues.[24]

Some associate the fifth great debate with the **complexity theory** that accounts for an interdisciplinary field of study that provides a valuable framework for understanding the challenges of global governance in a rapidly

---

24   For more information please see: Kunwar Rajeev. March 18, 2022. "Fifth Debate in International Relations Theory or an Enduring Grandeur," *Global South Colloquy*. Available at: </https://globalsouthcolloquy.com/fifth-debate-in-international-relations-theory-or-an-enduring-grandeur%EF%BF%BC/> [Accessed on 20/06/2023].

changing world by focusing on understanding complex systems and the emergence of new forms of governance that can be composed of multiple interacting elements exhibiting non-linear and unpredictable behavior. One of its representatives, **Emilian Kavalski**,[25] has made significant contributions to the field of complexity theory, particularly in the areas of global governance and the decentralization of international relations theory and practice, which relates to the growing prominence of non-Western (especially Asian) international actors and the noticeable impact of global climate change. In particular, he explores the nascent Asian normative orders, how they confront, complement, and transform established traditions, norms, and institutions, and the encounter of international relations with life in the Anthropocene, especially the conceptualization of and engagement with non-human actors. Kavalski contends that in both these areas, the concept and practices of relationality have essential implications for how global life is approached, explained, and understood.

The question we could ask ourselves at this moment is why we would engage in such theoretical deliberations that may seem quite abstract to many people. We do so to understand various angles of the debate related to managing regional conflicts of global importance. Our first principle with such a challenging task is to attain the best possible clarity in international relations. We don't engage in such abstract debate for its own sake. We do so because it will help us to understand a very complex global reality; we live in in the 21st century in a situation where regional and local conflicts are changing so rapidly that we cannot capture or properly describe them; we cannot tell people what's happening in various conflict zones. Hence, we must be very flexible in discussing specific global developments. Again, we are seeing this circle in all of these IR approaches, so imagine if we could get the best from all of the approaches. We can mix and match all the concepts, ideas, processes, and theories that have developed paradigms.

In this instance, the ontologist asks himself how to bring everyone to the table to discuss important issues. Imagine that **Immanuel Kant, Hans Morgenthau, Robert Keohane, Samantha Power, Kenneth Waltz, Charles Bates, Joseph Stewart Mill, and John Mearsheimer** are still alive, and many others. Imagine that we bring them together, and forget that some of them are dead. Let's use our imagination and bring the approaches that

---

25   For more information please see: Kavalski, Emilian. 2020. "Inside/Outside and Around: Complexity and the Relational Ethics of Global Life," *Global Society*, 34:4, 467-486, DOI: 10.1080/13600826.2020.1745158.

they represent, and, to achieve that, philosophy could be helpful to this ontology, in particular the study of being existence and the concepts of becoming and reality so the ontology *in statu nascendi* can start operating as a new hybridized merger of the IR theory and political philosophy that goes deeper into the nature of any given concept. In order to achieve this, we need to be adventurous in embracing this unique intellectual stimulus and motivation to be better scholars, and it is very important, especially for a beginning scholar, to be able to start his journey by taking into account the experiences of people before him and to use it in future debates related to the way the global architecture of power operates. Ask yourself what knowledge produced by the so-called positive-knowledge industry we can rely on and to what extent.

In this respect, the dedication to the constant evolution and self-perfection in ontology *in statu nascendi* is beneficial because we may not yet have the answers to our questions. Still, at least we know where to search for them. We don't need all the answers, but we need to start asking the correct questions. In this respect, the idea is that the common knowledge type of explanations would be eradicated by specific philosophical and IR-related approaches that will be a combo that will allow you to be better in your job. So, again, if we try to claim an IR type of mountain, let's be prepared to claim Mount Everest, meaning to do our utmost to befriend wisdom, even if this initially seems challenging. We can supplement those endeavors with the use of ontology *in statu nascendi*. This will clear the path towards something greater because you would avoid certain things that happened in the past because of oversimplifications and certain seemingly irrelevant developments. It was never meant to be easy to be an IR scholar; ultimately, your research must always be "in relation to" something. That is why I recommend embracing an ontological mode of thinking in IR theory, for this allows us to focus our attention on matters that matter so we can get things done.

There are no widely accepted sixth, seventh, eight, or ninth great debates in international relations, for they have not yet emerged. But they are likely to emerge soon, and they will relate to the way the IR theorist responds to the issues related to the impact of new technologies, artificial intelligence, and issues related to cybersecurity, cyber threats, the high speed of development in autonomous weapons systems, pandemics, the rise of non-state actors, asymmetric warfare, the changing nature of conflicts, the use of hybrid tactics such as disinformation campaigns, issues related to climate change, deforestation, water shortages, environmental degradation, exacerbated inequality, insecurity, and modern conflict. We will probably have to deliberate on the changing balance of power in the international system and deglobalization, especially after the events of 24 February 2022, which challenged many fundamental principles of international law and triggered the outbreak of a new Cold War between NATO and Russia and Belarus, and by extension, we would have to redefine the future demo-liberal international order that has been challenged by the rise of elitist authoritarian sympathizers—BRICKs— and China and Russia's more assertive policies. This debate will also center around how the new distribution of power will affect global governance, conflict management, and cooperation in the coming years.

We find ourselves in the 21st century, where everything is interchangeable. Ontology *in statu nascendi* wants to be at the forefront of those debates and to help elaborate a practical blueprint that will allow us to respond to the complex challenges and opportunities of the 21st century. To achieve that, I hope to supplement the existing IR theory with **Habermasian deliberative democracy** to attain a new horizon of investigation. Hegelian dialectics properly recollect the information that has escaped our attention in the previous phases of this project. The **Levinasian ontology of "the Other"** always compartmentalizes the available approaches, theories, and paradigms "in relation to" the living individuals that expect their knowledge to be as clear and approachable as possible. **Baumanian liquid modernity** and **Derridean deconstructive plasticity** bring together as many seemingly unrelated approaches as possible to ensure this project is as holistic as possible.

Dissemination of the results of this research

For the successful implementation of ontology *in statu nascendi*, we need to continuously drive-test the ontology in question by adopting a number of empirical, statistical, and analytical methods that will move this research in the desired direction and try to encourage all the necessary changes in policies and practices of prominent global policymakers, IR scholars, and field practitioners to attain the research goals and objectives.

Conclusion

The research into the nature of political ontology is not something new. We need to recall the work of Hans Morgenthau (1948), Roy Bhaskar (1979), Alexander Wendt (1999), and many other IR thinkers who set us on this journey before suggesting adopting the ontological mode of thinking in our IR-related debates. But as much as it is my firm conviction that the main elements of these debates remain pertinent to the way our discipline operates today, I am confident that contemporary IR theory can still benefit from more coordinated, frequent, and devoted exposure to the leading philosophical debates of today. This motivates this project because I claim that some preexisting limitations of IR theory have not been adequately worked through, despite various earlier attempts, on many levels.

To paraphrase Karl Theodor Jaspers, we must acknowledge that IR theory must seek better inquiry and verification paths that lie within global reality as it is conceived today in all its representations. In this respect, we need to pay extraordinary attention to clarity, truth, transparency, respect, and various ontological matters. As a political ontologist and political theorist, my role in this respect is to address those issues head-on. Given that the world and contemporary conflict zones are changing, we must do our utmost to acknowledge that so that IR theorizing can adjust to this completely new reality. As human beings, we are rather tragic creatures, for we are thrown into today's imperfect world, and the same is true of IR theory, for as much as we crave perfection, it is not attainable. Hence, we need to make the most of our existing resources. Still, despite the opinions of many scientists, IR theory is in relatively good shape, so we can effectively utilize its inherently diversified, pluralized methodology and scattered functionality and employ it to deal with complicated contemporary conflict zones, ongoing conflicts, and various vague concepts at hand. And we need to prepare ourselves for this exciting journey ahead, for, at one point or another, it will cause us some trouble on the conceptual level, for this is its beauty: IR theory has never meant to be unilateral, static, or dogmatic. On the contrary, by allowing so many different approaches to be part of this semi-scientific semi-philosophical megaproject that is inherently inclusive, we signal to the outside world that our tradition will always be ready to face the world out there from a different perspective.

Still, the same theory needs more assistance to adjust to the ever-changing circumstances of very elusive contemporary conflict zones and should accept all the help it can get, for the elusiveness and fluidity of specific soci opolitical dimensions in these conflicts deserve to be investigated adequately in the face of adversity and all of the conceptual challenges ahead. If we work harder together, we will overcome our limitations. This will be possible if we come to terms with the fact that IR theory is a scientific ontology that can be seen as compartmentalization and an evolutionary study of the existence and processes of being that coexists with, supplements, and enriches the old, traditional study of being, existing, and reality by incorporating various interdisciplinary elements from multiple schools, traditions, and studies. In essence, this project was designed to reevaluate our ideas, test our methods to make them more bullet-proof, and compare and expose them to different opinions, competing versions of reality, and pluralistic ontological modes of thinking.

Ultimately, ontology *in statu nascendi* also accounts for an invitation that hopes to transition itself into a platform for a new type of dialogue about the IR theorizing of the future, which will always be hungry for clarity and will always hope to ascertain the causes of things, test drive all theories, approach all paradigms to distinguish good from bad ones, and acknowledge all the main limitations of our discipline. It aims to apply this new rigor of thinking in different spheres of our social life. Still, it will not carry water or make excuses for those who cannot rise above their biases, prejudices, and misconstrued rationality. It recognizes that there is enough room here for those who hope to combine, synthesize, encapsulate, create a totally new paradigm, and test old dogmas and theories, and those who procrastinate and hesitate to embrace those more experimental approaches, new modi operandi, and the new plasticity of our elusive new post-positivist colleagues.

This ontology embraces the spirit of interdisciplinary collaboration, truth, and respect. It is open to embracing a new horizon of investigation. It shows our passion for academic excellence,[26] knowledge, wisdom, and humanity. It recognizes that nothing happens without reason and suggests that quality should be prioritized over quantity. In the meantime, however, ontology *in statu nascendi* is confident that IR theorizing cannot be judged by a standard that does not measure up to it, so instead of entrenching our positions, this project is meant to transition into an ontology of dialogue, finding common ground, and approaching our differences in a methodological, open-minded manner that respectfully disagrees with our opponents by recognizing where they are coming from. It requires us to secure a middle ground for a different horizon, enough space for those who want to introduce a new paradigm and those still driven by an old science that could be seen by some as dogma. Science creation is an evolutionary process and should recognize the limitations of time-space, location, background, kinds, modes, and attributes of any scientific and philosophical ontology or concept.

Ontology *in statu nascendi* essentially suggests that IR theory should not be used as a helpful catalog available for the methodological cherry-picking of the most popular ideas, theories, paradigms, and approaches, but rather should be used in a much more comprehensive, holistic, and contemplative manner that includes the element of constant change in the circular stream of becoming. In this respect, it is essential to emphasize that it is not a stream

---

26   In this respect, I understand academic excellence as an ability to demonstrate, perform, achieve, and/or excel in various scholastic initiatives, being able to produce knowledge, achieve high grades and superior performance, and the ability to collaborate with other like-minded individuals.

of becoming that resists human attempts to impose meaningful order on it. On the contrary, it is a stream that compartmentalizes various new ideas, theories, paradigms, branches of science, approaches, and traditions, a stream that can offer us a certain level of temporary certainty during the uncertain times of fragmented or even liquid reality. This study accounts for a genuine attempt to adopt a far more diverse portfolio of existing interdisciplinary work, approaches, methods, debates, and deliberations, boosted by the resilience of a new political ontology and a hybrid-type study that merges and blends several leading philosophical, political, and IR-related paradigms and approaches into an easily approachable ontology that provides the broader public with the tools to engage in much deeper ontological inquiry into the nature, origin, and genesis of any given concept. It offers a chance to be elaborated by the people and for the people in pursuit of actual objective truth and approach every object, every process, and every concept from the perspective of an actual humble observer of social reality at hand, who does not need to be concerned with any preexisting assumptions, or preexisting acceptable modes of analysis; they need to be persistent in their commitment to seeking truth in the realm of international relations.

It advocates strengthening our ontological thinking in our discipline. It suggests a considerable need for more frequent use of such a mode of thinking in various ad hoc investigations. Unfortunately, the problems we face today are rather serious, for our discipline exhibits the lack of a broader consensus about the systematic application of the IR theory as a consistent unit of in-depth analysis of various conflict-based situations, not to mention the nature of the disagreements over verifying the tangibility and truthfulness of our findings. For instance, according to Robert O. Keohane, "scientific success (by extension in IR theory) is not the attainment of an objective truth, but the attainment of a wider agreement on descriptive facts and causal relationships, based on transparent and replicable methods" (Keohane, 1998). This is not particularly characteristic of Keohane, for this type of thinking seems to be very characteristic of many IR scholars; Keohane has just chosen to be very transparent and straightforward in exposing the current mood and the prevailing opinion regarding what objectivity, clarity, and ideal truth account for in IR theory.

Undoubtedly, the truth in philosophical terms has to be absolute, and the ideal version of this truth should be undivided, unquestionable, and ultimate. So not every philosopher would be excited to embrace such an IR-type logic of interpreting the truth about international relations, but this is a part of our tradition and culture. Even if we compare the IR truth to a cake divided into various uneven parts, we need to acknowledge that the bearers of IR truth would belong to various IR approaches that would look after their individualistic interpretations of truth about international relations. According to this understanding, only when these approaches come together would they be able to present to the broader public the version of the truth about any given situation, concept, idea, or process that could be acceptable to both positivist and non-positivist research with all of the available characteristics, qualities, and axioms that would be open for a constructive and respectful debate in the field.

The difference in attitudes to constantly pursuing objective truth in the philosophical realm and settling for the prevailing opinion is more than evident here. As much as overcoming the current status quo may not be easy, this idea is worth pursuing, for we need to acknowledge that on some levels, Keohane may be right to try to respond to this challenge in the best possible manner by embracing our pluralistic worldview and heavily diversified horizons so our journey to discovery could begin, even if it does not offer us all of the answers straight away, for in the end we would still engage in pursuing the noble goal of pursuing truth, even if this seems to be a pretty naïve endeavor. Even if these attempts would be questioned by absolutists, meta-ontologists, or more metaphysically-oriented thinkers, we still can err on the side of caution by acknowledging all of the limits of this position so we can attain a more mature discourse and move it beyond the stage of becoming.

In the end, according to Merriam-Webster's Dictionary, the truth cannot be easily defined, for it can account for "a combination of the body of real things, events, and facts, as well as the state of being a transcendent fundamental or spiritual reality; a judgment, proposition, or idea that is true or accepted as true; the body of true statements and propositions; the property (as of a statement) of being in accord with fact or reality; or fidelity to an original or to a standard, and sincerity in action, character, and utterance."[27]

Suppose we apply this know-how in the realm of the IR theory. In that case, it would be used by both theoreticians and practitioners, so this could encourage them to formulate their research projects in the way that approaches a modern conflict most truthfully by recognizing that specific characteristics may have a slightly different nature, for they are to be defined both as "a combination of the body of real things, events, and facts, the state of being the case that is a transcendent fundamental or spiritual reality as fidelity

---

27   "Definition of Truth," Merriam-Webster Dictionary. Available at: </https://www.merriam-webster.com/dictionary/truth /> [Accessed on 20/05/2023].

in action, character and utterance" and "a state of being in accord with fact or reality, fidelity to an original or to a standard, and sincerity in action, character, and utterance."

From my perspective, IR theory will likely benefit from embracing such a pursuit because it triggers a much broader interdisciplinary debate that might help us attain a qualitative change in how our discipline progresses. We can accelerate this process by embracing all our diversified positions and selected philosophical approaches related to the field of ontology. Ultimately, I am confident that both of our disciplines can benefit from acknowledging the necessity of adopting an *in statu nascendi* type of studies and deliberations; this hope accounts for my own highly metaphorical defense of Westerplatte, for I see it as "some duty, some obligation, from which I simply cannot escape, and from which it is impossible to desert."[28]

---

28   A modern historian often emphasizes that the work the Solidarity trade union movement (led by Lech Wałesa) did in fighting the local communist regime in Poland was instrumental in dismantling the entire Warsaw Bloc and shaking the foundation of the *ancien régime*. But it must also be recognized that the Polish Catholic Church played a critical role in supporting this grassroots movement that ultimately freed Poland from Soviet domination in 1991. Particularly, the selected part of the Liturgy of the Word dedicated to the young people in Westerplatte peninsula, delivered by John Paul II in Gdańsk in June 1987, can be seen as a very motivational and inspirational speech to many people in Poland who needed this extra push in the last years of the struggle against the communist regime. It thought them not to be afraid, for when they worked together as one, they could change the course of the history of "this land." In his sermons and liturgies, the pope often referred to practical historical examples that could unite people to fight for their rights and freedom. I don't want to compare IR theory to the communist regime. Still, ultimately it can be as dysfunctional, and for these reasons, it deserves a better compartmentalization than the current one offers. I am ready to fight for it with a dedication similar to the defenders of the Polish outpost at Westerplatte in 1939. I am ready to fight a positive fight for it against those who love to cherry pick what they like in the IR theory and leave those parts that are less comfortable, for it is my firm belief that we can reform it in a way that it will become more apparent, more transparent, and more approachable to young adepts of international relations, who will see it as a joyful adventure of friendly approaches that work together for the common good, not a collection of inherently conflicted approaches, theories, paradigms and schools of thought.
In his Liturgy delivered in 1987 to Polish youth, John Paul II refers to the heroic defense of the Polish outpost at Westerplatte, one of the first battles of World War II, during which a small garrison of the Polish Army commanded by Major Henryk Sucharski and Captain Franciszek Dąbrowski (just 182 soldiers, five officers, and a doctor) defended the peninsula for seven days (from September 1 to September 7, 1939) against an overwhelmingly more substantial force of German invaders that in this particular battle was composed of 4000+ German Wehrmacht serviceman and supported by sustained artillery fire from the German battleship Schleswig-Holstein and air raids carried out by a group of Junkers Ju 87 dive-bombers and other heavy equipment. Despite those disproportions, the Poles did not back down from fulfilling the words of the soldier's oath in the moment of need; they succumbed to the ruthless attack and very often sacrificed their lives in the fight for a free and independent Poland (Hernik 2023).

Bibliography / Further Reading

Albertini, Tamara & Pietrzak, Piotr, "Clarity is what I seek first: An interview with Professor Tamara Albertini by Piotr Pietrzak," *In Statu Nascendi—Journal of Political Philosophy and International Relations 2020/2* (Vol. 3. No. 2).

Bhaskar, Roy. 1978. *A Realist Theory of Science.* 2nd Edition. Sussex: The Harvester Press.

Bhaskar, Roy. 1979. *The Possibility of Naturalism.* Sussex: The Harvester Press.

Bhaskar, Roy.1983. "Beef, Structure and Place: Notes form a Critical Naturalist Perspective," *Journal for the Theory of Social Behaviour* 13(1): p. 82–95.

Bhaskar, Roy. 1986. *Scientific Realism and Human Emancipation.* 2nd Impression. London: Verso.

Bhaskar, Roy.1989. *Reclaiming Reality.* London: Verso.

Bhaskar, Roy. 1993. *Dialectic: The Pulse of Freedom.* London: Verso.

Bhaskar, Roy. 1998. "Philosophy and Scientific Realism," in Archer, Margaret et al., eds., *Critical Realism: Essential Readings.* London: Routledge, pp. 16–47.

Cartledge Paul. 2006. *Thermopylae : The Battle That Changed the World.* Woodstock NY: Overlook Press.

Duarte Nuno Peralta, Helena Sofia Andrade N. P. Pinto, Nuno J. Mamede. 2003. "Reusing a Time Ontology." *ICEIS (3) 2003*: 121–128.

Elman, Colin, Miriam Elman. 2002. "How Not to Be Lakatos Intolerant: Appraising Progress in IR Research," *International Studies Quarterly* 46 (2): pp. 231–262.

Elman, Colin, Miriam Elman. 2003. "Introduction: Appraising Progress in International Relations Theory," in C. Elman, M. Elman, eds. *Progress in International Relations Theory. Appraising the Field.* Cambridge: MIT Press, pp. 1–18.

Elman, Colin, Miriam Elman. 1997. "Lakatos and Neorealism: A Reply to Vasquez," *The American Political Science Review* 91(4): pp. 923–926.

Elman, Colin, Miriam Elman, eds. 2003. *Progress in International Relations Theory. Appraising the Field.* Cambridge: MIT Press.

Evangelos, Koumparoudis. 2020. "Information Society and a New Form of Embodiment" *In Statu Nascendi -Journal of Political Philosophy and International Relations 2020/2*, pp. 41–58.

Griswold, Charles L. 2002. *Platonic Writings.* University Park: Pennsylvania State University Press.

Hartley III, Dean S. 2021. An *Ontology of Modern Conflict. Including Conventional Combat and Unconventional Conflict.* Springer.

Hernik. Jan, Defense of Westerplatte: The First Battle of World War II. Retrieved June 18, 2023. Available at: </https://warsawinstitute.org/defense-westerplatte-first-battle-world-war-ii/>[Accessed on 15th June 2023].

Kuhn, Thomas S. 1970. *The Structure of Scientific Revolutions*. University of Chicago Press.

Latifur, Khan & Feng, Luo, "Ontology Construction for Information Selection" *14th IEEE International Conference on Tools with Artificial Intelligence*, 2002. (ICTAI 2002). Proceedings. 122–127, 2002.

Mccarthy, Gabby. 2018. *Introduction to Metaphysics*. Edtech. http://www.vle books.com/vleweb/product/openreader?id=none&isbn=9781839473 654.

Pietrzak, Piotr. 2022. "Introducing the idea of Ontology in statu nascendi to the broader International Relations Theory" *International Conference Proceeding Series—International Conference on Economics and Social Sciences in Serik,* Turkey on 21–23 Oct 2022, pp. 570-585, https://eclss.org/publi cationsfordoi/pr0cNG118boo8kIE_SS2022_antalya.pdf.

Pietrzak, Piotr. 2022. "A Comparative Study of Russia's War in Ukraine (2014-, including its 2022 escalation), Russia's aggression in Georgia (2008), and Russia's Military Operations in Syria (2015-)" *International Conference Proceeding Series—VII. International Middle East Symposium: Political and Social Stability in the Middle East (May 10-11th, 2022, Online).*

Pietrzak, Piotr. 2021. *On the Idea of Humanitarian Intervention. A New Compartmentalization of IR Theories.* New York: Columbia University Press. https://cup.columbia.edu/book/on-the-idea-of-humanitarian-in tervention/9783838215921.

Pietrzak, Piotr. 2021. "Immanuel Kant and Niccolò Machiavelli's traditions and the limits of approaching contemporary conflicts -the case study of the Syrian Conflict (2011-present)" *In Statu Nascendi Journal of Political Philosophy and International Relations* 2021/2, pp. 53–84.

Pietrzak, Piotr. 2019. "On Human Rights in Syria: Deliberations on the universality of Human Rights and the International Community's Reaction to the Syrian conflict (2011—2019)" in: *Сборник "Универсалност и приложимост на човешките права".* Edited by Veselin Hristov Dafov, Ivan Kirkov, Tsena Zhelyazkova, Sofia 2020, ISBN: 978-954-07-4989-1.

Pietrzak, Piotr. 2019. "The Syrian Conflict (2011–ongoing): How a Perfectly Winnable Uprising Has Ended Up as a Ferocious Proxy War of Global Importance". In: *In Statu Nascendi Journal of Political Philosophy and International Relations* 2019/1, pp. 34–98. https://cup.columbia.edu/bo ok/in-statu-nascendi/9783838213095.

Pinto, H. Sofia. 1999. "Towards Ontology Reuse." In *Proceedings of AAAI99's Workshop on Ontology Management*, WS-99-13, pp. 67–73. AAAI Press.

Pinto, H. S., Gomez-Perez, A., and Martins, J. P. 1999. "Some Issues on Ontology Integration." In *Proceedings of IJCAI99's Workshop on Ontologies and Prob-lem Solving Methods: Lessons Learned and Future Trends*, 7.1–7.12.

Pinto, H. S. and Martins, J. P. (2001). "A Methodology for Ontology Integration." In *Proceedings of the First International Conference on Knowledge Capture*, K-CAP'01, 131–138. ACM Press.

Turner. J. 2016. "Metaontology." Oxford Handbooks Online. *Subject: Philosophy, Metaphysics, Philosophy of Language, Philosophy of Mathematics and Logic* Online Publication Date: Aug 2016. DOI: 10.1093/oxfordhb/9780199935314.013.25.

Wendt, Alexander. 1987. "The Agent-Structure Problem in International Relations Theory," *International Organization* 41(3): p. 335-370.

Wendt, Alexander. 1991. "Bridging the Theory/Meta-Theory Gap in International Relations," *Review of International Studies* 17(4): pp. 383–392.

Wendt, Alexander. 1992. "Anarchy is What States Make of It. The Social Construction of Power Politics," *International Organization* 46:2, pp. 391–425.

Wendt, Alexander. 1992. "Levels of Analysis. Agents and Structures: Part III," *Review of International Studies* 18:2, pp. 181–185.

Wendt, Alexander. 1994. "Collective Identity Formation and the International State," *The American Political Science Review* 88(2): 384-396.

Wendt, Alexander. 1995. "Constructing International Politics," *International Security* 20(1): pp. 71–81.

Wendt, Alexander. 1996. "Identity and Structural Change in International Politics," in Y. Lapid and F. Kratochwil, eds., The Return of Culture an Identity in IR Theory. London: Lynne Rienner Publishers, pp. 47–64.

Wendt, Alexander. 1998. "On Constitution and Causation in International Relations," *Review of International Studies* 24(5): pp. 101–117.

Wendt, Alexander. 1999. *Social Theory of International Politics*. Cambridge: Cambridge University Press.

Wendt, Alexander. 2004. "The State as Person in International Theory," *Review of International Studies* 30: pp. 289–316.

Wendt, Alexander. 2006. "Social Theory as Cartesian Science. An Auto-Critique from a Quantum Perspective," in S. Guzzini and A. Leander, eds., *Constructivism and International Relations*. Alexander Wendt and His Critics. London: Rutledge, pp. 181–219.

Wight, Martin. 1966. 1995. "Why is There No International Theory?" in J. Der Derian, *International Theory*. London: MacMillan.

**Academic Reviews of Pietrzak's Earlier Work related to the ontology
*in statu nascendi***

Prof. Dr. Veselin Dafov's review of Pietrzak's Ph.D. Dissertation, Sofia, Bulgaira, April 20, 2021. Available at: </https://www.uni-sofia.bg/index.php/bul/content/download/249691/1646163/version/1/file/Dafov.pdf/> [Accessed June 11, 2021].

Prof. Plamen Makariev's Review of Pietrzak's Ph.D. Dissertation, Sofia, Bulgaria, March 2, 2021. Available at: </https://www.uni-sofia.bg/index.php/bul/content/download/249695/1646179/version/1/file/Makariev.pdf/> [Accessed June 11, 2021].

Prof. Giorgos Kentas's Review of Pietrzak's Ph.D. Dissertation, Nicosia, Cyprus, 27 April 2021. Available at: </https://www.uni-sofia.bg/index.php/bul/content/download/249694/1646175/version/1/file/Kentas.pdf/> [Accessed June 11, 2021].

Prof. Dr. Hab. Arkadiusz Żukowski's Review of Pietrzak's Ph.D. Dissertation, Olsztyn, Poland, February 28, 2021. Available at: </https://www.uni-sofia.bg/index.php/bul/content/download/249696/1646183/version/1/file/Zukovski.pdf/> [Accessed June 11, 2021].

Assoc. Dr. Boris Grozdanov's Review of Pietrzak's Ph.D. Dissertation, Sofia, Bulgaria, April 14, 2021. Available at: </https://www.uni-sofia.bg/index.php/bul/content/download/249693/1646171/version/1/file/Grozdanov.pdf/> [Accessed June 11, 2021].

Book Review: On the Idea of Humanitarian Intervention: A New Compartmentalization of IR Theories—Australian Institute of International Affairs. (2022, June 15). Australian Institute of International Affairs. https://www.internationalaffairs.org.au/australianoutlook/book-review-on-the-idea-of-humanitarian-intervention-a-new-compartmentalization-of-ir-theories/> [Accessed January 11, 2023].

Interviews

Lachowski, Tomasz & Pietrzak, Piotr. 2023. Dr. Tomasz Lachowski's *in statu nascendi*. https://irinstatunascendi.wixsite.com/irtheorist/post/interview-with-dr-tomasz-lachowski.

Pietrzak, Piotr & Piskorska, Beata. 2023. Prof. Beata Piskorska's *in statu nascendi*—https://youtu.be/hXDYksw5EcA.

Astramowicz-Leyk, Teresa & Pietrzak, Piotr. 2023. Wywiad z Panią Prof. Teresą Astramowicz-Leyk na temat pomocy dla Ukrainy—https://youtu.be/mb2Q1_tn2c0.

Grabowski, Marcin & Pietrzak, Piotr. 2023. Prof. Grabowski on the Jagiellonian University's Assistance Offered to Ukrainian People after 2022—https://youtu.be/rKJC9da8KtA.

Pietrzak, Piotr & Tóth, Bálint László. 2023. Bálint Tóth"s *in statu nascendi*—https://youtu.be/KqSYNUg3ldg.

Pietrzak, Piotr & Żęgota, Krzysztof. 2021: "Interview with Krzysztof Żęgota, PhD on the Russian Federation's Geostrategic Imperatives and Vladimir Putin's future." In Statu Nascendi—Journal of Political Philosophy and International Relations Vol. 4, No. 1 (2021).

Albertini, Tamara & Pietrzak, Piotr. 2020. "Clarity is what I seek first: A scientific interview with Professor Tamara Albertini by Piotr Pietrzak," *In Statu Nascendi—Journal of Political Philosophy and International Relations Vol. 3, No. 2 (2020)*, p. 3–18, ISBN: 9783838214290.

Kojcic, Zoran & Pietrzak, Piotr. 2020. "Interview with Dr. Zoran Kojcic", *In Statu Nascendi—Journal of Political Philosophy and International Relations* Vol. 3, No. 1 (2020), p. 85–92, ISBN: 9783838214290.

Mehmeti, Sami & Pietrzak, Piotr. 2020. "Interview with Dr. Sami Mehmeti on the political situation in North Macedonia & Balkans in statu nascendi,", *In Statu Nascendi—Journal of Political Philosophy and International Relations* Vol. 2, No. 2 (2019), p. 109–116, ISBN: 9783838213392.

Dimitrova, Maria & Pietrzak, Piotr. 2019. "Interview with Prof. Maria Dimitrova on Emmanuel Levinas' Philosophy," *In Statu Nascendi—Journal of Political Philosophy and International Relations* Vol. 2, No. 1 (2019), p. 177–185, ISBN: 9783838213095.

Grabowski, Marcin & Pietrzak, Piotr. 2019. "Interview with Marcin Grabowski, Ph.D., on the Ever-Changing Political Situation of the Asia Pacific Region in General, and the Political Backdrop of North Korea in Particular," *In Statu Nascendi—Journal of Political Philosophy and International Relations* Vol. 2, No. 1 (2019), p. 3–32, ISBN: 9783838213095.

Pietrzak, Piotr & Trupia, Francesco. 2018. "Interview with Francesco Trupia on the Nagorno-Karabakh Conflict,", *In Statu Nascendi—Journal of Political Philosophy and International Relations* Vol 1, No 1, (2018), p. 117–128, ISBN: 9783838212296.

ABOUT THE AUTHOR

PIOTR PIETRZAK, Ph.D., eats and sleeps geopolitics every single day. He is a political thinker, author, and ontologist by training who takes pride in adding a pragmatic twist to IR theory, political philosophy, conflict management, security studies, and geoeconomics. He is a researcher with a strong background in political philosophy, conflict resolution strategies, international theories, and geopolitics. He has authored several articles and book chapters in peer-reviewed journals and edited volumes, including *On the Idea* *of Humanitarian Intervention: A New Compartmentalization of IR Theories.* 2021. He has also contributed articles to the online publication *Modern Diplomacy.*

Pietrzak teaches **Global Problems & Global Solutions** as part of a master's program titled "Political Pathologies of the Global World" at Sofia University "St. Kliment Ohridski." He was a Postdoctoral Researcher at Airlangga University in Indonesia (2022-2023) under the supervision of **Prof. Vinsensio Dugis** from the Faculty of Social & Political Sciences. He defended his Ph.D. Dissertation at Sofia University "St. Kliment Ohridiski" (2021) under the supervision of **Prof. Vasselin Dafov.** His second master's degree in international politics & international relations was obtained at the University of Manchester (2013) and was defended under the supervision of Prof. Yoram Gorlicki. His first master's degree Dissertation was defended at the University of Warmia and Mazury (2008) under the supervision of **Prof. Stefan Opara.** He was also awarded an Erasmus Scholarship to the University of Cyprus in 2007.

***

I want to show my gratitude to my intellectual home and the place where I was lucky to pursue my research—**Sofia University "St. Kliment Ohridski".** I would also like to express my deep gratitude to all those who inspired me and provided me with useful guidance, essential support, and all words of encouragement for the last two decades at **the University of Manchester, Cyprus University,** and my first *alma mater*, **University of Warmia and Mazury in Olsztyn.** The list of the people I want to thank the most begins with my Ph.D. supervisor **Prof. Veselin Hristov Dafov**, for his time, guidance, valuable suggestions, and of course, his infinite patience in seeing this project through. **Prof. Dafov** has been a constant source of encouragement to me. He pointed me in the right direction around several major issues encountered while preparing this research. I would also like to thank **Prof. Iskren Ivanov, Prof. Tsena Zhelyazkova Stoeva** from Sofia University, **Prof. Vinsensio Dugis** from Airlangga University, **Prof. Goran Ilik** from Bitola University for giving me the opportunity to present the collection of my elective courses to very eager to learn students from **Bulgaria, North Macedonia, Kosovo, Turkey,** and **Indonesia.**

Thank you to **Prof. Aleksander Gungov, Prof. Plamen Makariev** from Sofia University "St. Kliment Ohridski" **Prof. Giorgios Kentas** from

Nicosia University for they pointed me in the right direction in selecting the best possible academic texts that have opened my eyes to many pressing issues in some of the most up-to-date IR-related deliberations. My next compliments go to **Prof. Yoram Gorlizki, Prof. Veronique Pin-Fat** from Manchester University, **Prof. Inderjeet Parmar** from the City University of London. **Prof. Arkadiusz Żukowski, Prof. Selim Chazbijewicz,** and **Przemyslaw Piotrowski, Ph.D.** from University of Warmia and Mazury in Olsztyn, Poland for their contribution to my research.

I am forever indebted to all members and readers of the *In Statu Nascendi Journal of Political Philosophy and International Relation*s that I have had the privilege and honor of editing since 2017, especially to **Koubaroudis Evangelos, Ph.D., Stavros Panagiotou Ph.D., Hristiana Stoyanova, Prof. Marcin Grabowski, Ph.D., Galina Raykova, Sami Mohameti Ph.D., Joseph Milburn Ph.D., Prof. Krzysztof Zegota, Ph.D., Zoran Kojcic Ph.D., Venera Russo, Ph.D. Abiola Bamijoko-Okangbaye, Ph.D., Eliza Emily Campbell, Prof. Sophie Grace Chappell, Dimitris M. Moschos Ph.D., Nieves Turégano Muñoz, Prof. Malgorzata Tomala, Francesco Trupia Ph.D., Bálint László Tóth, Ph.D.** and **Matthew Gill.** Thanks to your support and useful guidance, I have explored a completely new uncharted territory of social science and was able to strengthen this project further.

Baba Seidu Abdul Rahman

Limiting the Negative Impacts of Economic Globalization on Africa's Economy Through Regional Economic Integration

Abstract: *Over several decades, the notion of Africa's integration became a talk of the day and still is.Some Schools of Thought believe that the commitment of African states to globalization would facilitate the realization of the benefits of economies of scale, through the expansion of markets and promote efficiency in the use of resources, encouraging the development and the sharing of new technologies and products, as well as the development of comprehensive strategies to enhance better bargaining capacity on the global scene which would result in improvements in the well-being of individual national economies. Unarguably, forces of globalization which have increased the interconnectedness of the world has brought with it both benefits and challenges. These forces, such as trade liberalization and technological advancement, whilst benefiting others, especially the developed states, have become a major challenge to developing countries, especially those in Africa. According to proponents of globalization, it is progress which developing countries must accept if they are to grow and fight poverty effectively. However, opponents of globalization claim that globalization has not brought the promised benefits to many developing countries but instead led to the marginalization of these countries. Thus, in the quest to benefit from globalization, while minimizing its being marginalized, Africa should resort to regional integration which has been considered to be the most appropriate measure to fight the challenges of globalization in developing countries. With the increasing perception that regional integration currently holds the key to Africa's development. This paper gives an overview of the extent to which Africa can limit the negative impact of globalization through regional integration.There has been several debates on the impact of globalization, especially financial and economic globalization on macroeconomic variables with some studies establishing positive impact, others negative relationship and yet others mixed effects. For instance, employing capital account liberalization as a measure of financial openness, Quinn (1997) and Klein and Olivei(2006) find a positive relationship between financial openness and economic growth. In contrast, Grilli and Milesi-Ferretti (1995), Kraay (1998), Rodrik (1998), and Edison, et al (2002) could not establish any relationship between these* *phenomena. Other studies, such as Arteta, et al (2003), Chanda (2005) and Ogunleye (2008a) find that the effect is mixed or fragile. Despite the expected laudable positive effects of globalization on the economies of developing countries, evidence abounds on its negative effects. For example, Levine and Schmukler (2003) posit that the internationalization of firms, a product of financial globalization, reduces the liquidity of the remaining firms in the domestic market. Globalization can also lead to crises given the imperfections in international financial markets. This is because integrated economies are more prone to crises and contagion spreads more rapidly in such economies as we have witnessed in the recent global financial and economic crisis. The imperfections in highly integrated markets can generate herding, bubbles and irrational behavior, speculative attacks and crashes among other things. Imperfections in international capital markets can lead to crises, especially balance of payments crisis even in countries with sound fundamentals. Further globalization has made most African countries dependent on foreign capital which creates financial difficulties and sharp economic downturn if there are sudden shifts and reversals in foreign capital inflows resulting from global activities. For example, when countries rely excessively on foreign capital inflows relative to their ability to generate financial resources in the domestic economy, they become vulnerable to sudden reversals of capital flows and, consequently, to liquidity crises. The importance of regional economic integration is a very pertinent issue in Africa, particularly in light of existing political and economic weaknesses. Africa is infested with the deepest levels of poverty, lowest share of world trade, and weakest development of human capital and infrastructure, to say the least. Thus the negative impacts of Economic globalization can be reduced when African countries acknowledge that regional economic integration is the best way to accelerate Africa's growth and development agendas. This is very important, because most of Africa's economies are currently faced with a plethora of challenges. These challenges range from dependency of most countries on agricultural exports, small and inefficient industrial bases, vulnerability to fluctuations in the world market, lack of compensation mechanisms, external debt etc. Of course, with all these challenges, the process of regional economic integration will not be easy, and the situation is further compounded by the globalization and liberalization of the world economy, greater integration of financial and money markets, and a shift towards the creation of large trading and economic blocs in North America, Europe, South-East Asia and China, which lead to Africa's risk of further marginalization in a multi-polar world. Indeed, regional integration in Africa has been viewed as the first step toward global integration. Generally, regional integration is often cast in the context and scope of deepening and widening (Weintraub 1994, Hoberg 2000, Gomez &Gunderson 2002). The objective of the article, therefore, is to demonstrate how Regional Economic Integration in Africa can reduce the negative impacts of economic globalization in Africa and promote intra-regional trade as well as the acceleration of development on the continent.*

Introduction

Globalization is a complex and multifaceted concept that has generated controversy from its meaning, its timeline, and its future as well as whether it is serving the interest of all or it is benefiting just a few countries or individuals in the world. Due to the fact that it cuts across almost all disciplines, each of the disciplines proffers varying definitions and interpretations for the concept. Although the existence of globalization has been demonstrated in empirical case studies, its definition remains vague, elusive, and even contradictory.

The lack of an essential definition has contributed, at least partially, to keep globalization as a highly contested subject (Acosta and Gonzalez, 2010). Cesare Poppi (1997: 300) notes that: The literature stemming from the debate on globalization has grown in the last decade beyond any individual's capability of extracting a workable definition of the concept. In a sense, the meaning of the concept is self-evident, in another, it is vague and obscure as its reaches are wide and constantly shifting. Perhaps, more than any other concept, globalization is the debate about it. Shenkar and Luo (2004: 199) refer to globalization as "the growing economic interdependencies of countries worldwide through the increasing volume and variety of cross-border transactions in goods and services and of international capital flows, as well as through the rapid and widespread diffusion of technology and information.

Globalization has also been defined to constitute the process of international integration arising from the interchange of world views, products, ideas and other aspects of culture. Advances in transportation and telecommunications infrastructure, including the rise of the telegraph and its development the Internet, are major factors in globalization, generating further interdependence of economic and cultural activities.

According to Adesina (2012), "Globalization involves economic integration; the transfer of policies across borders; the transmission of knowledge; cultural stability; the reproduction, relations, and discourses of power; it is a global process, a concept, a revolution, and an establishment of the global market free from sociopolitical control". It has helped to liberalize national economics by creating a global marketplace in which all nations must participate directly or indirectly: This undoubtedly led to growing activities and power of international financial investors mainly presented by multi-national corporations (Jaja, 2010).

Giddens (1990) defines globalization as "the intensification of world-wide social relations linking distant localities in such a way that local happenings are shaped by events occurring many miles away and vice versa". The implication of this definition is that globalization can be thought of as a process of integration of goods and capital markets across the world in which barriers to international trade and foreign investment are significantly reduced. Several drivers of globalization have been identified. These include technological developments that improve information flows and reduce transport costs, change in policy attitudes that favor liberalization of foreign investment rules, diminish protectionism, and ease migration trade, then FDI and finally financial flows.

The global economy, or world economy, is the economy of the world, considered as an international exchange of goods and services (McMillan Dictionary of world economy). In some contexts, the two terms are distinguished: the "international" or "global economy" being measured separately and distinguished from national economies while the "world economy" is simply an aggregate of the separate countries' measurements. It is common to limit questions of the world economy exclusively to human economic activity, and the world economy is typically judged in monetary terms, even if there is no efficient market to help valuate certain goods or services, or if establishing figures is difficult. Typical examples are illegal drugs and other black-market goods, which are a part of the world economy, but for which there is by definition no legal market of any kind. Market valuations in local currencies are typically translated to a single monetary unit using the idea of purchasing power.

In 2013, the largest economies in the world with more than \$2 trillion, €1.25 trillion by nominal GDP were the United States, China, Japan, Germany, France, the United Kingdom, Brazil, Russia, Italy, and India.

Economic globalization is the increasing economic interdependence of national economies across the world through a rapid increase in cross-border movement of goods, service, technology, and capital (Joshi. & Rakesh, 2009). Whereas the globalization of business is centered around the diminution of international trade regulations as well as tariffs, taxes, and other impediments that suppresses global trade, economic globalization is the process of increasing economic integration between countries, leading to the emergence of a global marketplace or a single world markets (Riley, 2005). Depending on the paradigm, economic globalization can be viewed as either a positive or a negative phenomenon. Economic globalization comprises the globalization of production, markets, competition, technology, and corporations and industries (Joshi. & Rakesh, 2009). Current globalization trends can be largely accounted for by developed economies integrating with less developed economies by means of foreign direct investment, the reduction of trade barriers as well as other economic reforms and, in many cases, immigration.

In 1944, 44 nations attended the Bretton Woods Conference with a purpose of stabilizing world currencies and establishing credit for international trade in the post-World War II era. While the international economic order envisioned by the conference gave way to the neo-liberal economic order prevalent today, the conference established many of the organizations essential to advancement towards a close-knit global economy and global financial system, such as the World Bank, the International Monetary Fund, and the International Trade Organization.

As an example, Chinese economic reform began to open China to globalization in the 1980s. Scholars find that China has attained a degree of openness that is unprecedented among large and populous nations, with competition from foreign goods in almost every sector of the economy. Foreign investment helped to greatly increase product quality and knowledge and standards, especially in heavy industry. China's experience supports the assertion that globalization greatly increases wealth for poor countries.

Regional integration is a process in which neighboring states enter into an agreement in order to upgrade cooperation through common institutions and rules. The objectives of the agreement could range from economic to political to environmental, although it has typically taken the form of a political economy initiative where commercial interests are the focus for achieving broader socio-political and security objectives, as defined by national governments. Regional integration has been organized either via supranational institutional structures or through intergovernmental decision-making, or a combination of both.

Past efforts at regional integration have often focused on removing barriers to free trade in the region, increasing the free movement of people, labor, goods, and capital across national borders, reducing the possibility of regional armed conflict (for example, through Confidence and Security-Building Measures), and adopting cohesive regional stances on policy issues, such as the environment, climate change and migration.

Intra-regional trade refers to trade which focuses on economic exchange primarily between countries of the same region or economic zone. In recent years countries within economic-trade regimes such as ASEAN in Southeast Asia for example have increased the level of trade and commodity exchange between themselves which reduces the inflation and tariff barriers associated with foreign markets resulting in growing prosperity. This idea is no different from the regional integration agenda of Africa.

Regional Economic integration according to Balassa (1961) is defined as *"the abolition of discrimination within an area"*. And according to Kahnert et al (1969) economic integration is *"the process of removing progressively those discriminations which occur at national borders"*. Therefore, scientifically, measures which merely diminish discrimination between countries are considered forms of cooperation not integration. According to Allen (1963, p.450) economic integration may mean something different to nearly everyone. That's why Allen (1963, p.450) argues that one of the many useful elements of the well-known Balassa (1961) book is that it evidently defines integration, clearly differentiating between it and cooperation.

Furthermore, Lipsey (1960, p.496) provided the following definition of the customs union theory (economic integration theory) as follows: *"The theory of customs unions may be defined as that branch of tariff theory which deals with the effects of geographically discriminatory changes in trade barriers* [among countries]"

An important question arises, and it is why study economic integration theories? Chou (1967) answered this question when he argued that the main reason behind studying the traditional theory of economic integration is to evaluate the desirability of a customs union from the world's welfare point of view using static effects as criteria. The new (dynamic) theory of economic integration has introduced dynamic effects of economic integration to this analysis. This is what we will study in-detail in section two of this paper.

One cannot talk about the different forms of economic integration without mentioning the work of Balassa (1961) which is considered the cornerstone of any work done on issues of economic integration. Balassa's book written in 1961, titled: *"The Theory of Economic Integration"* has been reviewed by many authors in internationally recognized journals. Some of these book reviews include Allen (1963, p.449-454) who described the book as an important contribution to an adequate understanding of economic integration. Havens (1962, p.47-48) also describes the book as making a worthwhile contribution to the theory of economic integration. In Ingram's (1962, p.612-614) review of the book, the author argues that Balassa has succeeded extremely well in explaining the theory of economic integration. Other book reviews of Balassa's work include Eastman (1962, p.466-467), Meyer (1962, p.389-391), and Hasson (1962, p.614-615). Balassa's book is widely cited in any book, article, or paper discussing economic integration—whether theory or policy.

According to Allen's (1963, p.450) review of Balassa's book: the basic ingredient of any integration form is the elimination of barriers to trade among two or more countries. Allen (1963, p.450) also stresses the point that although traditional international trade theory has dealt with the effects of reduction of trade barriers, a separate theoretical framework is needed to study issues of economic integration.

Economic integration can take many forms. According to Balasaa (1962) there are four different stages of economic integration. The first is a Free Trade Area (FTA), then a Customs Union (CU), then a Common Market (CM), and finally an Economic Union.

Panagariya (1998, p.2; and 2000, p.288) argue that the term PTA, whether used to stand for *Preferential Trade Area, Preferential Trade Agreement* or *Preferential Trade Arrangement,* has an advantage of being wider in that it can be used to describe FTAs, CUs and arrangements involving partial trade preferences.

Preferential Trade Arrangements (PTAs) usually entail lower tariff barriers among participating nations than with non-member nations. Panagariya (1998, p.2; and 2000, p.288) describe PTAs as an arrangement between two or more countries in which goods produced within the union are subject to lower trade barriers than the goods produced outside the union. The trade arrangement among the eight Muslim countries of the Developing 8 Organization is an example of a PTA. Bhagwati and Panagariya (1996, p. 82).

The impact of globalization—which implies the growth of a functional world market both penetrating and dominating so-called 'national' economies—has destroyed the 'nationless' of the fragile African economies, most of which are barely in functional order. Adherents to neoliberalism and globalization do not understand the operating principles of African economies. Globalization, therefore, does not have the same meaning for the people of the industrialized north, and the people of Africa. The major point here is that globalization has no theory of justice or equity, which means it cannot address the poor who constitute the global majority (Manboah-Rockson, 2000).

First, is the issue of divestiture and privatization as part of the economic logic of globalization. The issue of divestiture and privatization in Africa entails a few private companies and Multinational Corporations (MNCs) taking over the assets of states. The policies of the IMF and World Bank's ceiling on government spending have already led to the termination of most African economies' investment capabilities. The dollarization of the African local economies (a case in point is Ghana), and the regulatory and forced devaluation imposed by the international financial speculators have in themselves resulted in inflation. A case in point is Nigeria, where the Nigerian economy has been labelled a "rogue state." This, in turn, has resulted in layoffs, wage freezes, de-indexation of wages, and has caused the governments to eliminate minimum wage legislation and also to eliminate cost of living adjustments in collective bargaining agreements (Chossudovsky, 1997).

Secondly, globalization raises fears that the sovereignty of Africa's nation-states could be undermined. For, if sovereignty is defined as the ability of African states individually to exercise control without outside interference, then their nations, which are in embryonic stages will clearly experience diminishing sovereignty. These phenomena are troubling, as African countries have to convince themselves that pooling their resources will promote autonomous industrialization within the countries through the development of large intermediate and capital foods industries, the promotion of multinational enterprises, and especially the development of strategic natural resources within the sub regions (Manboah-Rockson, 2000).

Thirdly, participation in international organizations or the adoption of international agreements, which do not favor integration, limit policy options available to governments. They may even require modifications in long-standing and highly valued domestic policies and practices. The involvement and continued relationship of French-speaking countries in West Africa to their colonial metropolis is a clear example. France is one such 'colonial monster' which still practices a degree of economic and political integration with its former colonies in West Africa, who are members of ECOWAS, in pursuit of a cohesive regional development policy.

Also, In Africa, the emerging global free market works to set sovereign states against one another in geo-political struggles for dwindling natural resources controlled by colonial institutions. The effect of a laissez-faire philosophy, which condemns state intervention in the economy, also impels states to become rivals for control of resources that no institution has any responsibility to conserve. Similar to this is the current state of economic development theory demonstrated by the policies of the IMF and the World Bank regarding SAPs. Neither would the world economy that is envisaged and organized as a global free market be able to meet the universal human need for security in terms of ethnic conflicts and random cases of ethnic racism on the continent. The end result for African governments would culminate in their inability to protect their citizens and discharge their duties as engines for the realization of the now famous Abuja Treaty of 1994, which aims at the achievement of an African Economic Community (AEC) by the year 2025. A regime of global laissez-faire would prevent African governments from discharging this protective and development role; a failure of which will further plunge the continent into greater political, social and economic instability with varying consequences for the West (Manboah-Rockson, 2000). .

In addition, economic globalization is changing the way in which African governments operate in global commerce. The globalization of financial markets is just one aspect of this changed environment. The challenge to African policy makers is made more acute by a host of other 'internationalizations' under way, in such areas as crime, communications, drug smuggling, population movements, and product and service markets. International actors and events that national governments cannot hope to control, either individually or collectively, increasingly affect the so-called domestic issues that African governments are confronted with. This has evoked fears that national policy autonomy—or even national sovereignty—is being undermined. For sure, globalization raises many challenges for African policy makers. The structures of government and policy-making systems need to be adjusted if governments are going to function effectively in a global policy environment. Moreover, greater attention must be paid to the impact of globalization on the functioning and quality of democracy (Manboah-Rockson, 2000).

Finally, globalization will stifle progress because national governments will have no real option but to attempt to band together. If they try to modernize as the process of globalization forces most states to do, Africa will be robbed of its hopes to pursue and initiate a comprehensive and timeless development theory. As Hirst and Thompson (1996) put it, "globalization is a myth suitable for a world without illusions, but it is also one that robs us of hope…for it is held that Western social democracy and socialism of the former Soviet bloc are both finished." I could not agree more with Hirst and Thompson's assertion that the political impact of "globalization" on countries in sub-Saharan Africa will definitely result in the pathology of over-diminished expectations.

Finally, Ohmae (1995) suggests that such an anomaly provides an interesting and useful critique of these 'Western visions of the global.' "These 'global perspectives' tend to conceal a limiting, enclosed and particularly centered position that is characterized by historical and geopolitical amnesia." This attitude of forgetfulness is conducive to the preservation and continued development of a distorted 'world view', since it allows for the historical erasure of imperial politics, and in addition, represses the record of contemporary forms of western power over the non-western forms, which some authors refer to as the 'new imperialism.'

Regional economic integration refers to the agreement amongst countries within a certain geographic area for reducing and ultimately removing tariff barriers, making sure there is better flow of services or goods through the respective nations. The following paragraph looks at how regional economic integration in Africa can limit the negative effects on the Continent. The issue of financial stability is central to the survival of any financial. The regional financial markets have increasingly become integrated over the last decade. Interest rates in regional countries are much closer to each other than they were a decade ago. Also, cross-listed companies in regional stock exchanges currently account for nearly 60 percent of total market capitalization, up from zero a decade ago. Trinidad and Tobago, the financial hub of the region, has clearly played a leading role in bringing about greater financial integration by channeling its large oil windfall savings to neighboring countries.

While the deepening financial integration of the region is clearly encouraging in that it has the potential to make more capital available to the most efficient regional firms, this potential has not been fully tapped. From a macroeconomic perspective, reducing fiscal imbalances and the large debt burdens is a precondition for such resources to be directed to the private sector. In addition, there is uneven regulatory oversight of the financial sector and limited corporate governance in an environment of rapidly growing financial derivatives and increasing cross-border financial flows.

The stability of the financial sector would need to be safeguarded by enhanced supervision. With increasing linkages, there is a clear need for close coordination in regulation and supervision among country authorities, and possibly the creation of a regional oversight body. Reducing remaining entry barriers and capital controls and harmonizing taxation, regulatory and supervisory frameworks and improving market infrastructure will go a long way toward maximizing the benefits from financial integration. Extending financial integration beyond the region would also help reap the full benefits by diversifying risks and enlarging financing flexibility.

Regional integration can help Africa build regional value chains, and thereby tap into global value chains. Regional integration efforts, however, need to go hand in hand with competitiveness-enhancing policies as explored in other parts of the Africa Competitiveness Report. The importance of regional integration is being felt across the continent, as evidenced by African leaders now calling for a free trade area by 2017. Nevertheless, it still takes almost twice as long to trade across borders in sub-Saharan Africa compared with other regions, such as Latin America and the Caribbean and South-East Asia. Thus, much remains to be done to fully reap the benefits of regional integration for Africa.

With greater regional integration, economies of scale in production of goods that are not available to individual islands may be feasible for the region as a whole. Moreover, politically challenging policy changes can often be achieved through regional agreements. In addition, gains from specialization within the region can be realized by pursuing different strands of the value-added chain, as has been observed in the differentiations among African countries will lead to the development of higher quality locally branded products, such as Jamaican Blue Mountain coffee.

Member countries in a regional economic integration agreement have a wider choice of services and goods than were previously unavailable. They can also easily acquire products at lower costs following the removal or lowering of tariffs. This encourages more trade amongst member nations. Actually, the extra money got from purchasing cheaper products may be useful for buying even more goods and services.

The action plan for stimulating intra-regional trade and promotion of regional integration as a way of accelerating African development can be observed in four points (Njinkeu, D. &Fosso, B.P., 2006).

Taking commitments that can be fulfilled. African governments will not be taken seriously if they continue the proliferation of regional integrations that are poorly financed, with conflicting commitments or without concrete actions that would serve as its basis. It is urgent to carry out a rationalization of the regionalization process, deepening of the political reform on national and regional level to create dynamic regional markets, increase trade liberalization on the continent with special focus on intraregional trade and then on inter-regional trade. Transparent, predictable, and rule-based global trading and economic system supports growth and development of Africa. But a gradual approach towards liberalization is required. Given the current level of social and economic institutions vulnerability, the immediate implementation of international rules could negatively affect long-term development. African countries must ensure that integration into the global trends is in line with general development goals.

African trade is limited by market imperfections which explain high business costs. Coherent trade strategy with adequate sequencing between the creations of relevant exporting base before further liberalization on imports side is crucial. Regional integration should promote convergence of macroeconomic policies which will help in ensuring a stable frame. There are grounds for optimism in all sub-regions. Institutional frame should include mechanisms that encourage healthy business environment.

Dealing with the key problems of competitiveness. Significant constraint of African trade expansion is connected to the lack of infrastructure and other institutional deficiencies. There is a need to develop regional frame in key areas such as investments and competition, as well as the need for encouraging trade, regulation reforms and finance mechanisms. All regional integrations have projects of trade stimulation.

Interest has recently been growing in the "investment diversion effect" of regional integration as well. For example, in 1984 the EU received only one thirds of the direct investment that the United States did but by 1989 was at the same level. To foreign companies, the single, unified market that regional integration creates is also an attractive investment market, and the larger the integrated market, the greater the scale merits and therefore the attraction of locating there. However, in as much as investment resources are limited, this has the effect of diverting investment away from other countries.

Naturally, investment decisions are part of a company's business judgement, and the investment diversion effect should be seen as the result of this. But if regional integration brings with it trade policies that discriminate against products from outside the region, then it may distort the investment pattern between regions. (For example, if regional integration results in stricter rules of origin for non-regional products, then it will encourage direct investment in the region rather than exports to it.)

Economic integration not only leads to the creation of new and better technology, but it also encourages economic growth. As the respective countries trade freely, their GDP increases and therefore improves their economies. Nevertheless, regional economic integration usually requires that member nations give up their control over key policies such as trade, fiscal and monetary policies. (http://benefitof.net/benefits-of-regional-economic-integration/).

Several nations usually have a much larger political influence as compared to the influence that each individual country would have. This kind of integration is a vital strategy for addressing the issues of political instability and conflicts that might affect that particular region. Moreover, improved political cooperation due to regional economic integration is also vital for handling the economic and social challenges linked to globalization. (http://benefitof.net/benefits-of-regional-economic-integration).

Conclusion

In short, whatever the terminology, the process of regional integration in Africa is now inextricably linked to that of economic development (Asante, 1980). The lack of commitment to regionalism in Africa has manifested itself in member countries developing their own strategies, plans and priorities independently. The impact of globalization is thus manifested in a shift from a world of distinct national economies attempting to pool such economies together into a viable integration for development, to a global economy in which production is internationalized and financial capital flows freely and instantly between countries.

The negative impacts of Economic globalization can therefore be reduced when African countries acknowledge that regional economic integration is the best way to accelerate Africa's growth and development agendas. This is very important, because most of Africa's economies are currently faced with a plethora of challenges, which add to the external pressures.

Ensuring that regional economic integration succeeds in Africa is vital, not only because of the prospective benefits mentioned above, but also because the policies that are required to ensure its success are the same as those needed if Africa is to benefit from the process of globalization and integration into the world economy.

There are a number of theoretical studies that have addressed the importance of and/or necessity for regional economic integration, but most of them have focused on regions other than Africa. Regional economic integration is believed to be one of the means for increasing their welfare, and with it, countries may increase either the welfare of the integrated group, some countries within the group, or the world as a whole.

References

Abdel, J. T.1971. A review article: The relevance of traditional integration theory to less developed countries. *Journal of Common Market Studies* 9 (3): pp. 254-267

Acosta O. &Gonzalez J.I. 2010. "A thermodynamic approach for emergence of globalization", in Deng K. G. (ed.) *Globalization—Today, Tomorrow.* Croatia: Sciyo.

Albertin, G. 2008. *Regionalism or multilateralism? A political economy choice.* IMF Working Paper WP/08/65. Washington, D.C.: International Monetary Fund.

Balassa, B. 1961. *The Theory of Economic Integration.* Homewood, Illinois: Richard D. Irwin.

Balassa, B. 1975. Economic integration among developing countries. *Journal of Common Market Studies* 14 (1): pp. 37-55

Bhagwati, J. 1962. Review of An essay on trade and transformation, by S. B. Linder. *The Journal of Political Economy* 70 (5): pp. 516-517.

Bhagwati, J. 1971. Trade-diverting customs unions and welfare-improvement: A clarification. *The Economic Journal* 81 (323): pp. 580-587.

Bhagwati, J. 1993. Regionalism and multilateralism: An overview. Chapter 2 in New Dimensions in *Regional Integration*, edited by Jaime De Melo and Arvind Panagariya. Cambridge University Press.

Bhagwati, J., & Arvind P. 1996. The theory of preferential trade agreements: *Historical evolution and current trends*. The American Economic Review 86 (2): pp. 82-87.

Bhambri, R. S. 1962. Customs unions and underdeveloped countries. *EconomiaInternazionale* May 1962.

Greenway, D. 1981. Identifying the gains from pure intra-industry exchange. *Journal of Economic Studies* 9 (3): pp. 40-54.

Greenway, D., &Milner, C. 1990. South-South trade: *Theory, evidence, and policy*. The World Bank Research Observer 5 (1): pp. 47-68.

Haas, E. B. 1958. *The Uniting of Europe: Political, Social and Economical Forces* 1950-1957. London: Stevens for the London Institute of World Affairs.

Haas, E. B., & Philippe C. S. 1964. *Economics and differential patterns of political integration: Projections about unity in Latin America.* International Organization 18 (4): pp. 705 -737.

Heimenz, U., & Rolf J. L. 1990. *Regional integration among developing countries: Opportunities, obstacles, and options.* Tubingen, Germany: Westview Press.

Henderson, W. O. 1951. *Review of The customs union issue*, by Jacob Viner. The Economic History Review 3 (3): pp. 398-400.

Inotai, A. 1991. *Regional integration among developing countries, revisited.* Policy, Research, and External Affairs Working Paper no. 643. Washington, D.C.: World Bank.

Inotai, A. 1997. Interrelations between sub-regional co-operation and EU enlargement. *Chapter 4 in Part IV in Lessons from the Economic Transition: Central and Eastern Europe in the 1990s*, edited by Salvatore and Zecchini. Kluwer Academic Publishers.

Jaja, J. M. 2010. "Globalization or Americanization: Implications for Sub-Saharan Africa", in Deng K. G. (ed.) *Globalization—Today, Tomorrow.* Croatia: Sciyo

Joshi, A. B. & Rakesh M., 2009 *International Business,* Oxford University Press, New Delhi and New York ISBN 0-19-568909-7.

Kahnert, et al., 1969. *Economic integration among developing countries.* Paris: Development Center of the Organization for Economic Co-operation and Development, OECD.

Lipsey, R. G., & Kelvin L. 1956-1957. The general theory of second best. *The Review of Economic Studies* 24 (1): pp. 11-32.

Lipsey, R. G. 1957. The theory of customs unions: *Trade diversion and welfare.* Economica, New Series 24 February: pp. 40-46.

Lipsey, R. G. 1960. The theory of customs unions: A general survey. *The Economic Journal* 70 (279): pp. 496-513.

Manboah-Rockson, J. K. 2000. Regionalism and Integration in Sub-Saharan Africa: A Review of Experiences, Issues and Realities at the Close of the Twentieth Century. *Innovations: A Journal of Politics,* 3(1), 47-68.

Mikesell, R. F. 1965. The theory of common markets as applied to regional arrangements among developing countries. In *International Trade Theory in a Developing World,* edited by Harrod and Hague. New York: St. Martin's Press.

Panagariya, A. 1998. *The regionalism debate: An overview.* University of Maryland.

Panagariya, A. 2000. Preferential trade liberalization: The traditional theory and new developments. *Journal of Economic Literature* 38 (2): pp. 287331.

Poppi, C. 1997 "Wider Horizons with Larger Details: Subjectivity, Ethnicity, and Globalization", in Alan Scott (ed.), *The Limits of Globalization: Cases and Arguments.* London: Routledge.

Riley, T. 2005 *"Year 12 Economics"* Tim Riley Publications, p.9

Schirato, T. & Webb, J. 2003. *Understanding Globalization.* London: Sage Publications.

Scholte, J. 1997. "The Globalization of World Politics", in Steve Smith and John Baylis (eds). The Globalization of World Politics, Oxford: Universtiy Press.

Shenkar, O., & Luo, Y. 2004. *International Business.* New York: John Willey & Sons.

UNCTAD. 2007. Trade and development report 2007: *Regional cooperation for development.* UNCTAD/TDR/2007. Geneva: United Nations.

Viner, J. 1950. *The Customs Union Issue.* New York: Carnegie Endowment for International Peace.

World Economy.—*Definition.* American English Definition of with Pronunciation by Macmillan Dictionary. N.p., n.d. Web. 02 Jan. 2015

ABOUT THE AUTHOR

BABA SEIDU ABDUL RAHMAN—M.A Public Affairs, University of Ghana (2014-2015). M.A Economic Policy Management Program, University Of Ghana (Awaiting Certficate). Bachelor Of Arts In Economics And Political Science, University Of Ghana (2008-2013)

Yunus Emre Özigci

On the German Foreign Policy Sonderweg: The *Mittellage* and the *Mitteleuropa*

Abstract: *Current IR theorisation privileges its a prioris over the purely intersubjective, immediately given, lived/living praxis of the interstate environment and the interstate interactions. As such, the theoretical construct "precedes" the praxis in the study, which often becomes an effort to fit the praxis to the construct, presenting a distorted image of it. The concepts of the Husserlian phenomenology as adapted to the context through drawing from the more fitting aspects of the Heidegger's work, may provide a praxis-based, descriptive study of the IR field in general and of the state-actor's foreign policy in particular with viable tools. This article constitutes an attempt to outline this possibility through the study of one particular actor's foreign policy as to its nature, individual meaning ground, temporality and intersubjective environment. The choice of "Germany"-the line Brandenburg-Prussia, Prussia and Germany- as the subject of this attempt stems from already existing debates on the Sonderweg and Mittellage-Mitteleuropa, phenomenologically reducible to interactional individuality and meaning ground, in bracketing contents and judgments ascribed to them.*

Keywords: German foreign policy, Sonderweg, phenomenology, Mittellage, Mitteleuropa

Introduction

The term *Sonderweg* had been used to describe Germany's "unique" socio-political evolutionary course due to her "special circumstances". It was considered as a gratifying element in the XIXth and earlier in the XXth Centuries in Germany (Kocka 1999; Faulenbach 1980) but not without criticism (Mommsen 2004, pp37-72, 97-146).[1] During the late XXth Century, the history theses of Fischer and of Wehler (Wehler 1985; Fischer 1986) which focused on Germany's unique "modernisation" course and its political/policy consequences, re-initiated a debate on the *Sonderweg* (Kocka 1999; Faulenbach

---

1 Weber's depiction of the re-feudalised German bourgeoisie.

165

1994; Plessner 1959;[2] Mosse 1981;[3] Blackbourn and Eley 1984;[4] Blackbourn 1998).[5] This later debate focused rather on the Third Reich's nature as simply *the* end product of the *Sonderweg* or a negatively unique, almost accidental occurrence (Kocka 1999; Kocka 2018; Eley 1988).[6] The *Trauma* of the Shoah and of the Second World War directly and inevitably dominated this later debate. This significantly eclipsed the possibility to conduct a non-teleological study of the "special path".

In both periods, the comparison with "other" countries was inherent to the *Sonderweg* concept, underlining Germany's differentiation from "them", therefore incorporating *interaction* with "them" to its meaning ground. The *Sonderweg* was meaningful only "in interaction with others". The interaction and subsequent differentiation appear in foreign policy contexts: The *Sonderweg*'s given *subject* is "Germany", more clearly the "German state" and the "others" that become inherent to its meaning ground through interaction are *ipso facto* of the same nature. Consequently, the *Sonderweg* is fundamentally a concept of interstate interaction and as it depicts the differentiation of one particular State-actor from the others of the same nature within this interactional context, it depicts the *nature* of its "foreign policy".

Could the *Sonderweg* be discussed on this, preceding meaning ground with a wider, non-teleological perspective? As the ground of an individual actor's foreign policy contingencies, would it not then be still "alive"? Could it not have been providing other policy forms and contents than what it did in the past? Might such a discussion not be useful to define the existential *logos* of Germany's foreign policy? But how to study the *Sonderweg*?

This paper aims at proposing some answers to these questions. The possibility of a foreign policy meaning ground with ontological precedence over structures/ forms/ acts shall be debated in the first section. Here the first sub-section will outline the current IR theorisation's ontological "gap" in dealing with a purely intersubjective field. In the following sub-section, the phenomeno-ontology's possible use to close this "gap" will be discussed. The last sub-section will attempt to outline the German actor's foreign policy *(Sonder)Weg*'s preceding, existential features. There, the controversial-yet-

---

2   Centered on the nation-building.

3   Based on the unique rigidity of the political culture, social classification, and governmental structures.

4   For a neo-Marxist approach, discussing the German modernization and the political development of the German bourgeoisie.

5   Arguing that there was no straight line between 1848 or Bismarck and the Third Reich except the "infatuation with modern and cultural revolt against modernity".

6   On the reconciliation with Germany's past while keeping the Third Reich "unique".

fitting terms of *Mittellage* and *Mitteleuropa* shall be employed, in reduction of their various definitions/attributed meanings.

On this ground, in the second section, the German actor's multipolar and bipolar eras' *Mitsein* in its relatedness to the *Mittellage-Mitteleuropa* –as foreign policy *Sonderweg*- shall be outlined through the main events. The third section shall be reserved to a debate on the current (post-bipolar) horizon of the German foreign policy *Sonderweg* and forms/ acts it engenders. This debate will be conducted in two parts, which will be related to the early and the late post-bipolar eras.

I- The Foreign Policy of a State-Actor: The Theoretical Construct and the IR praxis

The ontological problem of the IR theorisation

Discussion on a state-actor's foreign policy reminds of Waltz's differentiation between the "theory of international politics" and the field of foreign policies (Waltz 1996). According to Waltz, the first one answers the question why actors "*similarly placed* (in a system) *behave similarly despite their internal differences*", whereas its twin question why actors "*similarly placed in a system behave in different ways*" is transferred to the quite vague domain of "their internal compositions" where the individualities of their foreign policies are shaped (Waltz 1996; Waltz 1979, pp. 122-123). The structural realist "dualism" here seems to have stemmed from the theory's basic concern of explaining the "system". It builds an objectivity-seeking power-relations model (Waltz 1979) based on the microeconomics (Waltz 1979, pp. 107-111), without the interference of individual incompatibilities (Waltz 1979; also see Fischer 2019 and Ripsman, Taliaferro and Lobell 2016, pp. 16-32). The sphere of the "internal compositions", researchable according to social, economic, cultural, geographical criteria and so on, is left out of the systemic field. This "purification" is criticisable for over-reducing parameters artificially. Still, its reason appears more ontological than methodological: The theory strives to delimitate and objectify an otherwise a purely intersubjective field with no direct correspondence in the "objective" reality. It tries to do so according to criteria it pre-assumes within its preceding *Weltanschauung*. The dualism appears as a symptom of this attitude, which itself constitutes an ontological impasse. The theory interprets the *praxis* and builds its causality narrative upon *its* criteria, gaining its explanatory power in its approach to occurrences and phenomena as such. However, within the intersubjective field of the IR, the theoretical construct's interpretation of phenomena becomes a closed circuit where the accuracy is assessed through the theoretical construct's own parameters. The theory builds a narrative on an objectivity it presupposes in a field that is existentially devoid of self-standing objectivity, in contrast to that of the positive sciences. Still and apart from this attempt to objectify, the theory's *assumptive* nature (such as the assumption of the state-actor as a single, self-standing entity) and its systemic approach (assuming the existence of a definable international system as reference) make the structural realist terminology essential to the current study, *after* an ontological debate.

Here, Katzenstein's emphasis on the identity, norms and culture (with historical perspective) in particular in relation with Waltz's "overlooked" question of why actors *"similarly placed in a system behave in different ways"* needs to be referred-to (Katzenstein 1996). At first glimpse, Katzenstein's work completes the actor's individuality ("inner compositions") *lacuna* of the structural realists with a constructivist approach, also dealing with the actor/ agency- environment relationship. However, his social/ cultural approach inevitably intervenes in the systemic sphere "purified" by the structural realists. Still, does the constructivist understanding of the international relations and of the foreign policy resolve the ontological problem mentioned above?

The constructivism emphasises the intersubjective nature of the IR field. Yet it is a *narrative* of intersubjectivity built on sociology and sociopsychology. As such, it has its *a prioris* which inherently reduce the *praxis*, the lived/living givenness to malleable material for the narrative. The very concepts of social construct and communicative processes repeat, with different parameters, the realist/ structural realist attempt to "objectivise intersubjectivity" (Onuf 1989, pp35-64; Onuf 2013, pp3-20; Wendt 1999). Moreover, the constructivist thought also covers the elements the realism/structural realism "assumes" and leaves intact. It thus further weakens the link with the givenness, the link the realist/ structural realist understanding of the IR preserves to a measure.

As to post-structuralism, the inherently "critical" de-centering puts forward its own *a priori* judgments for example on sovereignty, freedom, participation, oppression and so on, pre-conditioning as such the de-centering itself, thus creating another sort of narrative (Ashley 1984; Bartelson 1995, pp. 53-87; Allen 1982). This also includes the critical geopolitics (Lacoste 1976; Dodds 2005).

The criticism of the "assumption of objectivity" works against the study of the IR *praxis.* Instead of remaining within the pre-theoretical sphere and observing the modalities of the givenness of phenomena, the study either attempts to redesign the objectivity (the constructivist case) or to reduce the givenness and the criticised narrative together to *a priori* concepts of the decentring attempt (the post-structuralist case). The givenness becomes the material to be processed in order to fit in the "redesign" to the point that even the realist assumption of objectivity appears as a *partial* safeguard for the *praxis* against the current "theorisation of the intersubjectivity".

The ontological problem of the IR studies produces another complication: The theory's interpretation of the *praxis* requires a continuous reassertion of its own, preceding *Weltanschauung*[7]. The reassertion takes the content of the theoretical construct's definition of its object's "substance" at its *genesis/ genetic moment,* at its coming-into-being, which is the theory's immediate link with the specific object, phenomenon, occurrence that is being studied. The genesis is however imposed upon the object in its current, living, practical, immediate, *post-genetic* manifestation, which engenders a *temporal* distortion. The genetic moment of phenomena and occurrences is not necessarily identical to their living/lived, immediate givenness. The genesis as an event or process of its own does not necessarily equate to the post-genetically given meaning of the "object". Here the narrative inherently tends to juxtapose the past moment of another context onto the lived/ being lived experience, in its attempt to explain or "understand" or de-centre it in coherence with the theoretical construct. The actuality (also the past actuality) is attempted to be fit into the framework of the past *genesis.* The temporal distortion creates the risk to alter the practical, given, intersubjective meaning ground on which the (IR) phenomena and occurrences appear as they are.

The studies on the German *Sonderweg* reflect both facets of the ontological problem when they deliberate on its foreign policy problematic, in line with their differing theoretical *Weltanschauungen.* The "first level" of the experience of the intersubjective phenomena and occurrences, their immediate givenness, is eclipsed except when it is not "assumed" as objectivity (like the structural realist assumption of the state-actor). Also, concentrating the effort on the geneses of the phenomena and injecting them into the post-genetic "time", they risk temporal distortion. They progress teleologically, as the catastrophe of the Third Reich reversely defines the study's course, furthering the narrative of the geneses to the "temporal detriment" of the *praxis.*

---

7   The term is employed in Husserlian "criticism" here, indicating the view of the world constituted with involvement of belief, judgment, emotion and so on, differing from the "things themselves".

Phenomeno-ontology[8] of the IR praxis

Then how the Sonderweg may be studied within the IR praxis?

The *Sonderweg* stems from Germany's differentiation from the "others" on the grounds of "interaction". This interaction appresents as its consistent "subjects" the state-actors, therefore, appears as "interstate interaction". Here, the interaction, instead of being an *a posteriori* "act" separable from the subject's own existence in a way more akin to the Husserlian understanding of the experience of the other through empathy (Husserl 1982), appears as a fundamental element of the state-actor's meaningful givenness, "common" innerworldliness, here quite equivalent in *praxis* (and not in *genesis*) to *Mitsein* in Heideggerian terms (Heidegger 1996, p. 116) that enables and is enabled by *Mitwelt* (Heidegger 1996, pp. 111-112; Heidegger 1985, pp. 238-239). Thus the *Sonderweg* becomes, precedingly, the foreign policy/ IR *praxis* ground *of* Germany which presents uniqueness compared to those of the "others". The phenomeno-ontological study of the *Sonderweg* begins, therefore, by the ontology of "interaction", more clearly of the "subject-in-interaction", through a "phenomenological" approach aiming at dealing with the pre-theoretical, immediate, intersubjective givenness of it and of the environment within and in reference-to which it gains meaning.

Phenomenology's tools are reductions, either universal or eidetic (Husserl 1982, pp. 71-81; Husserl 1983, pp. 57-59, 220-221; Brainard 2002, pp. 68-74). The eidetic reduction to the experience of a particular object in a particular state gives its *"generic way of presenting itself, its Erscheinen"* (Taminiaux 1988, p. 62) while the universal reduction gives *intentio* and *intentum* within the subject's immanence. In our case, however, the reduction becomes one and same, since the state-actor is an intersubjectively constituted *simulacrum* of the true subject.[9] The reduction applied to the state-actor gives the generic way of presenting itself in limited forms/ contents: This is not that of "any" state-actor but of the specific actor as its *own generic way*, such as "Germany", "Japan" or "South Africa", in its basic individuality. Here, the reduction can but be eidetic and applied to a subject-*simulacrum*. Being so, it is also *pseudo-*

---

8   Phenomenological ontology depicts Heidegger's understanding of the phenomenology as the method of ontology, his transfer of the phenomenology from the domain of the consciousness to the field of existence. This is in fact in line with the Husserlian motto of "back to things themselves" and is the aim of this work. This does not mean discarding the Husserlian grounds, due to the intersubjective, co-constituted nature of the IR field where the "co-consciousness of things and events" is forthcoming, which brings us to a synthesis (Schrag 1958).

9   As a personality of higher order in Husserl's Vth Cartesian Meditation.

phenomenological: The residual forms and contents constitute the ground for the state-actor's positions and acts (or positions and acts intersubjectively ascribed to this subject-simulacrum in *praxis*), the "substance" of its *Mitsein*. These forms/contents are relative to others' given positions and acts, within and referring-to the intersubjective environment which should also be reducible to its fundamental contents. These "fundamentals" constitute the aim of the reduction in the study of the IR *praxis* (Heidegger 1985, pp. 238-239; Heidegger 1996, pp. 111-112).[10]

What will then be reduced and how the fundamentals of the state-actor's *Mitsein* will be expressed?

The reduction puts into perspective the theoretical attitude and related *a posteriori* judgments/predications pertaining to the state-actor (Brainard 2002, p54). It brackets not only the theory's *Weltanschauung* —which produces the ulterior narrative- but also its temporal distortion engendered by privileging the genetic moment over the *praxis*. This aims at displaying the fundamental and immediately given contents of the state-actor's *Mitsein*. These are not the elements of the state-actor's "inner composition" but its individual grounds of *Mitsein* within and in reference to the intersubjective environment/ international "system"/ *Mitwelt* as the milieu of the *Mitsein*. They are intersubjectively given "facts" that provide its interactions/ foreign policy acts with a meaning ground and with a horizon of contingencies. They are subject to a phenomenological *description* and not to a causal "explanation" which would repeat the IR theorisation's ontological problem.

The description of the actor's grounds of *Mitsein* needs conceptualisation and terminology. As regards the system and the actor-system relationship, the structural realist (polarity) terminology may be adopted due to its abovementioned "assumptive" nature. In this sense, the terms multipolarity, bipolarity and unipolarity/post-bipolarity for the given intersubjective environment/ *Mitwelt* of the interstate interactions appear valid in their strictly referential/ descriptive use, not involving the ensuing "objectifying" and "explicative" parameters of the theoretical construction. On the other hand, the expression of the state-actor's "generic way of presenting itself" requires *individual* conceptualisation. This replaces the structural realism's generalised "microeconomy mechanics", the constructivism's genesis-imposing social

---

10   Husserl describes the "personalities of higher order", including the state, as constituted through communicative processes, As such, he "regresses" from the immediate, post-genetic givenness to the genetic act.

processes, Husserl's also genetic description of the "personality of higher or-der" and Heidegger's "inauthenticity".

Suspending the theoretical attitude in order to reach to the givenness constitutes the first step of the reduction. Also, all contents of the actor's interaction with the "other", in all forms and appearances, which are further shaped by all predication, judgement, belief and emotion, are reduced toward irreducibility of the "generic way of presenting itself".

Secondly, the residuum is individual, in the sense of being expressible neither in theoretical generality nor as the actor's "inauthenticity" in Heideggerian sense, but as strictly its particular self -as the actor is not *Dasein* but a specific *Dasein-like* constitution-.

Thirdly, the residuum is but of the *Mitsein* to which the interacted others are inherent as their own eidetic content. Therefore, the eidetic reduction "applied to the actor's interaction with others" will not give the interactional content's "generic way of presenting itself" but that of the "other" within the framework of interaction from the perspective of the actor.

Lastly, to express the ground elements and subsequent forms/ contents of the state-actors' interactions in their "lived" temporality, Husserl's notions of retention-protention and anticipation are useful, yet the Heideggerian un-derstanding of temporality needs to be taken into account as well, in elabo-rating these two notions. The retention-protention appears *ultimately* as the subject's own lived actuality in its *Mitsein*. This is in contrast to the Husserlian phenomenology's more experience-centred understanding as in the example of a music piece, where conseqcutive notes are grasped as a meaningful whole in retention-protention (Husserl 1964, pp39-50). In line with the Heideggerian phenomeno-ontology, actuality means not only the retention-protention of specific experiences but more fundamentally, of the "subject"-as-it-experiences-the-thing in *Mitsein*. Heidegger's three temporal *extases* com-posed of having-been (with), dwelling-with and to be-with (Heidegger 1982, pp. 266-267) are directly defined *as Mitsein* as practical and given state of ex-istence. The terms retention-protention and anticipation in our work are still compatible with this, if they are taken as the innerworldy temporality of the actor/subject-who-experiences. The retention-protention in this sense en-compasses and fusions having-been and dwelling-with as the subject's mean-ingful "now". In other words, the retention-protention should *include* the rec-ollection as well, as an integral part of the subject's lived actuality, again con-trasting to Husserl's separative approach.

The anticipation becomes consequently the expression of the *subject's horizon* of contingencies in its *Mitsein*. This contrasts to Heidegger's anticipatory resoluteness due to its "horizontal" nature instead of an almost linear opening to the subject's own –undefined- "authenticity" (Heidegger 1996, pp. 351-352). With these reserves, the employment of the term's retention-protention and anticipation are useful in our study.

The Mittellage-Mitteleuropa as the fundamentals of the German Mitsein

"Germany" in this paper expresses the line Brandenburg-Prussia/ Prussia/ Germany as the temporal and factical appearances of one particular actor. Its "conservation of identity" is displayed by how its transformations were given/ referred-to: As *transformations*, from something into the transformed thing in a continuity, in reduction of the territories and states that were incorporated by it during its expansion, which is factually given as "its expansion" prior to any interrogatory attempt.

Then what does its reduction give as residuum? More clearly, what is given as fundamentally interactional for the German actor's Mitsein?

Mittellage and *Mitteleuropa*, despite their well-known connotations to the German history, are fitting to the description of the residuum. These terms' *vagueness* in the literature, as summarised in Schultz's account (Schultz 1989; also see Meyer 1946), indicates that their meaningful facticity was given *before* being defined, theoretically developed or criticised by geographers, political geographers and political-writers (Sievers 1916; Ratzel 1897; Guthe 1882; Brechtefeld 1996; Riemeck 1983).The exception is the *Mitteleuropa*'s more precise, geopolitical (Haushofer 1935) and "geo-cultural/ethnic" definitions on the Third Reich's line (Geyer 2001; Ditt 2001-the *Kulturraum(forschung-)*.

In any case, these also may be eidetically reduced. As such, the *Mittellage* gives the facticity of being situated *in the midst* of "others" as inherent to the actor's *Mitsein*. It is not a merely "objective" spatial/geographical situation, but the actor's interactional state given in spatial terms. As such, it is precedingly present in forms of and contents pertaining to interaction, in other words, to the foreign policy of the actor.

The *Mitteleuropa*, on the other hand, appresents "outwardliness" from the perspective of the German actor in its spatially expressed interactional environment. The literature's *a posteriori* attempts to define the notion through various parameters depict an environment of *actual* (retentional-protentional) fragmentation but *potential* (anticipatory) homogeneity in relation with the German actor.

In their reduced state, the two notions thus express the two *temporal facets* of the "German" *Mitsein*: The *Mittellage* as "the basic state of interaction" from its genetic moment onwards, is retentional-protentional. The *Mitteleuropa* gives the basic *anticipatory* state of the *Mitsein* that is co-present with the retentional-protentional *Mittellage*.

II- The Multipolar and Bipolar Praxis of the German Sonderweg

The German Mitsein during the Multipolarity

In structural realist terms, the multipolarity had long-time expressed the general shape of the international system characterised by a multiplicity of major powers which permitted flexible alignments and a large horizon of conflicts (Waltz 1979, pp161-163, 165-168). The bracketing of the *a posteriori* explanatory framework of the structural realism does not hinder this "givenness" of and reference-to the multipolar *Mitwelt* in its time. Berlin's foreign policy on its *Mittellage-Mitteleuropa* grounds during the multipolarity displays three basic features.

- 1- The *Mittellage* "imposes" a retentional-protentional *defensive* policy course to *mitigate* the current risks of encirclement. It mainly takes the forms of *non-neutrality* and *frequent* alignment changes:
- The Thirty Years' War period (1618-1648) (Parker 1997, pp.103-106, 148, 150-151; Schoellgen 1992, p.12).
- The First Northern War (1655-1660) (Bély 1992, pp.179-189)
- 1664-1672 period of French-Habsburg confrontations (Prutz 1897, pp. 42-84).
- 1674-1686 period of French-Habsburg confrontations: (Prutz 1897).
- The Great Northern War (1700-1721), from 1714 onward when the alignments' balance changes against Sweden (Schoellgen 1992, p15)
- The revolutionary/ Napoleonic wars: The disastrous participation in the IVth Coalition (1806-1807) to balance France already victorious over the IIIrd Coalition and the alignment change for the VIth Coalition after France's 1812 defeat.
- The Weimar Republic's erosion/ integration policy toward the Versailles regime including the 1922 Rapallo and 1926 Berlin Treaties with the also-isolated USSR; the 1925 Locarno Pact (Krüger 1993, pp.269-300), the participation in the League of Nations in 1926, the Briand-Kellogg Pact in 1928 and the Disarmament Conference (Duroselle 1993, pp.162-168).

- 2- The anticipatory *Mitteleuropa* policies aim at *suppressing* the *Mittellage* offensively, mostly with the aim of reducing one "opponent" at a time:

- The First Northern War: Flexibility between the Swedish and Polish alliances for territorial expansion, resulting with limited gains in the final Treaty of Oliva (Bély 1992, pp.179-189).

- The opportunistic late entry into the Great Northern War: Annexation of parts of the Swedish Pomerania with the 1720 Stockholm Treaty.

- The Austrian Succession War: Annexation of Silesia through the alliance with France and its preservation with two *separate* peace arrangements (1742 and 1745) with the Habsburgs (Anderson 1995, pp.7-11, 59-89, 112-135, 140-148, 210-213).

- -Participation in the 1772, 1793 and 1795 partitions of Poland, profiteering from the Polish-Russian wars (Lukowski 2014, pp. 52-81, 128-158, 159-182).

- Anti-Austrian alignment attempts of the "Potato War" (1777-1779) and the "Fuerstenbund" (1785) (von Ranke 1875, pp.253-288).

- Schleswig's annexation in 1864 through an opportunistic alliance with the Habsburgs (Breuilly 2014).

- The German Union (1866-1871): Escalation with, victory over and expulsion of Austria from Germany in 1866 after securing the French and Russian neutrality. Escalation and war with France, cementing the Prussian leadership leading to the German (Breuilly 2014).

- The pre-war political and territorial "successes" of the Third Reich's *Mitteleuropa* policies (Shirer 1991; Churchill 2002).[11]

- 3- In contrast to their aim, the *Mitteleuropa* policies often *reproduce* and *aggravate* the *Mittellage*:

- The Prussian conduct in the Austrian Succession War motivates the 1755 "Diplomatic Revolution" and the Seven Years' War of 1756-1763 (Bély 1992, pp. 537-560).

- The attempt to replace the German Confederation by the Prussia-led Erfurt Union isolates Prussia and leads to the 1850 Olmuetz Treaty (Bismarck 1991, pp. 83-117).

---

11   The denouncement of the Versailles obligations, the occupation of Rhineland, the naval agreement with the UK, the Anschluss, Munich Conference, and the occupation of Sudetenland, then of the rest of the Czech territory, of Memel and the signature of the Ribbentrop-Molotov Pact.

- The *Mitteleuropa*-policy product German Empire requires increasingly fragile/conflicting alignments to avoid encirclement such as the *Dreikaiserbund* of 1873[12] (Hildebrand 1994, p. 13, 97), the 1879 German-Austrian *Zweibund* of 1879 (Hildebrand 1994, pp. 8-12) and the 1887 *Rueckversicherungsvertrag*[13] (Hildebrand 1994, pp. 19-21).

- -1890-1918 period: The new *Mitteleuropa* policies of "intimidation" backfire: The termination of the *Rueckversicherungsvertrag* (Hildebrand 1994, pp.28-29) results in the Russo-French alliance in 1894 (Kennan 1984); Germany's naval and colonial expansion pushes Britain to the *Entente Cordiale* of 1904[14] and to the Reval settlement in 1907 (Williams 1966); The 1905 and 1911 Morocco crises transform the *Entente Cordiale* into a *de facto* alliance and set the course toward a general war.

- The Third Reich's every pre-war or wartime *Mitteleuropa*-policy "success" enlarges the anti-German coalition, leading to its ultimate defeat.

The German Mitsein during the Bipolarity:

At the end of the Second World War, the international system became reducible to the dialectic of *two* actors with a "qualitative edge over the others" (Waltz 1964). This *referential* change transformed the nature of interactions among the actors. The alignment mobility of the multipolar *Mitwelt* became extremely restricted (Waltz 1979, pp. 168-170), as the "otherness" gained a stable content through the said dialectic that replaced the multipolarity's "contingency horizon" of "others" for all actors including the "non-aligned".[15] In contrast to the multipolar *Mitwelt*, the actor's reference to the bipolar dialectic appresented a particular *Weltanschauung*—as ideological attitude—that further stabilised its foreign policy positions in retention-protention and on the anticipatory horizon.

The *nascent* Federal Republic's horizon in the bipolar *Mitwelt* consisted of three possibilities. 1) A united, neutral and demilitarised Germany as

---

12   Three Emperors' Treaty with Austria and Russia (June 18, 1881) GHDI—Document. (n.d.). GHDI—Document. https://ghdi.ghi-dc.org/sub_document.cfm?document_id =1858.

13   Secret Reinsurance Treaty with Russia (June 18, 1887). GHDI—Document. (n.d.). GHDI—Document https://ghdi.ghi-dc.org/sub_document.cfm?document_id=1862

14   The Entente Cordiale Between England and France—April 8, 1904. Great Britain, Parliamentary Papers London, 1911, Vol. CIII, Cmd. 5969 Formally titled, the 'Declaration between the United Kingdom and France Respecting Egypt and Morocco, together with the Secret Articles Signed at the Same Time.' The Franco-British Declaration, 1904. https://avalon.law.yale.edu/20th_century/entecord.asp.

15   As the "non-alignment" gains meaning on the bipolar dialectic.

foreseen by the 1952 Note (Ruggenthaler 2011) or the denuclearised coexistence of West-East Germany in line with the Rapacki Plan (Albrecht and Vale 1983) 2) A western-anchored Federal Republic. 3) European integration.

The first option was firmly refuted by the Adenauer government, which displayed a political reflex on the grounds of the *Mittellage-and even-Mitteleuropa*. The adopted second course validated Germany's division, the Federal Republic's opting for a "frozen" alliance based on a *Weltanschauung*, facing an equally frozen counter-alliance and another *Weltanschauung* yet mitigating the *Mittellage*. The European integration course was pursued as the complementary part of this fundamental position, differing for example from France, which developed a rather different perspective between the two policy courses.

As to immediate forms and contents of this foreign policy framework: The Federal Republic spared no effort to join NATO and to obtain the western permission to (re)build the *Bundeswehr* (Bradley 1992). With its NATO membership in 1955, the Federal Republic became –in contrast to France– one of the most cooperative members of the Alliance (Larres and Wittlinger 2018).

Bonn *pioneered* the European integration in tandem with its alliance-policies. The integration efforts from the 50s onward stabilised Europe in a way to facilitate the Alliance policies and the Alliance-provided security facilitated the European integration. On this ground, Bonn initiated with Paris the European Coal and Steel Community in 1951-1952,[16] and contributed to the establishment of Western European Union in 1954.[17] The European Economic Community and the Euratom followed in 1957.[18]

As regards precedence between Bonn's Alliance and European policies, the episode of the 1963 Treaty of Elysée[19] is exemplary, since it confronted

---

16   *Traité instituant la Communauté Européenne edu Charbonetd e l'Acier* (April 18, 1951). Available at </https://eur-lex.europa.eu/legal-content/FR/TXT/PDF/?uri=CELEX:11951K/TXT&from=EN/>.

17   *Traité de Bruxelles modifié (Paris, 23 octobre 1954)*. (n.d.). CVCE.EU by UNI.LU. https://www.cvce.eu/obj/traite_de_bruxelles_modifie_paris_23_octobre_1954-fr-7d182408-0ff6-432e-b793-0d1065ebe695.html/>.

18   *Treaty establishing the European Economic Community (Rome, 25 March 1957)*. (n.d.). CVCE.EU by UNI.LU. Available at: </https://www.cvce.eu/en/obj/treaty_establishing_the_european_economic_community_rome_25_march_1957-en-cca6ba28-0bf3-4ce6-8a76-6b0b3252696e.html/>.

19   Council, A. (2013, January 22). *Text of the Elysee Treaty (Joint Declaration of Franco-German Friendship)*. Atlantic Council. https://www.atlanticcouncil.org/blogs/natosource/text-of-the-elysee-treaty-joint-declaration-of-francogerman-friendship/>.

the German bipolar *Mitsein* with the French one, which had been seeking the "independence" of the European structures from the transatlantic Alliance. The Bundestag ratified the Treaty only with the addition of a preamble underlining NATO's role as the venue of the West's collective defence and the indispensability of close cooperation with the US.[20] As such, Bonn preserved its priorities *with and despite* an already centrifugal France.

As to the anticipatory *Mitteleuropa* within the bipolar *Mitwelt*, the Federal Republic pursued, during the initial decades of the bipolar era, a policy of isolating the GDR and of achieving the German union under Bonn, known as the Hallstein Doctrine (Gray 2003). Bonn did not recognise the Oder-Neisse line and did not drop the issue of the Germans expelled from Poland and Sudetenland (see Hughes 2005; Allen 2003). Such contents of the anticipatory *Mitteleuropa* clearly did not offer a horizon of becoming retentional-protentional/actual in the bipolar *Mitwelt*. On the other hand, this form of the *Mitteleuropa*-policy "completed" the German bipolar *Mitsein at the retentional-protentional time.*

The German *Mitsein* also synchronised with the *détente.* As early as the end of the Cuban Crisis, Bonn began to soften the Hallstein Doctrine[21] and quitted it as the *détente* started. With the 1970 Moscow and Warsaw Treaties, Bonn recognised the current national borders in Europe, including the Oder-Neisse Line.[22] With the Basic Treaty of 1972, the two German states recognised each other (Pfetsch 1993, pp. 178-181). With the 1973 Prague Treaty, Bonn dropped ethnic-Germans issues.[23] The "German *détente*" dramatically reflected on the German exports to the Eastern Bloc (Pfetsch 1993, p. 183).

However, Bonn's policy course quite strictly followed the evolution of the central dialectic of the bipolarity on the grounds of the *Mittellage-Mitteleuropa.* When new bipolar tensions arose, in particular with the Soviet occupation in Afghanistan and the anti-regime movements in Poland, Bonn automatically adjusted its attitude accordingly, as in the example of hosting the

---

20   *Preamble to the Élysée Treaty ratification Bill (Bonn, 15 June 1963).* (n.d.). CVCE.EU by UNI.LU. https://www.cvce.eu/en/obj/preamble_to_the_elysee_treaty_ratification_bill_bonn_ 15_june_1963-en-cb4f6630-4187-436a-922b-f14f13a2ea2e.html/>.

21   Conclusion of trade agreements with Poland, Romania, and Hungary in 1963, Bulgaria in 1964, Czechoslovakia in 1967, establishment of diplomatic relations with Yugoslavia in the same year.

22   Die Verträge mit Moskau und Warschau, Presse- und Informationsamt der Bundesregierung, Bonn 1971, pp. 9-32.

23   The Treaty of Prague (11 December 1973). Available at: </https://www.cvce.eu/cont ent/publication/1999/1/1/0714c937-28b6-452a-86d2-ed164f64fcae/publishable_en. pdf/>.

Pershing-IIs without procrastination when the SS-20 missiles were deployed in East Germany (Pfetsch 1993, p. 197).

III- The Post-Bipolar German Mitsein

Early post-bipolarity: The temporal linearity of the Mittellage and the Mitteleuropa

The collapse of the USSR and of its alliance network "ended" bipolarity in the sense of the omnipresence of an intersubjective reference to a central dialectic and certainly not through the material disappearance of the forces' balance (Waltz 1993). This also appeared to be the case for Moscow (Tsygankov 2016, p.86 for his term "liberal westernist euphoria"). Yet, the post-bipolarity did not nullify all aspects of the bipolar *Mitwelt*. The Western structures were preserved and expanded toward the ex-Warsaw Pact members. During the enlargement of NATO and the EU in particular, Russia was held at a controlled distance (Lašas 2010, pp74-77; Simón 2013, p. 195) –as in the examples of the PfP, the NATO-Russia Founding Act and then the NATO-Russia Council-. Some of the main bipolar structures and practices were also preserved, such as the P-5 of the UN Security Council or the West-Russia bilateralism in matters of conventional and nuclear arms' control. Also referring to this "preservation", Russia increasingly claimed a status akin to bipolar counterpart (Light 2009). Moscow invented the "near-abroad" concept as a sort of "outward" sovereignty (Olcott 1995). In other words, the post-bipolarity began rather as an alteration of the bipolarity, with its partial retention. It appeared as reducible to an assertion of validity-if not-superiority of one "pole" over a referentially maintained "other". This retentional-protentional givenness *ipso facto* appresented an anticipatory horizon with the contingency of the dialectic's re-emergence. An important example to this intersubjective "temporalisation" is NATO's retentional-protentional transformation/reform through adoption of new roles and procedures (Webber, Sperling and Smith 2012, pp. 27-28), while preserving the classic/ bipolar collective defence identity toward an anticipatory horizon.

The German reunification occurred as an immediate product of the *passage* into the post-bipolarity. It took the form of the absorption of the East by the Federal Republic at a period when the retentional-protentional invalidation of the bipolarity was acute and Moscow's resistance was but feeble. On the other hand, through the *passage*, the *Mitteleuropa* regained viability, in other words, the perspective of becoming retentional-protentional. Germany's attachment to the Western Alliance and to the EU, otherwise confined to the *Mittellage* during the bipolarity, began to provide the *Mitteleuropa* with a valid horizon. Germany quickly became a pioneer of the NATO and the EU enlargements toward the ex-Warsaw Pact members (Lašas 2010, pp. 69-70; Wood 2020), accompanied by intense bilateral efforts to promote reforms in these countries. During the transitory period of the first half of the 90s, Germany led the EU efforts and occupied the first place in bilateral support for structural transformation[24] (Lemasson 1997, pp. 84-85). Germany immediately became the most important trade partner and FDIs source of the Central-Eastern European countries (Carroué 1992; Lemasson 1997, p.89). It is of note that the investments in the region became *"complementary to German production, investments and employment* (Tueselmann 1998).

Germany's good neighbourhood/ cooperation agreements concluded in 1991 and 1992 with each country of the region were of particular importance as the process committed Berlin to promote their—then still non-existent—EU membership processes (Lašas 2010, p106). Regardless the reluctance of many EU members on the matter of enlargement, the German-led enthusiasm had the US's "outsider" support as it coincided with its post-bipolar policy of securing the ex-Warsaw Pact countries within the framework of the NATO enlargement. It also coincided with these countries' desire for security within NATO and the EU (Lašas 2010, pp. 104-105). They therefore entered into a symbiotic relationship with Germany. As such, the post-bipolar Mitwelt favoured not only the Mittellage facet of the German foreign policy but also the Mitteleuropa as it coincided with the anticipatory horizon of the Western Alliance and that of the ex-USSR countries of Europe in general.

Germany generally avoided any appearance of unilateralism in this period, continuously seeking consensus among the EU and NATO partners (Crawford and Olsen 2017). In doing so, she stressed the normative corpus of democracy, human rights and fundamental freedoms (Wolff 2013) on one hand and her attachment to her alignments on the other. Yet two exceptions occurred: At the start of Yugoslavia's disintegration, Berlin *unilaterally* recognised the Slovenian and Croatian independences, creating a *fait accompli* (Crawford 1996). Secondly, in contrast to her taking action during the Kosovo crisis and the Afghanistan operation, she stayed outside of the Second

---

24   Transform- das Beratungsprogramm der Bundesregierung für Osteuropa: die Beratung Mittel- und Osteuropas beim Aufbau von Demokratie und sozialer Marktwirtschaft, Konzept und Beratungsprogramme der Bundesregierung, Fortschreibung 1997.

Iraqi War and of the Libya intervention (Miskimmon 2012; Dettke 2009): Berlin appeared to be capable of taking *unilateral* action or moving with her allies "as needed". In other words, Berlin's post-bipolar *Mitsein* on the meaning ground of the *Mittellage-Mitteleuropa* had ontological precedence over its "values" or *to a reasonable degree*, alignments. It is of note that the "avoided" *politically controversial* (objected-to by Moscow) Second Iraqi War and the Libya intervention had no relationship with the *Mittellage-Mitteleuropa* policy ground, while the participated-in Afghanistan operation at least "proved" Germany's alignment loyalty on a *non-controversial* (not objected by Moscow) issue which also did not contradict the German "normativist and multilateralist tradition" (Maull 2011; Crawford and Olsen 2017).

The post-bipolar symbiosis between the Mittellage-Mitteleuropa and the alignment loyalty (with the abovementioned exceptions) also facilitated Berlin's building a special relationship with Russia without substantial hindrance (Forsberg 2016), since Germany became "less visible" among its allies during the NATO/EU enlargements and the "unipolar/unilateral interventions". For example, Germany's military participation in the Kosovo intervention was eclipsed by NATO institutionally and by the US individually, which bore the burden of confrontation with Russia (Norris 2005).

Later post-bipolarity: The evolving environment of the German Mitsein

Displayed by the Western Alliance's enlargement and intervention policies as well as Russia's increasingly vocal objections, expectations of the equal counterpart status and recovery attempts in the near-abroad, the *anticipatory* facet of the early post-bipolar *Mitwelt* began to gain retentional-protentional properties. This may most likely be placed at Putin's famous speech at the 2007 Munich Security Summit.[25] The Russian President's strong warning about the NATO enlargement had the tone of a bipolar-counterpart's threat of retaliation. It found echo during the 2008 NATO Bucharest Summit as Germany and France blocked the grant of MAPs to Ukraine and Georgia (Arbuthnot 2008). In the same year, Russia confronted and heavily defeated Georgia as the latter intervened in the Russian-backed South Ossetia (Desseyn and Tchantouridze 2012). The "West" protested but did not sanction Russia. Moreover, the "unipole" initiated the "Reset" the following year, which, at least from Moscow's perspective, reinforced the Russian claims of "equal"

---

25   Speech of the Vladimir Putin and the Following Discussion at the Munich Conference on Security Policy. Available at:</http://www.en.kremlin.ru/events/president/transcripts/ 24034.

status and the Russian "rights" in its near-abroad (Hahn 2013). Even the Reset's collapse presented a "bipolar" character much akin to the end of the *détente*, following the Arab Spring movements in 2010 and NATO's intervention in Libya in 2011 (Perra 2016; O'Sullivan 2018) as the "West" acted in negligence of the Russian claim to bipolar-like counterpart status.

In sharp contrast to the Orange Revolution times (Mitchell 2012), the "post-Munich" Russia intervened in Ukraine in 2014 as the pro-Russian government was overthrown (Kalb 2015). Crimea was annexed, Lugansk and Donetsk seceded and the "West" sanctioned Russia, furthering the new temporalisation of the West-Russia relations in the post-bipolar *Mitwelt*.

The once-anticipatory bipolar-like setting's re-emergence had a visible impact on the German foreign policy meaning ground. The *Mittellage* and *Mitteleuropa* policies of the post-bipolar era were arguably "achieved" (Crawford 2007, pp. 20-55) when the 2007 Munich Security Conference was held. The exceptions, at different degrees for each, had been those countries under Russia's direct (such as Belarus and in part the pre-2014 Ukraine) or indirect (through the separatist entities in Moldova and Georgia) influence. The NATO-EU enlargement and the normative expansion had annulled Berlin's chronic security concerns stemming from the *Mittellage*. This reduction was furthered by Germany's special relationship with Russia (Zverev 2012). The East European countries' symbiosis with Germany further reinforced Berlin's position in the EU policy making. In a way, the *Mitteleuropa* policy horizon was completed, the anticipatory contents of its *Mitsein* had become retentional-protentional, therefore the *Mitteleuropa* and the *Mittellage* had merged temporally.

The *novel* temporal linearity of the German *Mitsein* depended on the retentional-protentional invalidation of the bipolar-dialectic and its *contingent* re-emergence of it on the anticipatory horizon. Thus the "turning point" of 2007 and the subsequent events contradicted with this temporal linearity.

Germany's reaction to this re-temporalisation seems to have taken the form of appeasement initially, in blocking (postponing) the MAPs for Ukraine and Georgia. Germany then emphasised the "Eastern Neighbourhood" which would hold these countries at arm's length and not "provocate" Russia (Fix 2021, p. 69, 88). This attitude continued with the Georgian events, when Germany avoided reactions that would risk her special relationship with Russia (Fix 2021, pp.63-65). Instead, Berlin unilaterally initiated and actively led the EU to her own "Reset" with Moscow: "The EU-Russia Partnership for Modernisation" (Fix 2021, pp.67-90) from 2009 onward adopted the discourse of reforming Russia "in the long run". Furthermore, the "Meseberg

Initiative" aimed at responding to Russia's call to establish a "new European Security Treaty", through a "Political and Security Committee" between Russia and the EU, but it failed in resolving the Transnistria issue (Fix 2021, pp. 91-97).

Berlin tried to maintain a balance between its alignments and its Russia-policy in the non- "systemic" issues of the Arab Spring and the Libya intervention, with a rather passive attitude. When the 2014 Ukrainian crisis erupted, Germany went along with the EU sanctions regime with a legalistic/normative discourse yet played an important role in preventing them to reach to unaffordable levels for Russia (Fix 2021, pp. 133-145; Wood 2020). Moreover, she took initiatives like the Nord Stream II, limiting the damage to the Berlin-Moscow relations (Forsberg 2016).

After 2014, the German position regarding Russia had been dissociating from some of the East European actors, in particular Poland and the Baltic States which had increasingly been adopting anti-Russian positions (see Yoder 2018). German "balancing" seems to have been decreasing its political credibility in its *Mitteleuropa* area". The German "reluctance" on the matter of stationing of NATO forces in East European countries *despite* their insistence or the initial German obstructions to the "lethal" arms aid to Ukraine further aggravated this process (Fix 2021, pp. 146-148). gradually deteriorating the German *Mitsein*'s achieved temporal "linearity".

The ongoing Russian invasion of Ukraine constitutes perhaps the most important event in the process of the post-bipolarity's re-temporalisation. At the start of the war, face to Russian onslaught, Kiev seemed to be ready to accept constitutional neutrality and make territorial concessions through plebiscites in Crimea, Donetsk, and Lugansk.[26] When the Russians had to evacuate the Kiev front, this attitude began to change and with the success of the counteroffensives at the Kharkov and Kherson fronts, disappeared. Russia, on the other hand, engaged herself more and more in the war, through

---

26   Please refer to: **1.** Ukraine has offered neutrality in talks with Russia—what would that mean? Available at: </https://www.theguardian.com/world/2022/mar/30/ukraine-of-fer-neutrality-meaning-constitution-russia-what-does-neutral-status-country-mean-how-would-it-work; **2.** "Ukraine War: Zelenskyy Says Ukraine Is Willing to Consider Declaring Neutrality and Offer Security Guarantees to Russia." **3.** Ukraine and Russia explore neutrality plan in peace talks | Financial Times. "Ukraine and Russia Explore Neutrality Plan in Peace Talks," March 16, 2022. https://www.ft.com/content/7b341e46-d375-4817-be67-802b7fa77ef1. **4.** McDade, Aaron. "Russia Claims Dispute Over Crimea, Donbas Has Been 'Settled' With Ukraine." Newsweek, March 30, 2022. https://www.newsweek.com/russia-claims-dispute-over-crimea-donbas-settled-ukraine-1693474. **5.** Saul, "Russia-Ukraine Talks: Ukraine Hints at Progress on Crimea, While Both Sides Optimistic on Putin-Zelensky Meeting."

the partial mobilisation[27] and the annexation of the Ukrainian regions partially or totally under occupation.[28]

The immediate consequence of the invasion has been the imposition of *now-crippling* "Western" sanctions on Russia, unlike those of 2014. The EU and consequently Germany have a central role in maintaining the sanctions.[29] This has been accompanied by providing military and financial aid to Ukraine to sustain the war. Therefore, unlike the previous "re-temporalisation crises", the Western coherence appeared to be quite solid, with the prospects of Ukrainian success. For Germany, the erosion of the "achieved" temporal linearity of *Mittellage-Mitteleuropa*, which had been mitigated between 2007 and 2022, has become unavoidable with the war in Ukraine. The war seems to have made the German alignments and the Germany's Russia-policy *dialectical* at the retentional-protentional time. This situation was further amplified by the increased criticism of the German reluctance in helping Ukraine,[30] in particular from the East European/ *"Mitteleuropean"* NATO/EU members. In consequence, Germany finds herself dragged into a more forthcoming

---

27   Ellyatt, Holly. "Putin Mobilizes 300,000 Troops for War in Ukraine and Warns He's Not Bluffing with Nuclear Threat." CNBC, September 21, 2022. https://www.cnbc.com/2022/09/21/russia-ukraine-war-putin-announces-partial-military-mobilization.html.

28   Please refer to: **1.** BBC News. "Russia to Formally Annex Four More Areas of Ukraine," n.d. https://www.bbc.com/news/world-europe-63072113. **2.** dw.com. "Russia Annexes Four Ukrainian Regions—DW—09/30/2022," n.d. https://www.dw.com/en/russia-putin-announces-illegal-annexation-of-four-ukrainian-regions/a-63292049. **3.** Reuters. "Putin to Annex Seized Ukrainian Land, U.N. Warns of 'Dangerous Escalation.'" Reuters, September 29, 2022. https://www.reuters.com/world/europe/russia-set-annex-ukraine-territory-west-warns-new-sanctions-2022-09-29.

29   Please refer to: **1.** "Implementation of the Sanctions on Russia—Overview—Federal Ministry of Finance—Issues." Bundesministerium der Finanzen, March 18, 2022. https://www.bundesfinanzministerium.de/Content/EN/Standardartikel/Topics/Europe/War-in-Ukraine/implementation-of-the-sanctions-on-russia.html. **2.** Website of the Federal Government | Bundesregierung. "EU Agrees on Sanctions against Russia | Federal Government," July 26, 2022. https://www.bundesregierung.de/breg-en/news/eu-sanctions-2008438.

30   Please refer to: **1.** Germany's Chancellor Has 'a Lot' for Ukraine. But No Battle Tanks. https://www.nytimes.com/2022/09/25/world/europe/olaf-scholz-germany-ukraine-war.html; **2.** dw.com. "Kyiv Decries Berlin's 'disappointing Signals' on Weapons—DW—09/13/2022," n.d. https://www.dw.com/en/russia-ukraine-updates-kyiv-decries-germanys-disappointing-signals-on-weapons/a-63101592. **3.** BBC News. "Ukraine War: Germany's Conundrum over Its Ties with Russia," n.d. https://www.bbc.com/news/world-europe-61118706. **4.** Foreign Affairs. "Germany's Ukraine Problem," August 10, 2022. https://www.foreignaffairs.com/germany/germanys-ukraine-problem. **5.** Judy Dempsey, German Ambiguity Is Deciding Ukraine's Future. https://carnegieeurope.eu/strategiceurope/87215. **6.** Ellyatt, Holly. "Germany Promised Ukraine Weapons but Hasn't Delivered. Now, Anger toward Berlin Is Rising." CNBC, September 16, 2022. https://www.cnbc.com/2022/09/16/ukraine-slams-germany-for-failing-to-send-it-weapons.html. **7.** Hoyer, Katja. "Germany Is Failing Ukraine." The Spectator, May 30, 2022. https://www.spectator.co.uk/article/germany-is-failing-ukraine/.

position in sanctioning Russia and materially helping Ukraine, therefore attracting Russian countermoves as in the example of the energy embargo.[31] Yet the war has been prolonged and current dynamics may evolve further.

A Russian victory over Ukraine with the replacement of the Kiev regime with a pro-Russian one is susceptible to engender a bipolar-like systemic rigidity not only from the perspective of the western alignment structures but also by making a "successful" Russia an "antithetic" political/normative centre of gravity.[32] Such a return to a bipolar-like environment would once again make the *Mitteleuropa* a component of the retentional-protentional *Mittellage*.

A Russian defeat is susceptible to return Moscow to the wake of the USSR's disintegration. In this case, another anticipatory horizon of *Mitteleuropa* could appear and detach it from its linearity with the *Mittellage*.

On the other hand, a "separate peace" with Ukrainian concessions of territorial or constitutional nature (neutrality) would probably suppress the ground of the Western sanctions and synchronously validate the "Russian near-abroad", making the *Russian* post-bipolar anticipatory horizon retentional-protentional, at least in part. Yet, this is likely to preserve the temporal linearity of the *Mittellage-Mitteleuropa*, providing Germany with ground for evasion/mitigation policies akin to the 2007-2022 period. Judging from the German policies of the said period, such a "peaceful settlement of the Ukrainian crisis through diplomacy", if it appears, could logically have Berlin's support and facilitation regardless of its consequences on the international system of which Germany is a part.

Conclusion

The term *Sonderweg* was employed to express Berlin's *fundamental* differentiation from "Others". The *Sonderweg* debate was later centred on the causal/

---

31   Please refer to: **1.** Gas flows to Europe won't resume until sanctions lifted: Russia | Russia-Ukraine war News | Al Jazeera. "Gas Flows to Europe Won't Resume until Sanctions Lifted: Russia," September 5, 20225. https://www.aljazeera.com/news/2022/9/5/russian-gas-flows-halted-until-europe-lift-sanctions. **2.** BBC News. "Nord Stream 1: Russia Shuts Major Gas Pipeline to Europe," n.d. https://www.bbc.com/news/world-europe-62732835. **3.** Meredith, Sam. "Russia Has Cut off Gas Supplies to Europe Indefinitely. Here's What You Need to Know." CNBC, September 6, 2022. https://www.cnbc.com/2022/09/06/energy-crisis-why-has-russia-cut-off-gas-supplies-to-europe.html. **4.** Russia switches off Europe's main gas pipeline until sanctions are lifted financial times https://www.ft.com/content/2624cc0f-57b9-4142-8bc1-4141833a73dd. **5.** Reuters. "Putin Says Russia to Stop Supplying Energy If Western Price Caps Imposed." Reuters, September 7, 2022. https://www.reuters.com/business/energy/putin-blames-germany-west-nord-stream-1-shutdown-2022-09-07/.

32   Or a valid co-center of gravity with Beijing, on the ground of the fast-developing strategic cooperation between the two actors.

historical roots of the Third Reich. Being reducible to "differentiation from", it might, however, have evolved more in line with its own meaning ground, which is "interaction"/ interstate interaction, appresents foreign policy. Such a debate to be conducted on phenomenological/ existential grounds has the potential of contributing to the study of the German foreign policy beyond a relatively narrow time period delimited by a specific *regime* or a series of events but in continuity, defining the irreducible elements of the actor's interactions.

In this vein, the *Mittellage* and the *Mitteleuropa* appear not only as mere concepts of a period of the German actor's foreign policy but the meaning grounds which engender forms and acts of it in relation with different intersubjective environments/ international systems. They have a *temporal* character specific to the German actor, the former being valid in actual/ retentional-protentional time and the latter defining the anticipatory horizon of the interaction. Their relationship varies in differing phases of multipolarity, bipolarity and post-bipolarity, sometimes having separate validities, sometimes one being secondary to the other in detriment to its own validity and sometimes merging into one temporal linearity. On these grounds, the ongoing war in Ukraine is susceptible to create a new, yet long postponed turning point for the German actor, within the general process of transformation of the post-bipolar interstate intersubjectivity.

Bibliography

Albrecht, Ulrich and Vale, Michel 1983. "The Political Background of the Rapacki Plan of 1957 and Its Current Significance". *International Journal of Politics*, 13(1/2): 117-133.

Allen, W.F. 1982. "Hannah Arendt: Existential Phenomenology and Political Freedom". *Philosophy&Social Criticism* 9(2): 170–190.

Allen, Debra J. 2003. *The Oder-Neisse Line: The United States, Poland, and Germany in the Cold War*. Westport: Praeger.

Anderson, Matthew Smith 1995. *The War of the Austrian Succession 1740-1748*. London: Longman Publishing Group.

Arbuthnot, James 2008. "The Bucharest Summit and the Future of NATO". *The RUSI Journal*, 158(3): 40-44.

Ashley, R.K. 1984. "The Poverty of Neorealism". *International Organization*, 38(2): 225-286.

Bartelson, Jens 1995. *A Genealogy of Sovereignty*. Cambridge University Press.

Bély, Lucien 1992. *Les relations internationales en Europe: XVII-XVIIIeme siécles*. Paris: PUF.

von Bismarck, Otto 1991. *Düşünceler ve Hatıralar* (Gedanken und Erinnerungen). ME Basımevi Cilt I.

Blackbourn, David and Eley, Geoff 1984. *The Peculiarities of German History: Bourgeois Society and Politics in Nineteenth-Century Germany.* Oxford: Oxford University Press.

Blackbourn, David 1998. *The Long Nineteenth Century: A History of Germany,1780-1918.* Oxford: Oxford University Press.

Bradley, Dermot 1992. "The Bundeswehr and German Reunification, 1955-91". *Irish Studies in International Affairs* 3(4): 53-66.

Brainard, Marcus 2002. *Belief and its Neutralization: Husserl's System of Phenomenology in Ideas-I.* Albany: SUNY.

Brechtefeld, Joerg 1996. *Mitteleuropa and German Politics: 1848 to the Present.* NY: St Martin's Press.

Breuilly, John 2014. *Austria, Prussia and The Making of Germany: 1806-1871.* Oxon: Routledge.

Carroué, Laurent 1992. «L'Allemagne en première ligne pour la conquête des économies de l'Est», *Le Monde diplomatique,* Janvier 1992: 12-13.

Churchill, Winston 2002. *The Gathering Storm.* NY: Rosetta Books.

Crawford, Beverly and Olsen, Kim B. 2017. "The Puzzle of Persistence and Power: Explaining Germany's Normative Foreign Policy". *German Politics*, 26(4): 591-608.

Crawford, Beverly 1996. "Explaining Defection from International Cooperation: Germany's Unilateral Recognition of Croatia". *World Politics*, 48(4): 482–521.

Desseyn, Ryan; Tchantouridze, Lasha 2012. "Realpolitik and the Russia-Georgia War: Three Years On", *Central Asia and Caucasus*, 131: 111-119.

Dettke, Dieter 2009. *Germany Says No: The Iraq War and the Future of German Foreign and Security Policy.* Washington DC: Woodrow Wilson Centre Press

Ditt, Karl 2001. "The Idea of German Cultural Regions in the Third Reich: The Work of Franz Petri". *Journal of Historical Geography*, 27(2): 241-258.

Dodds, Klaus J. 2005. *Global Geopolitics: A Critical Introduction.* Doechester : Pearson Prentice Hall.

Duroselle, J.Baptiste 1993. *Histoire diplomatique de 1919 à nos jours.* Paris: Dalloz

Eley, Geoff 1988. "Nazism, Politics and the Image of the Past: Thoughts on the West German Historikerstreit 1986-1987". *Past & Present*, 121:171-208.

Faulenbach, Bernd 1980. *Die Ideologie des deutschen Weges: Die deutsche Geschichte in der Historiographie zwischen Kaiserreich und Nationalsozialismus*. Muenchen 1980.

Faulenbach, Bernd 1994. "Deutsche Sonderwege: Anmerkungen zur aktuellen Diskussion über das deutsche historisch-politische Selbstverständnis". *Comparativ*, Heft(1):14-30.

Fischer, Fritz 1986. *From Kaiserreich to Third Reich: Elements of Continuity in German History, 1871-1945*. London-NY: Routledge.

Fischer, Marcus 2019. "On the Ontology of the Structural Realism". *Open Journal of Political Science* 9(1).

Fix, Liana 2021. *Germany's Role in European Russia Policy*. Cham: Palgrave Macmillan.

Forsberg, Tuomas 2016. "From Ostpolitik to 'Frostpolitik'? Merkel, Putin and German Foreign Policy towards Russia". *International Affairs* 92(1): 21-42.

Geyer, Dietrich 2001. "Ostforschung im Dritten Reich". *Osteuropa*, 51(6): 733-739.

Gray, William Glenn 2003. *Germany's Cold War: The Global Campaign to Isolate East Germany 1949-1969*. The University of North Carolina Press.

Guthe, Hermann 1882. *Lehrbuch der Geographie*. Hannover: Hahn.

Hahn, G.M. 2013. "Russia in 2012: From Thaw and Reset to Freeze". *Asian Survey*, 53(1): 214-223.

Haushofer, Karl 1935. *Weltpolitik von Heute*. Berlin: Zeitgeschichte Verlag und Vertriebs Gesselschaft.

Heidegger, Martin 1996. *Being and Time*. Albany: SUNY.

Heidegger, Martin 1985. *History of the Concept of Time: Prolegomena*. Bloomington: Indiana University Press.

Heidegger, Martin 1982. *The Basic Problems of Phenomenology*. Bloomington: Indiana University Press.

Hildebrand, Klaus 1994. *Deutsche Aussenpolitik 1871-1918*. München: Oldenbourg Verlag.

Hughes, Gerald 2005. "Unfinished Business from Potsdam: Britain, West Germany and the Oder-Neisse Line: 1945–1962". *The International History Review*, 27(2): 259-294.

Husserl, Edmund 1982. *Cartesian Meditations*. The Hague:Martinus Nijhoff

Husserl, Edmund 1970. *The Crisis of European Sciences and Transcendental Phenomenology*. Northwestern University Press.

Husserl, Edmund 1983. *Ideas Pertaining to a Pure Phenomenology and to a Phenomenological Philosophy*. The Hague: Martinus Nijhoff.

Husserl, Edmund 1964. *Leçons pour une phénoménologie de la conscience intime du temps*. Paris: PUF.

Kalb, Marvin 2015. *Imperial Gamble: Putin, Ukraine and the New Cold War*. Brookings Institution Press.

Katzenstein, Peter J. 1996. *The Culture of National Security: Norms and Identity in World Politics*. New York: Columbia University Press.

Kennan, George F. 1984. *The Fateful Alliance: France, Russia and the Coming of the First World. War*. New York: Pantheon Books.

Kocka, Juergen 1999. "Asymmetrical Historical Comparison: The Case of the German Sonderweg". *History and Theory*, 38(1):40-50.

Kocka, Juergen 2018. "Looking Back on the Sonderweg". *Central European History*, 51:137-142.

Krüger, Peter 1993. *Die Aussenpolitik der Republik von Weimar*. Darmstadt: Wissenschaftliche Buchgesselschaft.

Larres, Klaus and Wittlinger, Ruth 2018. "A Fragile Friendship: German-American Relations in the Twenty-First Century". *German Politics*, 27(2): 152-157.

Lacoste, Yves 1976. *La géographie, ça sert d'abord à faire la guerre*. Paris: Maspéro

Lašas, Ainius 2010. *European Union and NATO Expansion*. NY: Palgrave Macmillan.

Lemasson, Sylvie 1997. "La Mitteleuropa". In François Bafoil, ed., *Les strategies allemandes en Europe centrale et orientale: Une géopolitique des investissements directs*. Paris: L'Harmattan.

Light, Margot 2009. "Russia and Europe and the Process of EU Enlargement". In Elana Wilson-Rowe and Stina Torjesen, eds., *The Multilateral Dimension in Russian Foreign Policy*, pp83-96. Oxon: Routledge.

Lukowski, Jerzy 2014. *The Partitions of Poland 1772, 1793, 1795*. Oxon: Routledge

Maull, Hanns W. 2011. "Deutsche Außenpolitik: Orientierungslos". *Zeitschrift für Politikwissenschaft*, 21(1): 93-117.

Meyer, Henry C. 1946. "Mitteleuropa in German Political Geography". *Annals of the Association of American Geographers*, 36(3): 178-194.

Miskimmon, Alister 2012. "German Foreign Policy and the Libya Crisis". *German Politics*, 21(4): 392-410.

Mitchell, Lincoln 2012. *The Color Revolutions*. Philadelphia: University of Pennsylvania Press.

Mommsen, Wolfgang 2004. *Max Weber und die Deutsche Politik:1890-1920*. Tuebingen: Mohr Siebeck.

Mosse, George 1981. *The Crisis of German Ideology: Intellectual Origins of the Third Reich*. NY: Schocken Books.

Norris, John 2005. *Collision Course:NATO, Russia, and Kosovo*. Westport: Praeger

Olcott, Martha B. 1995. "Sovereignty and the Near-Abroad". *Orbis*, 39(3): 353-367.

Onuf, Nicholas G. 1989. *World of Our Making*. Columbia: University of SC Press

Onuf, Nicholas G. 2013. *Making Sense,Making Worlds*. NY: Routledge.

O'Sullivan, Susannah 2018. *Military Intervention in the Middle East and North Africa: The Case of NATO in Libya*. Oxon: Routledge.

Parker, Geoffrey 1997. *The Thirty Years' War*. Oxon: Routledge.

Perra, Antonio 2016. "From the Arab Spring to the Damascus Winter: The United States, Russia and the New Cold War". *Contemporary Review of the Middle East*, 3(4): 1-24.

Pfetsch, Frank 1993. *Die Aussenpolitik der Bundesrepublik 1949-1992*. München: W.Fink.

Plessner, H. 1959. *Die verspaetete Nation*. Stuttgart: W.Kohlhammer Verlag

Prutz, Hans 1897. *Aus des Grossen Kurfuersten letzten Jahren: Zur Geschichte seines Hauses und Hofes*. Berlin: Reimer.

von Ranke, Leopold 1875. *Die Deutsche Geschichte und der Fuerstenbund*. Leipzig:Dunker und Humblot.

Ratzel, Friedrich 1897. *Politische Geographie*. Muenchen: R.Oldenburg Verlag

Riemeck, Renate 1983. *Mitteleuropa: Bilanz eines Jahrhunderts*. Frankfurt: Fischer Taschenbuch Verlag.

Ripsman, Norrin M.; Taliaferro, Jeffrey W. and Lobell, Steven E. 2016. "Neoclassical Realist Theory and the Limits of Structural Realism" in *Neoclassical Realist Theory of International Politics*. NY: Oxford University Press.

Ruggenthaler, Peter 2011. "The 1952 Stalin Note on German Unification: The Ongoing Debate". *Journal of Cold War Studies*, 13(4): 172-212.

Schöllgen, Gregor 1992. *Die Macht in der Mitte Europas*. München:Verlag C.H.Beck.

Schrag, Calvin 1958. "Phenomenology, Ontology, and History in the Philosophy of Heidegger". *Revue Internationale de Philosophie*, 12 44 (2): 117-132.

Schultz, Hans-Dietrich 1989. "Fantasies of Mitte: Mittellage and Mitteleuropa in German geographical discussion in the 19th and 20th centuries". *Political Geography Quarterly* 8(4).

Shirer, William 1991. *The Rise and Fall of the Third Reich*. London: Arrow Books

Sievers, Wilhelm 1916. *Die geographischen Grenzen Mitteleuropas.* Giessen: Otto Kindt.

Simón, Luis 2013. *Geopolitical Change, Grand Strategy and European Security.* Basingstoke: Palgrave Macmillan.

Taminiaux, Jacques 1988. "Immanence, Transcendence, and Being in Husserl's Idea of Phenomenology", ed. Sallis J.C., Moneta G., Taminiaux J., *The Collegium Phaenomenologicum: The First Ten Years,* p. 62. Dordrecht: Kluwer Academic Publishers.

Tsygankov, Andrei P. 2016. *Russia's Foreign Policy Change and Continuity in National Identity.* Rowman & Littlefield.

Tueselmann, Heinz-Josef 1998. «Standort Deutschland: German Direct Foreign Investment-Exodus of German Industry and Export of Jobs?". *Journal of World Business,* 33(3): 295-313.

Waltz, Kenneth 1996. "International Politics is not Foreign Policy". *Security Studies,* 6(1):54-57.

Waltz, Kenneth 1979. *Theory of International Politics.* Addison-Wesley Publishing

Waltz, Kenneth 1964. "The Stability of a Bipolar World". *Daedalus* 93(3): 881-909.

Waltz, Kenneth 1993. "The Emerging Structure of International Politics". *International Security,* 18(2): 44-79.

Webber, Mark; Sperling, James; Smith, Martin 2012. *NATO's Post-Cold War Trajectory: Decline or Regeneration?.* Basingstoke: Palgrave Macmillan.

Wehler, Hans-Ulrich 1985. *The German Empire 1871-1918.* Oxford-NY: Berg

Wendt, Alexander 1999. *Social Theory of International Politics.* Cambridge University Press.

Williams, Beryl J. 1966. "The Strategic Background to the Anglo-Russian Entente of August 1907". *The Historical Journal* 9(3): 360-373.

Wolff, Jonas 2013. "Democracy Promotion and Civilian Power: The Example of Germany's 'Value-Oriented' Foreign Policy". *German Politics,* 22(4): 477-493.

Wood, Steve 2020. *Germany and East-Central Europe: Political, Economic and Socio-Cultural Relations in the Era of EU Enlargement.* Oxon: Routledge.

Wood, Steve 2020. "Understanding for Russia in Germany: International triangle meets domestic politics". *Cambridge Review of International Affairs,* DOI:10.1080/09557571.2019.1703647.

Yoder, Jennifer 2018. "Good Neighbourliness in a Tense Neighbourhood: German-Polish Relations, 1990 to the Ukraine Crisis". *German Politics,* DOI:10.1080/09644008.2018.1429409.

Zverev, A. 2012. "Economic Cooperation Between Russia and Germany". *Problems of Economic Transition* 55(1): 51-62.

ABOUT THE AUTHOR

YUNUS EMRE ÖZIGCI holds a PhD degree in Political Sciences from the Université catholique de Louvain. He graduated from the Galatasaray University (International relations) and completed his MA studies at the University of Ankara (International relations). His research interests and publications cover the IR theory and phenomenology. Since 2000, he has been working as a diplomat in the Turkish Ministry of Foreign Affairs and served, besides various departments of the Ministry, in Algeria, Belgium, Switzerland and Russia. Currently, he is the First Counsellor of the Turkish Embassy in Nairobi and Deputy Permanent Representative to UNON (UNEP and UN-Habitat).

Note: This article is personal work. It does not reflect the official views of the Turkish Ministry of Foreign Affairs where the author works.

ORCID: 0000-0003-3388-7149
Tel: +254 0110020521
Email: emremisik@icloud.com

Begüm Burak & Piotr Pietrzak

Interview with Dr. Begüm Burak

Piotr Pietrzak (PP) *Dear readers of In Statu Nascendi. Today it is my great pleasure and privilege to interview with Dr. Begüm Burak a Turkish independent researcher who defended her Ph.D. thesis in 2015. she collaborated with various universities in Italy, the United Kingdom, Bosnia and Herzegovina, and Spain. Dr. Burak is interested in modern history, Turkish studies, discourse analysis, media, and politics, democratization, matters related to religion and politics, secularism, democratic theory, , matters related to military coups particularly the ones in Turkey, as well as political culture in Turkey How do you do, Dr. Burak?*

Begüm Burak (BB) I'm fine thank you very much. it's a real pleasure to be here.

(PP) Thank you very much for accepting our invitation. My first question is related to your Ph.D. dissertation which you defended in 2015, that was subsequently recently published as a book in 2022. Could you tell us a bit more about your thesis and what kind of a change took place since that time in Turkey? Could you tell me if the thesis in your study is still relevant in your country?

(BB) First of all I want to thank you very much, Dr. Pietrzak, for your kind invitation it's an honor to be here in your channel and thank you for giving me the opportunity to talk about my studies. Yes I defended my PhD almost 8 years ago and it was published as a book: *The Image of the Undesired Citizens in Turkey: A Comparative Critical Discourse Analysis of the Hürriyet and Zaman Newspapers* (2022) by Generis Publishing House. And yes lots of things have changed as you mentioned in Turkey since that time after my graduation. A failed military attempt took place in Turkey in 2016 and unfortunately, some the uiniversity where I made my PhD was one of these institutions which got closed down after the failed military coup attempt but luckily I had defended my thesis earlier and I had the Ph.D. degree officially and I became a doctor and I had the chance to publish my thesis as a book.

I focused on the main concept of undesired citizenship in my thesis—this concept has been addressed by many scholars while talking about the inequality discussions in Turkey and what kind of citizens faced discrimination in Turkey. This is a really dynamic issue to discuss because things have changed in Turkey ever since I completed my thesis.

In this research, I classified four different types of undesired citizenship, the first one is the Kurdish citizens, the second is the Muslim/pious citizens the other is the Alvi people and the other group was the non-Muslims but this can be classified as the undesired citizenship in Kemalist republican rhetoric. As you know, the regime was promoted in the early Republican period so when Turkey was founded as a secular Republic, the identity of Turkey was supposed to be Sunni, Muslim, Turkish &secular, so the practicing Muslims and non-muslims like the Armenians and also Alavi people who don't adopt Suni Islam, all these groups were seen as the "others". But as you said many things have changed since 2002 ever since the AKP regime has started ruling Turkey.So the practicing Muslims are no longer undesired people, wearing scarf can be seen in the public offices. The non-muslims are still seen as undesired citizens so yes I agree the things have changed. In this publication I tried to analyze the major media discourses (Hürriyet and Zaman newspapers) about these citizenships.

For instance I discussed some key events like the capture of Abdullah Öcalan, the leader of the Kurdistan Workers' Party (PKK), and I tried to analyze the Kurdish Identity my thesis is very long it is around 500 pages long so I selected many key events related to each identity and I used critical discourse analysis, I incorporated the discussion on the two newspapers in terms of the circulation one was the Zaman newspaper who reacts as you know and the other side was Hürriyet and it was one of the best selling dailies at that time period so I chose this two newspapers and I tried to analyze them in terms of content it seems a bit you know undesired according in Turkish Academia but I thank you very much for asking me this question and to you know thanks for letting me tell about my study yes you've mentioned Zaamn Daily got closed in the aftermath of the failed coup d'etat.

(PP) Could you please tell me about the background behind this decision? Also, please inform our readers about life as an academic in your country. How hard it is to be an independent academic in Turkey when you are also a grassroots activist who happens to have more liberal views than the ruling elites?

(BB) Thank you this is a really good question and it's really important. Just a very short time after the failed d'etat attempt in two top back in 2016 ,the government you know the state's discourse argued that this failed attempt was orchestrated by Fethullah Gülen and his followers. So the Gülen Community (so-called Hizmet movement) which once was seen as a moment of Intercultural dialogue was named as a terrorist organization but actually a long time ago , in late 2013 there was this conflict between the government and the Gulen community because of various corruption scandals and other issues related to governance. So the picture is still not very clear. To be honest the reports from local centers, government and that of international organizations have not been you know completely released about the background of the coup d'ettat but many institutions like the newspapers and the universities affiliated with Gülen network now called as a terrorist group. . The state can start scrutinizing you because you for instance graduated from a particular university or your research focuses on something which is inconvenient. In respect of the newspaper I was working for—this newspaper was one of the best-selling dailies—it was a legal paper you know circulated all around turkey and also abroad but now it is seen as a terrorist group's paper so it's really challenging and many things have changed as a result. Some Gulen-linked schools got closed down, the same with newspapers. The authorities just shut down Gulen-linked banks such as Bank Aysa, and many other local financial institutions. You know this is really complicated so maybe we could dedicate another video to this particular issue.

(PP) Definitely, Dr. Burak. Thank you very much for your answer. I really appreciate it. To the best of my knowledge, your most recent research relates to cyberspace and online Freedom. Could you tell us more about internet freedom in Turkey and cyberspace discussions? How free are you to conduct your research in a free and unconstrained manner?

(BB) In terms of freedom, I am free to conduct any kind of research, but in terms of publishing it or, you know, in terms of talking about some specific details in the research, this could cause me some trouble. let me give an example to illustrate this: I published a paper one year ago about online freedoms in cyberspace online surveillance, and the erosion of online freedoms in Turkey. This theme of cyberspace has attracted my attention for like a couple of years and I try to focus on these issues issue and I think among other Scholars it's a rising trend in the Academia: cyber security, metaverse etc.

I can say this online freedoms also have been under threat in the recent years because turkey has adopted a presidential regime a unique presidential regime because it's unlike the American type of presidential regime because there are no proper you know checks and balances system there's only one man rule, to be honest maybe it's also not very good to talk about this but this one man, the president controls many most of the things in Turkey so in terms of online freedoms if you criticize for example the regime in press yes it's also not very recommended in Turkey but if you also circulate your ideas on Twitter you don't have to have many followers or you don't have to be very impactful social media profile the thing is that if someone doesn't like you for example, they can just get a screenshot of your Twitter posts and you don't have to say anything embarrassing or you know anything of a criminal content but if you criticize maybe some people can get this as an attempt to jeopardize your career.

(PP) Have you ever come across any of thesems of punishment yourself?

(BB) I did not experience any retaliation from the hands of the government, but just like hundreds of thousands of Turks, I try to exercise a form of self-censorship so sometimes when I post things online. I always ask myself whether something could have some harmful consequences for me. At times I come to the realization that some posts could be misread and I chose to delete them, so that is why I exercise this self-imposed censorship. It is a very important issue for both academics and also academic journals in Turkey. Please refer to my article on criticizing a president in Turkey, which can be seen as a criminal activity. For my article please visit (Burak et al., 2022). These types of discussions are important in Turkey, and it is my recommendation that people analyze this issue from various perspectives such as a Democratic Theory, the freedom of speech. It is important to ask to what degree our constitutional rights are exercised. To what degree can we enjoy the same freedom of speech as for instance our colleagues in Europe? You see exercising our online freedoms can also be tricky for in recent years Turkey has passed a comprehensive law that impacts the way social media operates in my country. For instance, it is not clear to me who will decide what information I can post online is legal or illegal. Why would the government interfere in this sphere of life? Who gave the government the right to decide whether this idea is acceptable, correct or authentic? These are all really important issues that we discuss that will have an impact on our everyday lives.

(PP) Dr. Burak, thank you for your answer. I always try to encourage my colleagues to speculate a bit about the future. So could you please tell me more about the future of Turkey not under the Erdoğan regime? But when the current president will retire from active

politics? In other words, given that just like Putin, he has been in active politics ever since 1999, so what would be the likelihood of Erdoğan retiring from politics, and how would that impact your country?

(BB) Yes, you are right, President Recep Tayyip Erdoğan has been in politics since the early 1990s. He started his career in politics as the mayor of Istanbul and hold this office for the major of the 1990s, so if we combine local and national politics he has been active for more than three decades. You see, this question can be answered in two different ways because in May 2023 Turkey will witness elections. Those are very important elect, and I am not sure if they will result in changing the regime. But in any event, I need to say that whoever wins, there are broader constitutional issues that need to be discussed Turkey is a presidential republic. You see the changes that have been introduced by AKP (The Justice and Development Party is officially abbreviated as AK Party) have been opposed by the majority of the opposition parties. From the perspective of the opposition parties, the current Erdoğan-like twist of presidentialism is hardly democratic. That is why the opposition party leaders suggest that they will return to the parliamentary regime at the first opportunity, which is more democratic and suitable for Turkey.

From my perspective, the Erdoğan regime is facing a massive challenge. Even though today's Turkey is not free, he controls media and makes it extremely difficult for the opposition parties and a truly civic society to function in the public sphere. So not all opposition parties are even allowed to take part in the election, they don't have equal access to the media. But his regime cannot hide massive economic problems that impact the lives of ordinary people, skyrocketing inflation, and massive unemployment, especially among young people. All of those problems will have a great impact on the future of Turkish politics. I personally think that the Erdoğan regime is not also as strong as it used to be. Based on recent opinion polls, the main opposition block enjoys an important degree of support and in some other reports published by independent organizations so I think Turkey will face a radical change after the 2023 elections.

(PP) Thank you for this comprehensive response, if you allow, can I ask you one more question about Turkish foreign policy?

(BB) Sure go for it.

(PP) Could you tell me more about the Turkish role in helping the Syrian refugees, ever since the beginning of the Syrian Uprising in 2011, What's your view on the way the government is handling this issue? Especially given the recent deal with Russia, and the reaproachemet with al-Assad, that happened above the Syrian heads.

(BB) Thank you for this question, but you see actually the migration issue is something that I didn't focus on too much in my research. But I can acknowledge that Turkey hosts more than four million Syrian refugees in Turkey. This has been an ongoing issue. When we approach this from the domestic perspective, refugees have been on the agenda for quite some time. Some members of Turkish society criticized the government's involvement in Syria. Because of rising unemployment and inflation in Turkey some people think that these refugees are a burden for the Turkish people. I agreee with that to some degree and I wonder what your opinion is in this respect Dr. Piotr? I think, you have more expertise this issue, given your research background.

(PP) Thank you for redirecting a question. I suppose that when it comes to Turkey and Poland, we have pretty much similar situations when it comes to certain politics toward refugees. These days Turkey hosts more than 4 million Syrian refugees; meanwhile, Poland ever since February 2022, has hosted more than 3 million Ukrainian refugees, so on some levels, our countries meet certain obligations towards the neighboring populations that happen to be exposed to various forms of violence from their countries of origin. In the Syrian case from the hands of a local despot, the authoritarian regime of Bashar al-Assad. In the Ukrainian case, the refugees were escaping the brutalities inflicted upon them by the Russian military serviceman and Russian serving affiliated mercenaries. Still, this is just a part of an argument. The issue is more complicated than when we look at it closely (…).

If I may ask the final question, could you tell me more about the Turkish drone production? Turkey is exporting latest Bayraktar TB2 drones to Ukraine, how important is that in warming up Turkish image around the world? The Ukrianian people even wrote a song about this drone, on the other hand the same drones were expored to Azerbejan and used in a rather instrumental manner against Aremnia in the latest major escalation the Second Nagornokarabakh War? What's your intake on that?

(BB) This question is very interesting, for it is yet another really important topic that I covered in my recent research. I made a conference presentation about this. Analyzing the impacts of this drone production, the exports to other states, is important as it impacts the image of Turkey and its foreign policy image. I presented a paper in a conference and discussed the way the Bayraktar drones contributed to Turkish foreign policy image. It is also important to acknowledge that Selçuk Bayraktar the manufacturer of these armed drones is President Erdoğan's son-in-law, so it is very interesting how this topic has been covered by the Western media. Mr. Bayraktar has been interviewed by big western media outlets. This is important not only from the perspective of the use of these drones in Ukrianie but as you mentioned it also seems quite instrumental in giving Azerbaijan a considerable advantage over Armenia. More than 20 different countries bought these drones to so far. This is one way of approaching this topic. The other is the fact that the overall perception is very positive, for it projects a picture of Turkey as a country that is not dependent on foreign infrastructure, or technology but an actual player that is capable of producing such sophisiticated piece of modern weaponry that is an export hit among everyone. The current demand surely cannot be met. Countries are lining up to buy those drones based on my reading of government-close media outlet reports

(PP) Clearly, the nature of modern conflict is changing in a breathtaking speed; the use of Bayraktars clearly changed the course of even such seemingly uneven confrontation as the war between Ukraine and Russia. Clearly, Azerbaijan benefited heavily from one of their investment in those drones, and so did the reputation of Turkey, you never know… maybe once day Selçuk Bayraktar will take over from President Erdogan.

Dr. Burak, thank you very much for this interview. Thank you so much for your time, and I wish you all the best in your research, and I hope that our academic collaboration will extend beyond this interview.

(BB) Thank you so much for giving me this space to introduce your readers to my research. It is a real pleasure and a real opportunity. Thanks a lot, Dr. Pietrzak. I do appreciate it.

(PP) Thank you very much.

Interviewee:

BEGÜM BURAK, Ph.D. is a Turkish independent researcher, who defended her Ph.D. degree in 2015. Her academic collaboration extends to the universities in Italy, the United Kingdom, Bosnia and Hercegovina, Bulgaria, Georgia, and Spain. In 2018, she became one of the founding members of www.ilkmade.com.Dr. Burak is interested in matters related to Modern History, Turkish Studies, Discourse Analysis, Media and Politics, Democratization, Cyberspace, online freedom, Internet Freedom, Religion and Politics/ Secularism, Democratic Theory, Comparative Democratization, Political Culture, Matters related to the military coup of 2016.

Links:

- https://independentresearcher.academia.edu/BegumBurak
- https://www.youtube.com/@begumburak
- https://moderndiplomacy.eu/author/begumburak/

Interviewer:

PIOTR PIETRZAK, Ph.D. specializes in the politics of the Middle East and the Islamic world, focusing his attention on the theory of International Relations, political philosophy, geopolitics, international law, and conflict resolution strategies.

ORCID: http://orcid.org/0000-0003-0464-1991
E-**mail**: Pietrzak_IR@hotmail.com

Further reading:

Burak, Begüm., ve Nezih Onur Kuru, A. B., Saygın, P. M., Kartal, R. N., Başkan, B., Çelebi, B., & Uzun, B. (2022, June 27). An Analysis of Unending Prosecutions: The Crime of Insulting President—Daktilo 1984. Daktilo 1984. https://daktilo1984.com/d84intelligence/an-analysis-of-unending-prosecutions-the-crime-of-insulting-president/

Burak, Begüm. 2022. The Image of the Undesired Citizens in Turkey: A Comparative Critical Discourse *Analysis of the Hürriyet and Zaman Newspapers:* Generis Publishing.

Burak, Begüm. "Human Rights Violations in Cyberspace: Internet Censorship and Online Surveillance in Turkey." | Begum Burak, PhD—Academia.edu. Accessed December 7, 2022. https://www.acad emia.edu/70046112/human_rights_violations_in_cyberspace_internet _censorship_and_online_surveillance_in_turkey.

Burak, Begüm. "A Weak State with a 'Strong State' Tradition: The Case of Turkey." E-International Relations, August 8, 2012. https://www.e-ir. info/2012/08/08/a-weak-state-with-a-strong-state-tradition-the-case-of-turkey/.

Burak, Begüm. "Quo Vadis Turkish Politics?" Begin-Sadat Center for Strategic Studies, April 4, 2021. https://besacenter.org/quo-vadis-turkish-politics/.

Burak, Begüm. "Teaching nation-building and nationalism: a critical perspective of Turkish academia" Journal of Applied Learning & TeachingVol.5 No.1 (2022) http://journals.sfu.ca/jalt/index.php/jalt/index

BOOK REVIEWS

Violeta Nikolova on Peter Frankopan's *the Silk Roads: A New History of the World* (Alfred A. Knopf, 2019).

The Silk Roads: A New History of the World shifts the center of historical importance of the Western (American, European) reader from their own region to the glorious past of the far territories of the East. Peter Frankopan opens the doors to, in my opinion, neglected moments in history in the nowadays political rhetoric that heavily predetermined the course of present events and distribution of world powers. The author makes a clear link between the ancient times of history to nowadays to present a holistic and new interpretation of world history, economy, and international relations. Would history repeat itself and is the author hinting to another redistribution of power that would repeat the triumphs of the East? These are some of the questions a reader is addressing to him/herself, while immersing in the book. Relating some of the book stories to my personal experience, I found, for example, the storyline of the chapters "The Road of Gold" and "The Road of Silver" (Frankopan, 2015) interestingly relevant to my daily routine. In those passages, Frankopan is describing the setting of the 15th century and the great geographical explorations of the Spanish and of the Portuguese sailors. Apart from the already familiar road from the shores of Western Europe to America, the author is offering a detour — the newly established road to Asia, revealing little known worlds to multiple European travelers and respectively tempting their trading instincts. Following the discovery of gold and silver in Central and Southern America, Europe was getting richer and richer with the massive transportation of goods coming across the Atlantic. In the same period another significant event changed global trade—Vasco da Gama explored a sea road to Asia, where Chinese porcelain, silk and precious spices were expecting their now wealthy consumers from the West. By the end of the 16th century Manila was founded by the Spanish people and the district became a significant link on the road between the Americas and Asia, without the need to

cross through Europe and Africa. These events could help explain some of the still Spanish-sounding names of the local population in the Philippines with whom I communicate and work daily from far Bulgaria and could contribute to the raising image of the country as a significant workforce in the current corporate world. Can we draw a parallel here between the conquistadors of the past and the current corporations? We can see how in both cases we can speak of globalization and of easier and faster ways to transport goods and services across the globe. Of course, these shortened paths that connect the world come at a very high price and often involve the cost of human life. Only time would show if the Philippines were on another raise as a significant trade point of the world, but history could make us foresee some of those events and could also help us prepare for any potential consequences. Of other major topics discussed in the book, such as the history of the Middle East, including the rise and fall of the Persian and Ottoman Empires, as well as the hardships of the Jewish population, the echo could be heard more and more vividly nowadays, given the current tensions between nations or the political ambitions of certain politicians over other states. Most notably it illustrates how war and trade often go hand in hand, where the new silk roads not only open the doors to an individual to explore the world but also bring significant threats. Lastly, the journey from antiquity to nowadays that Peter Frankopan had offered me personally as a reader has served as a massive foundation for the courses of my current Master program—Political Pathologies of the Global world. As my main and only critique to the "The Silk Roads: A New History of the World" is that the voice of the author can be loudly heard throughout the narrative, instead of leaving the author stay immersed in the historical episodes. In a way, the book sounds as a criticism to the West world and mostly to its ignorance, encouraged by their educational systems by neglecting the past achievements of the East. One should indeed gather all viewpoints to get enlightened on a specific topic, but these should not exclude the local history and development of one's nation.

Bibliography

Frankopan Peter. 2019. *The New Silk Roads : The Present and Future of the World* First American ed. New York: Alfred A. Knopf.

ABOUT THE AUTHOR
VIOLETA NIKOLOVA is an early researcher and master's student taking a course in the **Political Pathologies of the Global World** program at Sofia University. Her dissertation deals with the questions related to the Ukrainian Orthodox Church's attempts to speed up the process to a fully autocephalous institution. At the same time, Violeta is a Project 205 Violeta Nikolova is Analyst in a large pharmaceutical company and

has occupied different roles in the IT and Insurance sectors. The spark that brought her into Political Science was her Debating Society at her High School, located at the heart of her beloved Sofia.

E-mail:
violetanikolova21@gmail.com

Dobromir Gyulev on Peter Zeihan's *the End of the World Is Just the Beginning: Mapping the Collapse of Globalization*. First ed. New York NY: Harper Collins Publishers. (2022)

Peter Zeihan's *The End of the World Is Just the Beginning—Mapping the Collapse of Globalization* is a journey that covers huge stretches of territory from a historical, geographic, demographic and economic perspective. Zeihan picks apart all major sectors of the global economy such as transportation, manufacturing, finance, mining, agriculture etc. with the ultimate goal of warning us about the imminent collapse of the global interconnected world as we know it.

Zeihan masterfully develops his ideas by starting with the development of the human economic activities since prehistoric times and explains how the systems we currently take for granted developed. For example, when writing about the development of the current transportation systems Zeihan starts with the use of boats and rafts along inland waterways, goes through ocean shipping via sailing ships constantly threatened by pirates and reaches to the massive container ships of today that can only fit in the biggest of ports.

The key point in Zeihan's narrative is the notion that the world has enjoyed a period of unprecedented peace and prosperity after the end of World War II thanks largely to the security imposed by the U.S. military and more specifically naval power. The global trade boomed and reached unprecedented levels thanks largely to the development of transport (both on land and on water) and the relative stability and lack of threats.

The industrial revolution and the urbanization of the countries over the past hundred years have generated enormous wealth and have brought billions of people out of poverty. However, these prosperous times are coming to an end due to various factors, but the most important of them in Zeihan's view is the ageing population across most of the globe. The fact that over the past 50 years, every new generation in the developed world is smaller than the previous one is the key reason why the current model of global economy and extreme interdependency cannot last.

Zeihan is convinced that the inevitable disruption in the extremely delicate global supply chains, caused by the lack of sufficient workers at all levels of production, research and development, trade etc., will ultimately bring the current global model to a halt.

Examples such as the COVID-19 pandemic, the blockage of the Suez Canal, the disruptions in wheat and fertilizer trade by the war in Ukraine are some of the examples that Zeihan uses to illustrate what lies ahead of us.

The biggest loser in this new global order would be China due to two main factors—the devastating effects of the one-child policy enacted by the Chinese Communist Party combined with the inevitable decline in births caused by the fast industrialization of China on the one hand; and on the other, the extreme dependence of the Chinese economy on imported raw materials, foods, technology etc. A slight disruption in the global trade and supply chains risks pushing as much as 500 million Chinese people in a situation of significant food shortage within a year, Zeihan warns.

Another country that faces the biggest risk of collapse under the new world order is Russia, whose demographic situation is even worse than that of China. Still its vast territory with sufficient energy resources and enough fertile land to produce food may allow the country to avoid a collapse like China.

Still, the book is much more than a simple doomsday warning. Zeihan takes his time to explain how regional alliances such as those between countries in South-East Asia, or those of the NAFTA members (U.S., Mexico and Canada) as well as some individual countries such as Argentina or France would be able to weather the storm much better than the rest of the world. In Zeihan's view these countries' robust demographic outlook, their manufacturing capacity, and their ability to produce enough food to feed their populations are the key factors that will most likely make them the new centers of prosperity and development in the fragmented world that we will see in the second half of the 21st century.

Although the book is comprehensive and attempts to look at the global economic and political stage from various perspectives, the predictions the author makes are too bold and not fully supported by evidence. For example, Zeihan takes for granted the fact that North America and the United States in particular will emerge as the leaders of the new global stage after the end of the process of deglobaization, but fails to take into account the deep political divides in the current US politics and the risks they pose for the integrity of the federation. The extreme left or right political views have been moving from the fringes to the mainstream over the past ten years and have had a growing impact on the actual political landscape of the different US states. The rift between the states with the most liberal and left-wing policies such as California and the more conservative and right-wing ones such as Florida has been growing exponentially and the notion of secession definitely does not sound as absurd as it sounded a couple of decades ago.

On the other hand, the prognosis that China's economy will collapse, and its population will decline by half until 2050 does not take into account the possibility of the Chinese people deciding to revise Beijing's current political doctrine in the face of internal strives and risks of a catastrophic economic crisis. The control of the Chinese Communist Party may appear as unchallengeable at the moment, but so was the grip of the Communist Party of the Soviet Union until the economic crisis of the late 1980s and early 1990s and the war in Afghanistan. A possible invasion of Taiwan by China may trigger the same unstoppable chain of events that led to the collapse of the USSR some 30 years ago…

The large technological and social shifts of the past few years are also somewhat overlooked by Zeihan. The ability of one global player to obtain enormous military or economic advantage over its rivals thanks to the development of Artificial General Intelligence (AGI) may easily result in a completely different picture that could be even grimmer than the one painted by Zeihan.

Despite these shortcomings, the book is a must read for people who are interested in international relations and want to have an overlook of the current state of the globalized world. It can also serve as a warning that the intricate economic and political systems that we take for granted are in fact very delicate and must be protected and upgraded to function properly and guarantee a prosperous life for the human population.

Bibliography

Zeihan Peter. 2022. *The End of the World Is Just the Beginning : Mapping the Collapse of Globalization* First ed. New York NY: Harper Business an imprint of Harper Collins Publishers.

ABOUT THE AUTHOR

DOBROMIR GYULEV has a Bachelor of Arts in Italian Philology from Sofia University St. Kliment Ohridski and is currently pursuing a **Master of Arts in Political Pathologies of the Global World** at the Political Science department at the same university. Gyulev is professionally engaged in risk & compliance, risk assessment and media analysis. His primary interests relate to global and national politics and social developments, international relations and conflict resolution. Gyulev regularly comments on topics related to national politics and international relations in Eastern Europe and the Black Sea region.

E-mail:
dobromir.gyulev@gmail.com

Previous Editions of the Journal

Issue 2021:2 comprises, amongst others, the following interviews & articles:

- United Nations Peacekeeping Missions in Haiti (1993–2019),
- Immanuel Kant and Niccolò Machiavelli's Traditions and the Limits of Approaching Contemporary Conflicts—the Case Study of the Syrian Conflict (2011–Present),
- The Mental Health of UCAV Drone Operators and Deployed Soldiers: a Comparative Study of PTSD and Moral Injury Using an Example of US Soldiers,
- The Economic Partnership Agreement in the Context of Globalization and Africa's Development the Opportunities and the Threats,
- Spillover-effects in International Railway Cooperation: The Case of V4 Countries,
- Aristotle's Phronesis and Socratic Skepticism: A Starting Point for the Development of Applied Ethics,
- Literature as a Modern Art (Letërsia si art modern),
- Culture as Understood in the Thought of Emmanuel Levinas and Hans-Georg Gadamer,
- Hegel's Notion of Recollection in Comparison to Agnes Heller's Notion of Imagination,

Issue 2021:1 comprises, amongst others, the following interviews & articles:

- Constructivism in the Study of Sustainable Development,
- "Why should Russia not be gifting Kaliningrad Oblast to Ukraine?" (Interview with Dr Krzysztof Żęgota),
- 'Democracy to come': Derrida's 'undecidability' and Laclau's 'Ethical' as Investment Everydayness,
- Every-no-where: A brief comparison of Paul Ricoeur's "Imagination in discourse and in action" (1994) with Hegel's philosophy of imagination as expressed in Donald Phillip Verene's Hegel's Recollection: A Study of Images in the Phenomenology of Spirit (1985),
- A Hidden Tenderness for the World: Reconstructing Marx's Ethics,

Issue 2020:2 comprises, amongst others, the following interviews & articles:

- "Clarity is what I seek first": An interview with Professor Tamara Albertini,

- Reinventing Politics: An Epistemic Conversion of Information Technologies,
- Information Society and a New Form of Embodiment,
- The Analysis of the Economic and Political Determinants of the Venezuelan Presidential Crisis since 2019,
- Balance of Power and the 21st Century Iron Law of International Relations or an Outdated Idea,
- North-South Railway Construction Projects in the Visegrád Four Countries (V4),

<u>Issue 2020:1</u> comprises, amongst others, the following interviews & articles:

- Interview with Dr. Zoran Kojcic on his unique form of philosophical counselling,
- Paul Tillich's Critical and Political Theology and his Critique of Modernity,
- The Phenomenology of Women. On Female Discourse in Julia Kristeva's and Simone de Beauvoir's work,
- The Implications of Relativity in Translation and vice versa,
- The Republic of Korea—United States of America's "Strategic Patience": A counter measurement of the Alliance in Responding to Democratic People's Republic of Korea' Nuclear Development Program (2013—2017),
- Dueling with Disinformation: Disinformation and Information and Communication Technologies in the Middle East,
- How would Realists Interpret People Republic of China's wish to "cultivate the image of a responsible great power"?

Issue 2019:2 comprises, amongst others, the following interviews & articles:

- Donald J. Trump's policy toward North Korea and the Islamic Republic of Iran—a Comparative Study,
- Contrariwise and inconsistent positions on Turkey´s EU membership—Do party politics matter in German foreign policy?
- Charity Begins at Home: Resolving the Tensions of Liberalism(s), "White Privilege" and African Corruption via Rawls and Transnational Digital-Communitarianism,
- Lukács, Kojève and Verene's interpretations of Hegel's recollection in his *Phenomenology of Spirit,*
- Madonnas and whores or blood and gore? Roles for women in the so-called Islamic State,

<u>Issue 2019:1</u> comprises, amongst others, the following articles:

- Interview with Prof. Marcin Grabowski on the Political Situation in Asia in general and North Korea in particular,
- Cecin'est pas Artemis Papachristou,
- The EU and The Migration Crisis' 'The EU-Turkey Deal': policy effectiveness and challenges of implementation
- The Syrian Conflict (2011–2017): How a Perfectly Winnable Uprising has been transformed into a Civil War, Only to End up as a Ferocious Proxy War,
- Under what circumstances Ukraine can get the Crimean Peninsula back from the Russian Federation?
- Interview with Prof. Maria Dimitrova on continental philosophy in general, and Emmanuel Levinas' Philosophy in particular,
- Patristic Tradition, Criterialism and Levinasian Quasi-Theological Conditions of the Self,
- Reconsidering the Notion of Creative Genius in Postmodern Philosophy and Art,

<u>Issue 2018:1</u> comprises, amongst others, the following articles:

- Corporate Instrumentalization of Deliberative Democracy in Global Governance,
- A Comparative Study between Levinas and Kierkegaard on Subjectivity and the Self,
- The Kremlin's Reaction to the St. Petersburg Metro Attacks seen through the Prism of Russian Intervention in Syria,
- Donald Trump's visit to Saudi Arabia, Saudi Iranian Relations, and the Future of the Iranian Nuclear Deal,
- The United Kingdom on the Verge of a "Constitutional Crisis": Between the Possibility of a Second Referendum on the Membership in the European Union and a Potential Second Vote on Scottish Independence,
- Was it Greece last decade (2007—2017) or just a culmination of the process that has led Athens to the brink of the economic collapse.

From the Editor's desk

Dear Readers,
Dear Members of the Editorial Board,
Dear Members of the Advisory Board,
Dear Publishers,
Dear Colleagues,

Sofia, 30 June 2023,

Some six years ago, we established *In Statu Nascendi—Journal of Political Philosophy and International Relations*. This marked the beginning of one of the most productive, dynamic, and fascinating periods in my professional career. I will be forever grateful for the opportunity to serve you in my current capacity, for I've enjoyed my time here to the fullest.

I will always cherish this experience, for what we have managed to achieve together in such a short period of time has surpassed my wildest expectations. I am particularly thankful to the people who comprised an integral part of this periodical, our readers, authors, members of the editorial board, academic advisors, editors, copyeditors, translators, proofreaders, fine-tuners, and naturally, our publisher. All of you did an incredible job! Thanks to your hard work, dedication, and professionalism, we published six incredible volumes, contributing immensely to expanding our conceptual and ontological horizons. So, in my last act as an editor of *In Statu Nascendi*, I would like to congratulate you for your amazing achievement of being instrumental in helping to publish almost 150 robust academic articles and some of the most fascinating book reviews, for I am certain that their influence will resonate in the decades to come. Well done!

I would also like to kindly inform you that I recently decided to vacate the position of editor-in-chief of *In Statu Nascendi*. This wasn't an easy decision, but it was necessary due to an increase in my other professional commitments. Sadly, we have not found a replacement for my position, and our **editorial board** decided to terminate the contract with the publisher.

This ultimately means that the publication of this volume is this periodical's final edition.

In a way, the dissolution of our **editorial board** is surely an unfortunate event, for it marks the Hegelian/Fukuyamian end of this periodical's existence as we know it. But I am very optimistic about what the future holds, for it is only natural for us to continue on the path that we embarked upon in 2017. The end of this project does not mean that we will stop testing the more established doctrines, approaches, theories, and paradigms that are too often considered to be unquestionable or absolute. On the contrary, our network will continue the journey that aims to dig deeper into the essence of our existence. Indeed, the spirit of *our network* dictates that we contribute to the main currents of the academic debates of the future, for we know that we still have a lot of work to do when it comes to fighting dogma, misinformation, and various forms of bias and prejudice that also exist in the academic world.

Ultimately, the end of this project marks just the beginning of our non-profit's speedy transition to ***In Statu Nascendi—Think Thank***, which will continue to positively surprise you in the decades to come, for it is designed to provide advice and ideas on specific issues related to geoeconomic, political, and socio-economic problems. We perform research and advocacy concerning international law, social policy, political strategy, economics, military technology, artificial intelligence, green technology, and culture.

In other words, I would like to signal that as an organization we are now ready to move beyond the stage of becoming, recollect our experience, and approach it from a totally different, more mature perspective.

Wishing you all the best in your future endeavors.

Yours sincerely,

Piotr Pietrzak, Ph.D.

Co-editor of this volume, Former Editor-in-Chief of *In Statu Nascendi
Journal of Political Philosophy and International Relations*
Co-founder of **In Statu Nascendi—Think Thank**
Pietrzak_IR@hotmail.com